IMAGES
of America

THE 1972 FLOOD IN NEW YORK'S SOUTHERN TIER

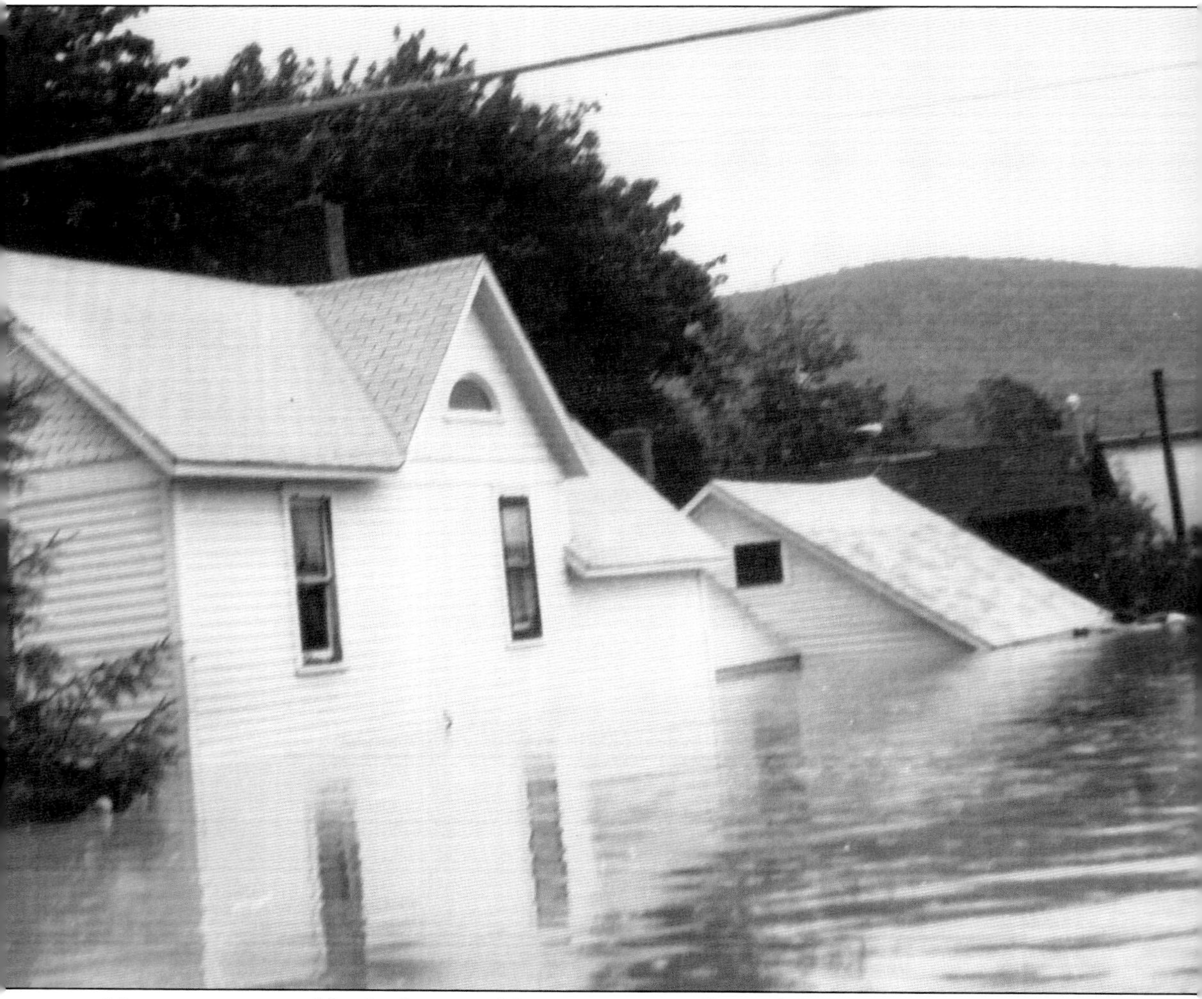

Houses, garages, public facilities, and businesses were all awash literally overnight in the 1972 flood. This image, taken from a rocking boat (to judge by the angle), suggests the community's sudden precariousness. (Courtesy of Corning-Painted Post Historical Society.)

On the Cover: When the Penn Central Railroad Bridge collapsed in Corning, it added to local problems and put constrictions in the national rail net. (Courtesy of Corning-Painted Post Historical Society.)

IMAGES
of America

THE 1972 FLOOD IN NEW YORK'S SOUTHERN TIER

Kirk W. House

ARCADIA
PUBLISHING

ISBN 978-0-7385-7678-7

Published by Arcadia Publishing
Charleston, South Carolina

Printed in the United States of America

Library of Congress Control Number: 2011934462

For all general information, please contact Arcadia Publishing:
Telephone 843-853-2070
Fax 843-853-0044
E-mail sales@arcadiapublishing.com
For customer service and orders:
Toll-Free 1-888-313-2665

Visit us on the Internet at www.arcadiapublishing.com

Almost 35 years ago, I dedicated my first book to my wife, with thanks for all the help she had given me. In another state and another century, with our then unborn children now grown men, she has helped me through Addison's disease, post-traumatic stress disorder, a master's degree, and 15 books. So here and now, as there and then, this is for Joyce.

Contents

Acknowledgments

Several agencies and individuals shared their collections and their recollections to help in the preparation of this book. It is always invidious to single out particular people, when so many have contributed. But, Owen Franks, reference librarian at the Chemung County Library District Steele Memorial Library in Elmira, connected me with his predecessor Ann Brouse, who graciously shared her photographs documenting the devastation of the library and the community. Liz Turissini shared her family's slides and their experience. Ginny Wright, as always, kindly shared about the experience at the Museum of Glass. Mike Connor went the extra mile with railroad photographs. Jill Thomas-Clark and others made it possible to include the outstanding Museum of Glass images. Kristine Gable of Corning Incorporated helped steer me straight on proper 1972 terminology and personnel at the Glass Works. At the historical societies, many thanks go to Rachel Dworkin (Chemung County), Ron Wyatt and Nedra McElroy (Steuben County), plus Sheri Golder and "Doc" Cavallaro (Corning-Painted Post).

For sharing their stories, special thanks go to Dot Cornell, Lorraine Loomis-Konig, Ian Mackenzie, Jane Shadel-Spillman, Liz Turissini, John van Zanten, Gary Waldo, John Weaver, Millie Weaver, Nancy Weaver, and Ginny Wright. For their help, thanks also go to Corning mayor Richard P. Negri and to my photographer son Joshua B. House.

Though 40 years have passed, "the flood" is still a living memory and still referred to without any additional descriptor needed. The ongoing success of the region is a testimony to the spirit and strength of its people and to the nationwide efforts of the American community.

Each image caption ends with an abbreviation identifying that image's source. I myself have memberships in the Steuben, Chemung, Tioga, and Corning-Painted Post Historical Societies. Membership in any of these agencies preserves history and builds community. Please consider joining. The following is a key for identifying the image sources: Ann Brouse (AB); Chemung County Historical Society Booth Library (CC); City of Corning (CoC); Corning Incorporated, Department of Archives and Record Management (CI); Corning Museum of Glass Rakow Library (CMOG); Corning-Painted Post Historical Society (CPP); Erie Lackawanna Historical Society (EL); Steuben County Historical Society (SCHS); Steuben County Historical Society, Robert and Elizabeth Turissini Gift (RET); Steuben County Historian (SCH); and Tioga County Historical Society (TC).

INTRODUCTION

For centuries, the people of New York's Southern Tier simply lived and died with floods. Historic events include the Pumpkin Floods (1786, 1817, and 1860), the Great Inundation (1833), the Big Flood (1857), and the Tremendous Flood (1861). But by the middle of the 20th century, new technology and new attitudes toward government enabled action. After catastrophic inundations in July 1935, New Deal programs created flood-control systems to manage the problem.

Still, there are floods and *floods*. In June 1972, the remnants of Hurricane Agnes drifted overland from New Jersey, parked along the New York–Pennsylvania state line, merged with another low-pressure system, and poured out rain in tropical torrents for 50 hours.

The waters rose, and the rivers rolled, causing "the most destructive and widespread flooding on record in New York State," according to the *Encyclopedia of New York State*. Fourteen Empire State counties became disaster areas, and New York suffered 24 deaths, with 18 of them in the Corning area. It was America's costliest mainland hurricane up to that time, with New York's damage alone over $700 million, and there were well over 100 dead nationwide. The name *Agnes* was retired from future use for hurricanes. In addition to the storm's earlier damage in Virginia and Florida, catastrophes stretched from New York City and Long Island in the east to the Allegheny River in the west, not to mention reaching New Jersey, Pennsylvania, Maryland, Quebec, and Ontario.

This book focuses in more closely on Steuben and Chemung Counties in New York's Southern Tier and their neighbors to the east—the hard-hit stretch where the Chemung and Susquehanna Rivers exploded past their banks and attacked the communities that had grown up depending on them. Recovery took months, even years. Ever since then, the region's history (both public and personal) has been divided into the time before and the time after the Hurricane Agnes flood of 1972.

The biggest story of this period is the one that did not happen. Corning Glass Works, the region's largest employer, suffered extensive damage from the flood. It could well have decided to take leave of its namesake city, and relocate its headquarters and major production to one of its many other facilities. But Glass Works officials quickly determined, and announced, that they would not only stay in Corning but also take a leading role in rebuilding the region. Without that commitment, this would be a very different story.

And, of course, the story never ends; each community needs to find that resolve again and again. Significant floods came to the region again in 1975, 1996 (from rapidly melting ice), 1998, and 2006. In September 2011, as this book was being prepared, Chemung and Steuben Counties were little affected; but some of Broome County suffered even worse than it had in the Agnes flood. Once again, it started with a hurricane—Irene, in this case. After the remnants of Hurricane Irene drenched the region, the remnants of Tropical Storm Lee did the same a few days later, forcing the Susquehanna out of its channel. Binghamton evacuated 20,000 people and downstream Pennsylvania, 100,000 more.

Better forecasting, better communications, and better preparation made the difference. Many of those improvements were built on the hard lessons learned from Hurricane Agnes.

The following are some notes on nomenclature used in the book:

Southern Tier refers to the seven counties, from Chautauqua to Broome, running almost 200 miles along the east-west state line between New York and Pennsylvania.

Northern Tier refers to the corresponding Pennsylvania counties along the "underside" of that line.

Twin Tiers refers to the two regions together, lying like two courses of bricks, one atop the other.

Finger Lakes is the 14-county region of New York that includes the 11 Finger Lakes. Keuka Lake reaches into Steuben County. Seneca Lake lies just north of Chemung County, and Cayuga Lake is just north of Tioga County.

Corning Glass Works was already well over a century old in 1972. Corning Glass Works was (and is) the major employer in the Corning-Elmira area. It is now the high-technology Corning Incorporated.

Corning Glass Center was in 1972 a multiuse facility, including the Corning Museum of Glass. All those features are now encompassed in the much larger Corning Museum of Glass.

Hurricane is a cyclonic storm, originating in the tropics, with sustained winds of at least 74 miles per hour.

Tropical storm refers to a similar storm with sustained winds between 39 and 73 miles per hour. The Agnes system was technically a tropical storm, just short of hurricane strength, when it made landfall in the state of New York.

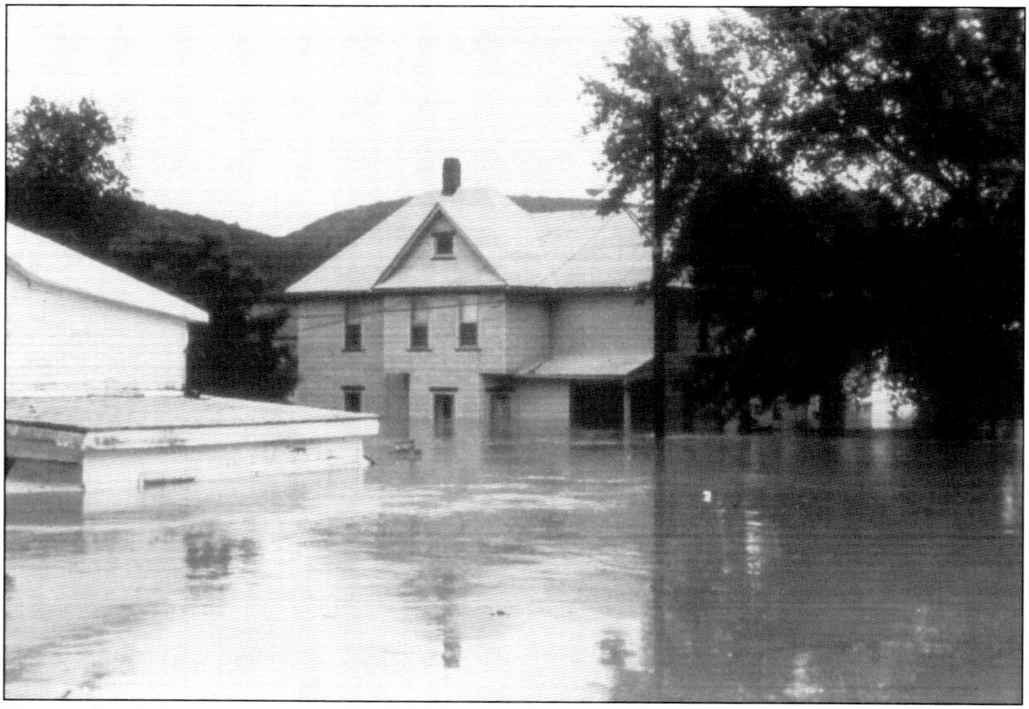

Houses flooded, contents ruined, lives lost: effects from the 1972 flood still reverberate 40 years later. (RET.)

One

Steuben County

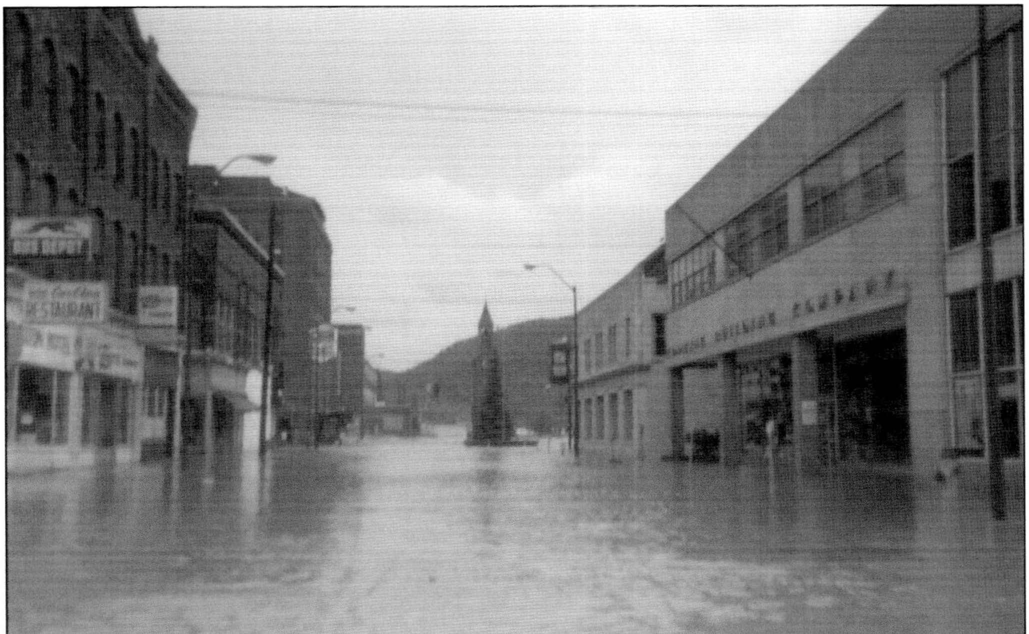

The Conhocton, Canisteo, and Tioga Rivers all rose when the Hurricane Agnes rains came. They have their confluence and form the Chemung where Corning meets Painted Post. In the early morning hours on June 23, 1972, all three tributaries crested at that point pretty much simultaneously. (CPP.)

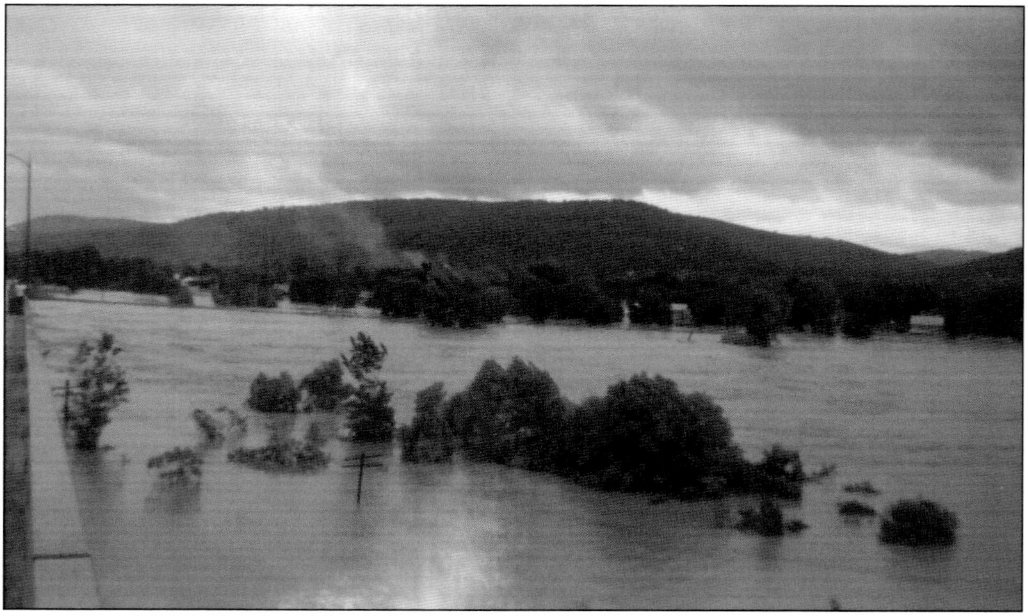

Eighteen people died—three-fourths of the deaths that occurred in New York. Corning was cut off from the rest of the world. (CPP.)

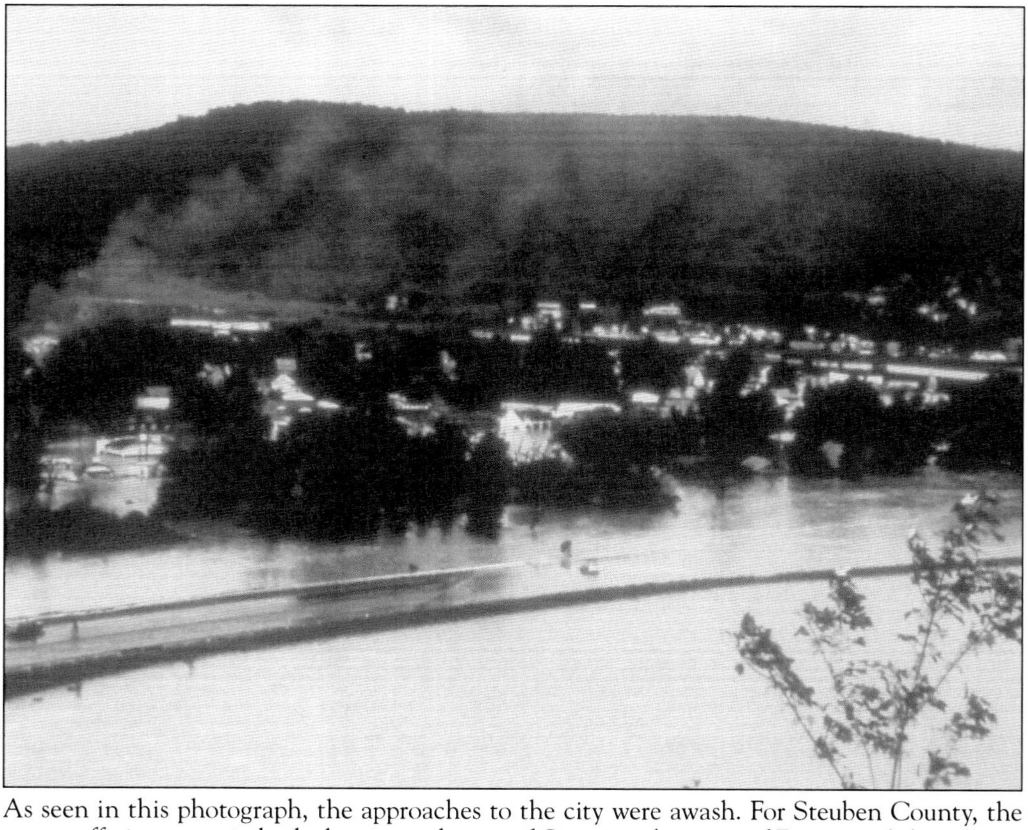

As seen in this photograph, the approaches to the city were awash. For Steuben County, the worst suffering came in both the city and town of Corning, the town of Erwin, and the villages of Riverside, Painted Post, and South Corning. (RET.)

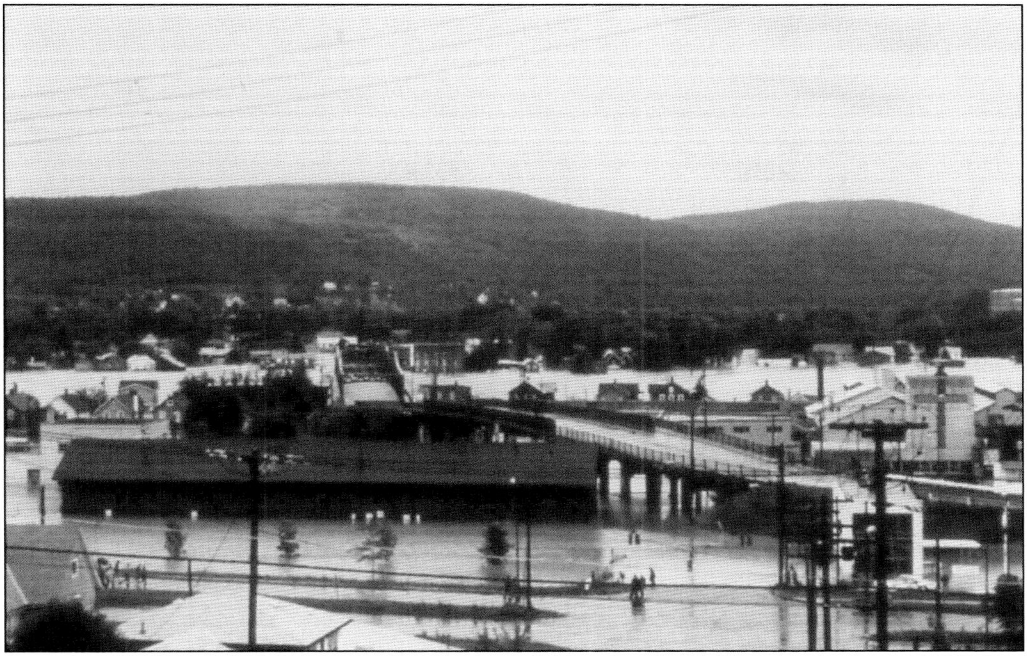

Upriver towns, such as Addison, Bath, and Hornell, suffered from the floods, as did the Keuka Lake communities. But, Corning area residents could not get in; they could not get out; they could not get around inside. The Northside was largely underwater. Even those Northside neighborhoods not flooded were still cut off from "The Hill" and the Southside. (RET.)

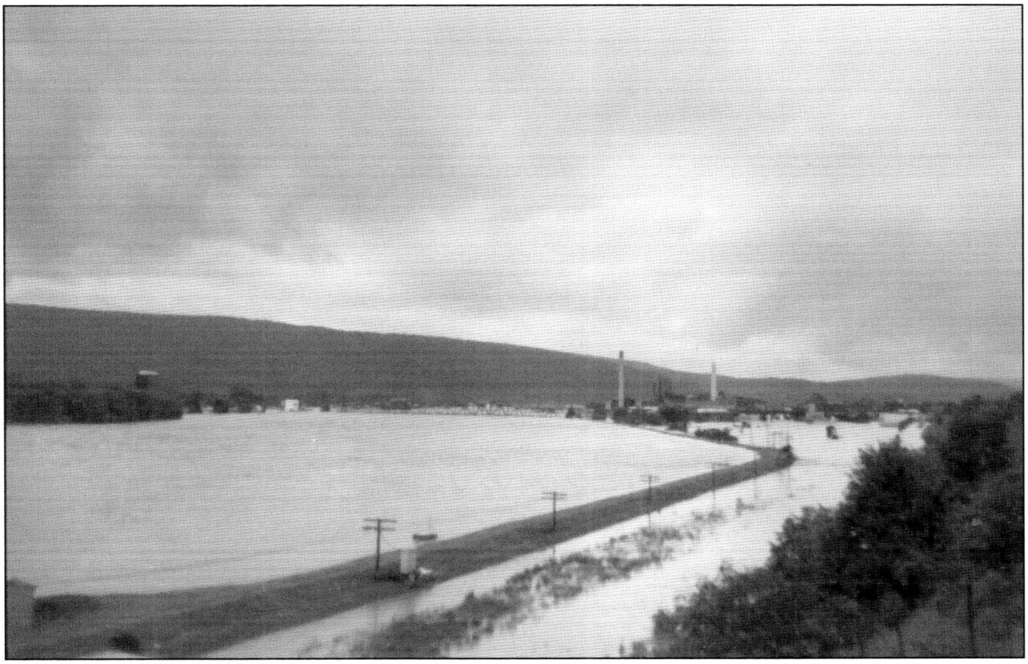

The rivers drowned their banks and rose to meet the bridges. On the right are the smokestack and shot tower from the Glass Works, and on the left is an office tower for the Glass Works. The Glass Works main plant manager shut the place down at 2:30 a.m. and sent the night shift home. This turned out to be an excellent decision. (CPP.)

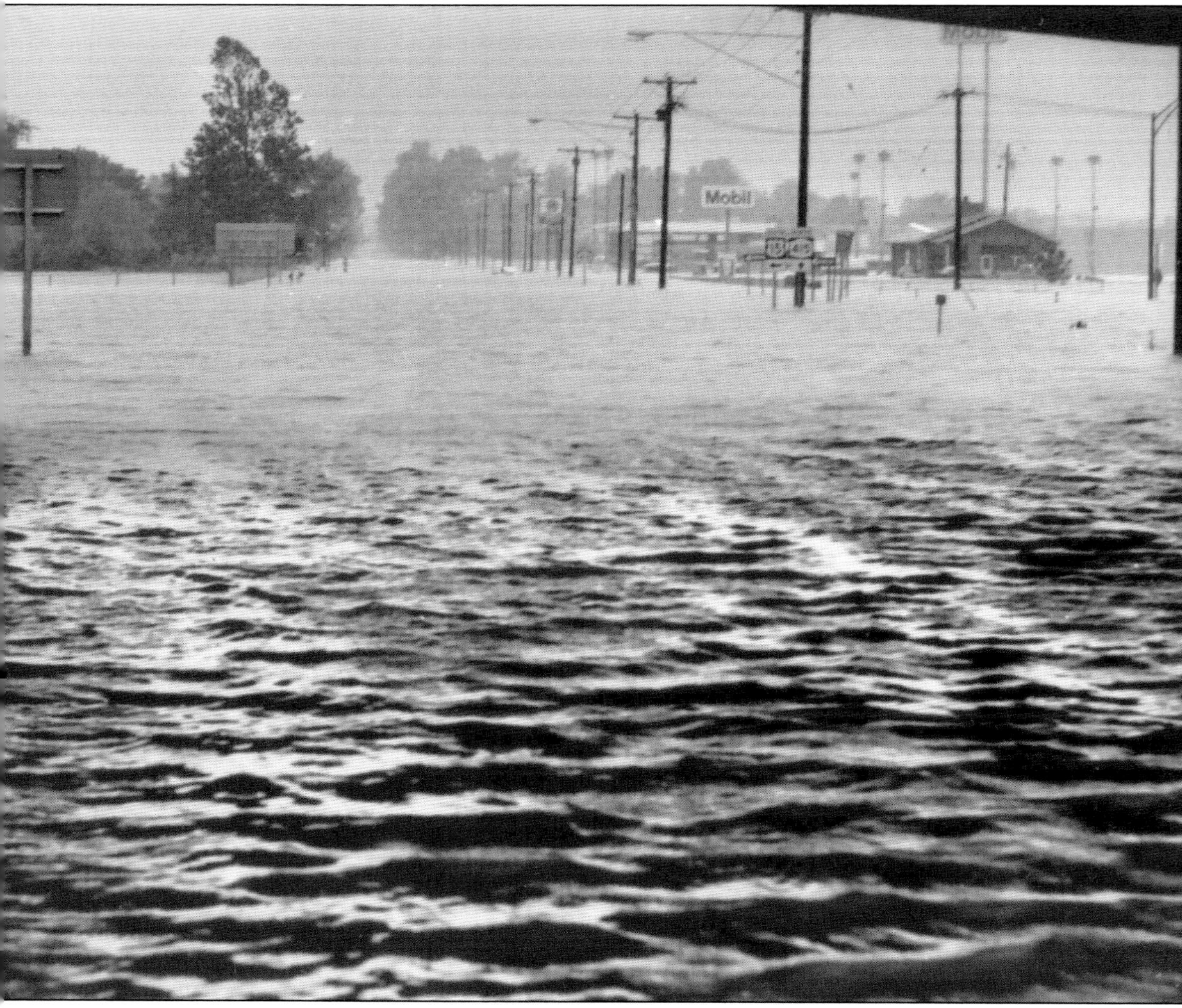

Waters rose quickly in Painted Post, shown here. The upriver county seat of Bath was largely saved by government construction, but not, ironically, by specific flood-control features. Berms bearing the limited-access Southern Tier Expressway acted as dikes for Bath. (CPP.)

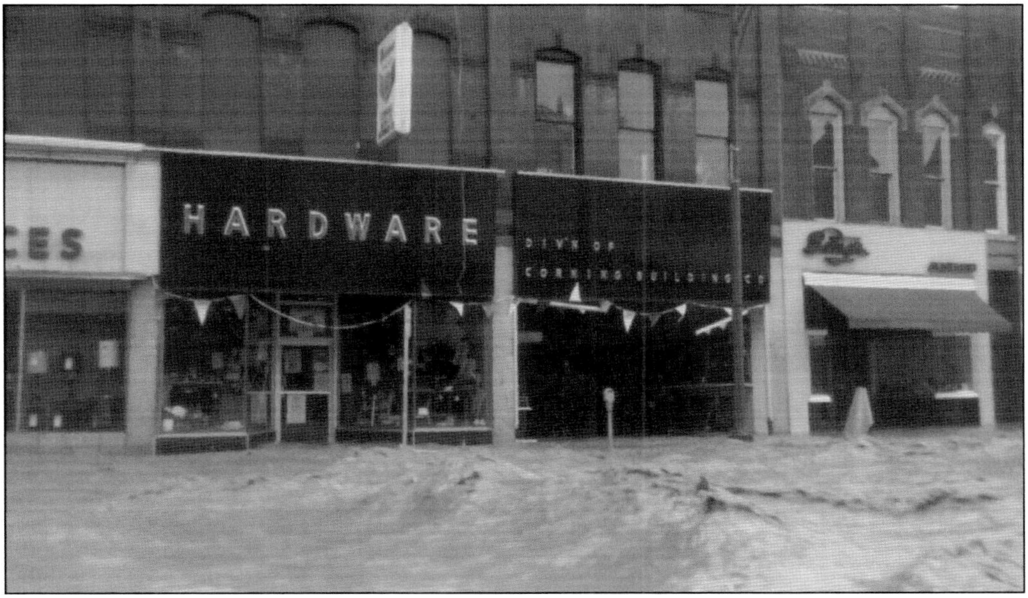

Corning's Market Street shopping district on the Southside was one of the first to be hit and one of the worst to suffer. Department store owner Bob Rockwell stayed in his business overnight but might as well have gone home. In the morning, he opened the doors and watched $250,000 worth of stock float out, along with the clerks' comfortable shoes. (CPP.)

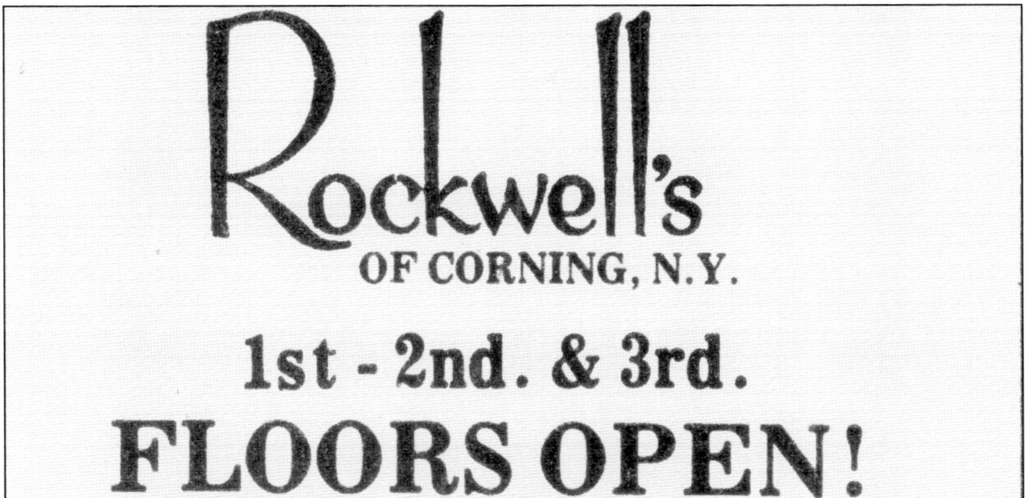

It was not "business as usual," but Bob Rockwell's store was back in action within the week. Rockwell, who died in 2009 at the age of 97, personally operated a retail establishment on Market Street almost to the end—he was very much the dean of Corning's business community. (SCHS.)

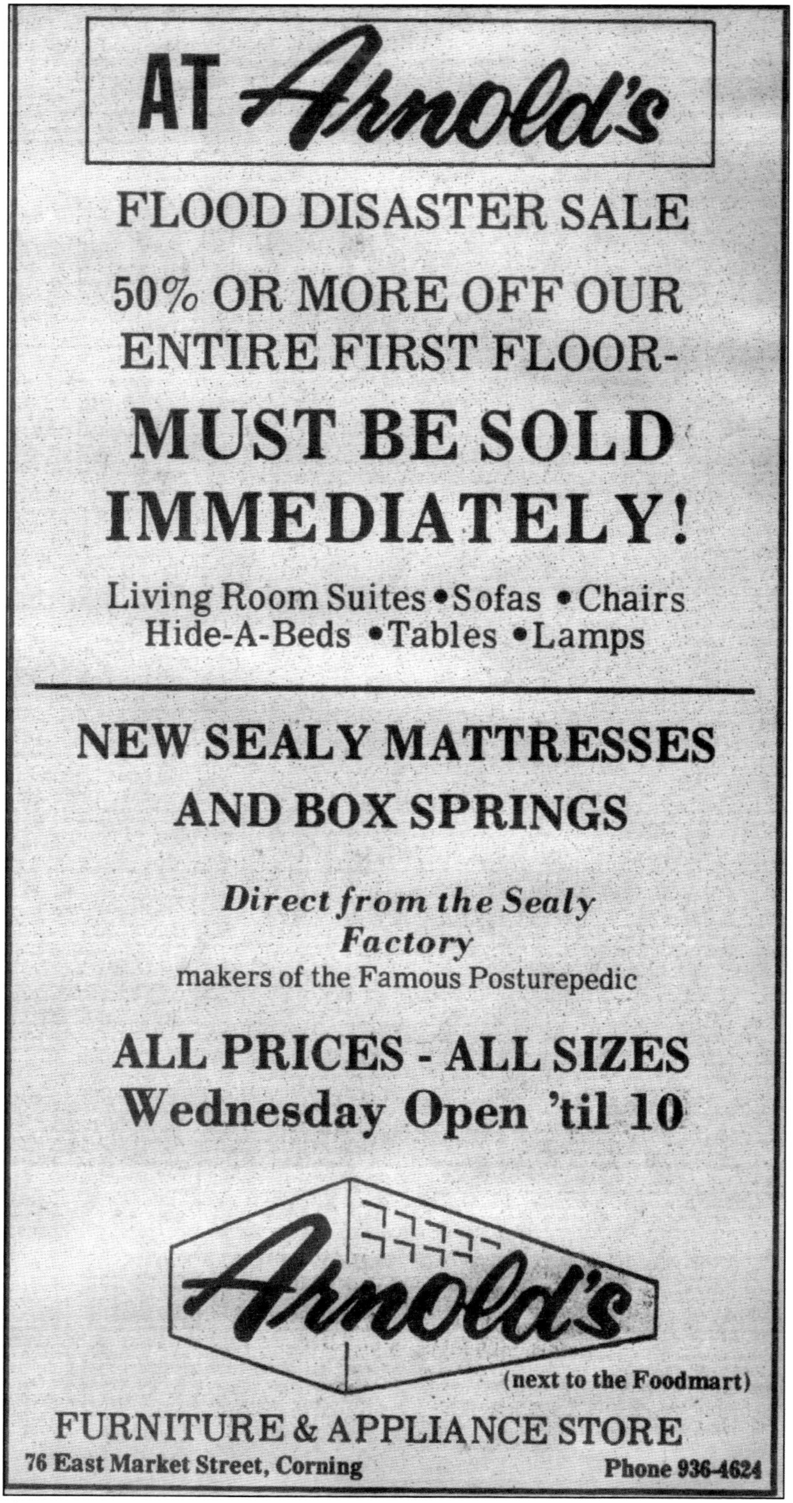

Hundreds of owners and operators had to struggle to save their businesses, even as they strove to restore their homes. (SCHS.)

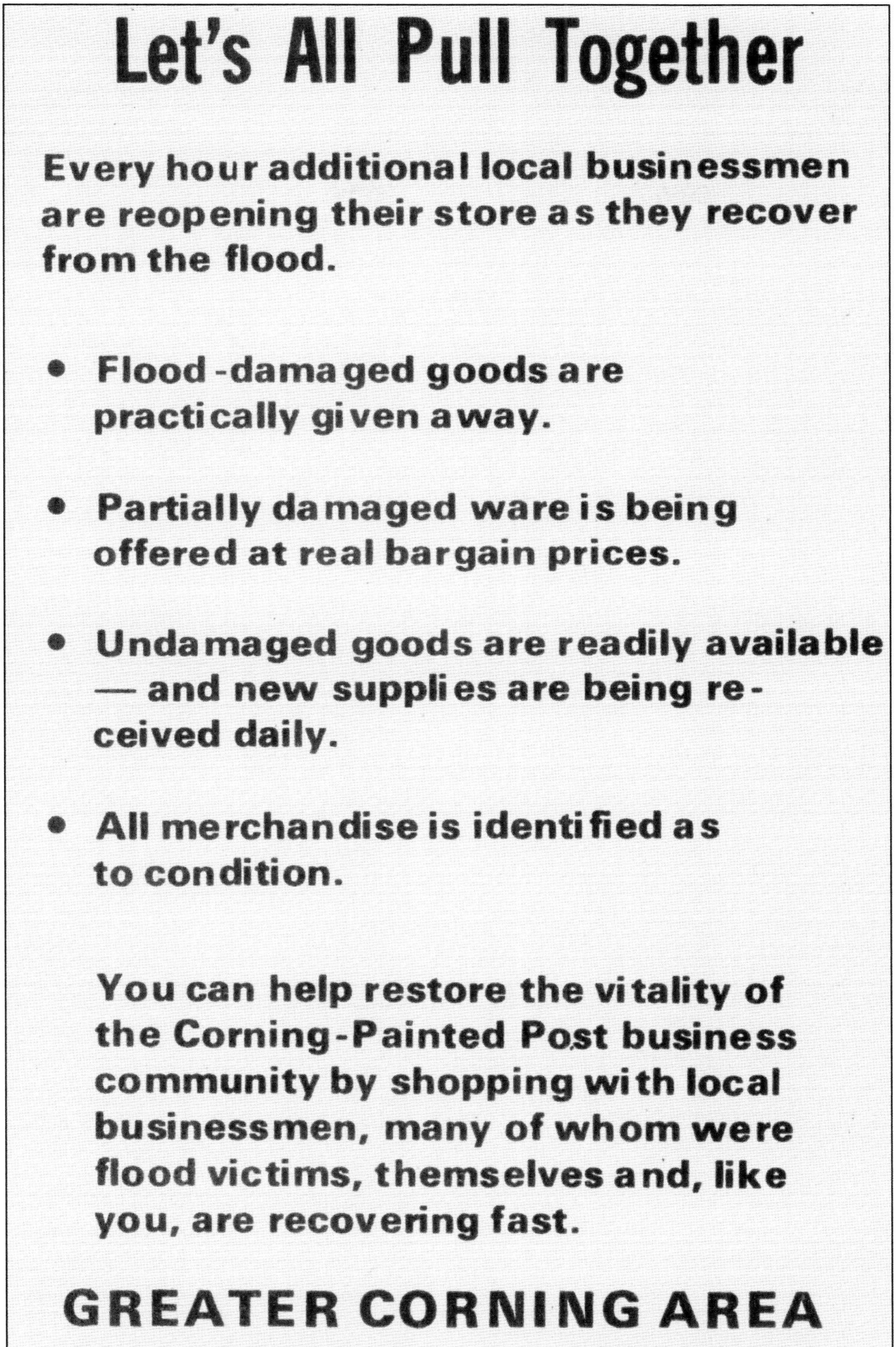

Many could not help but wonder if the city and its commercial life would survive. The answer was yes, but that gratifying fact would take years to become clear. (SCHS.)

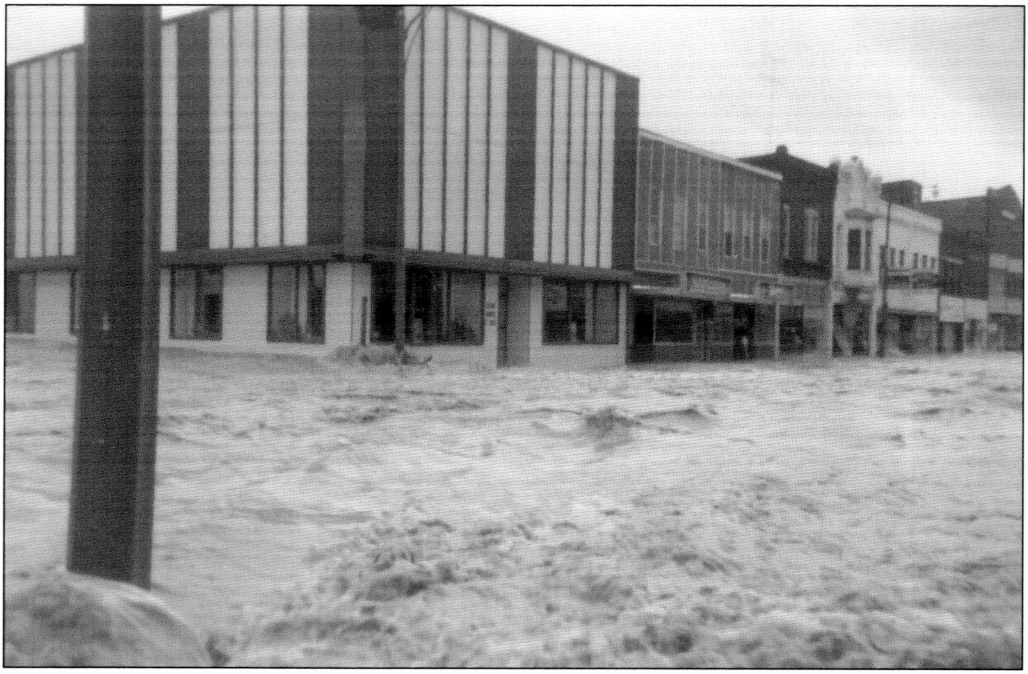

When the waters overflowed, it was not just a gentle rise. That river came up in a rush, fast and dangerous. This scene was captured at Market and Cedar Streets, just below today's Rockwell Museum of Western Art. (CPP.)

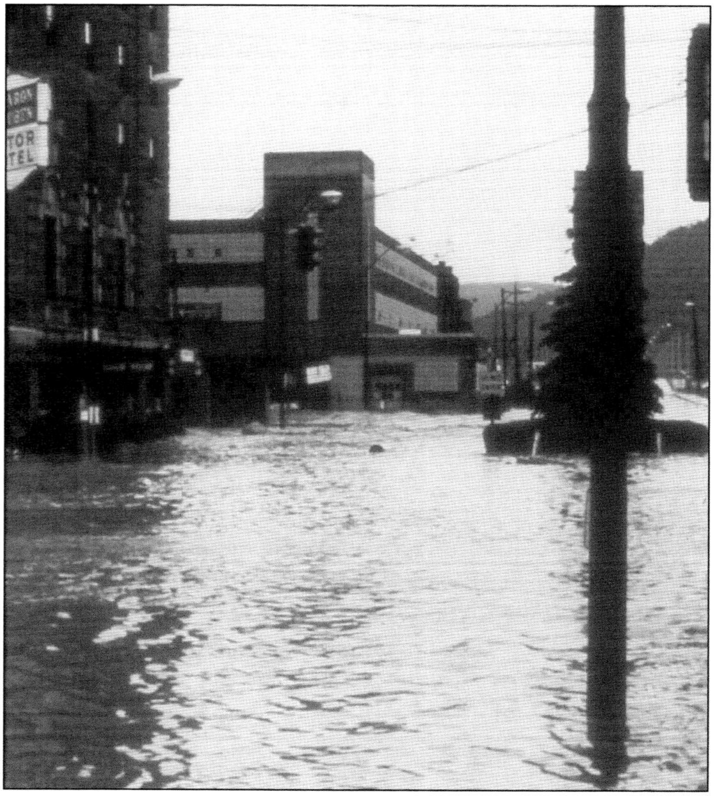

The old Baron Steuben Building still stands by the Centerway Square, but a parking garage now takes the place of the Glass Works production facilities in the background. The landmark Centerway Bridge is now for pedestrians only. The flood weakened it too much for heavy traffic. Vehicular traffic uses a new bridge several blocks down on Cedar Street. (RET.)

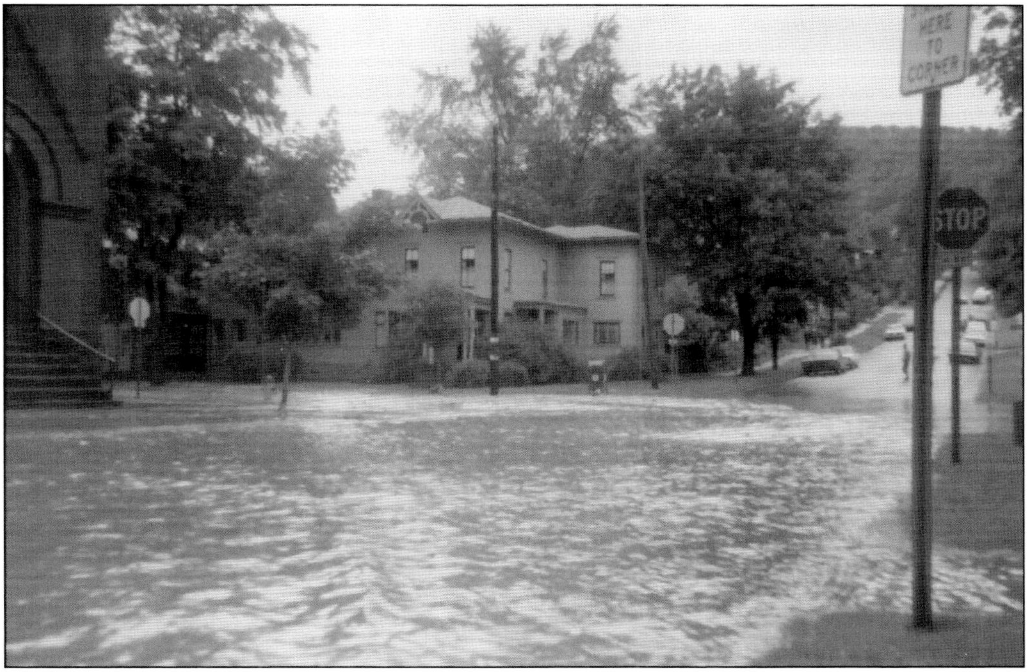

Residential districts were not doing any better. "The Flat" in Corning, both the Northside and the Market Street–Denison Parkway section of the Southside, was flooded. "The Hill," seen rising here on the Southside, was spared the worst of it. This is the First United Methodist Church on Cedar Street. (CPP.)

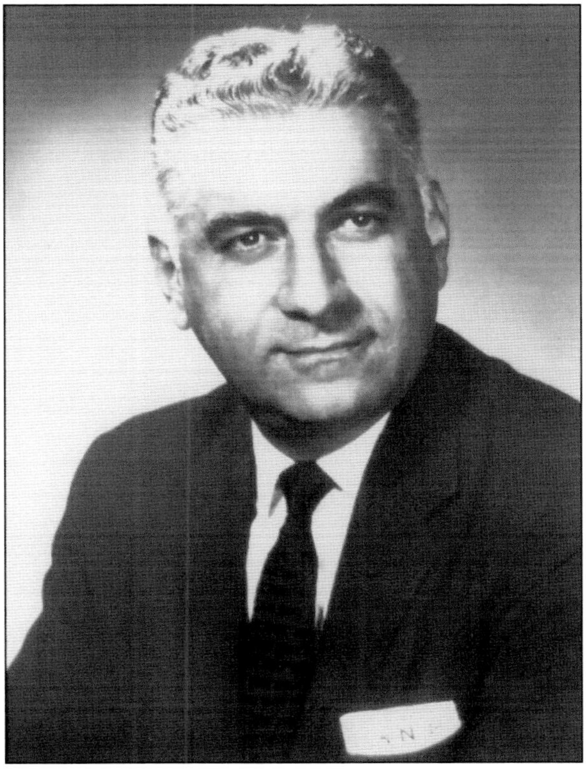

The river rose quickly, and it rose overnight, while many folks were sleeping. Sirens and whistles wailed, and Mayor Joseph J. Nasser (shown here) sent local National Guardsmen out to bang on doors and get the sleepers moving. A hundred people attending a graduation party wound up on the roof of the St. Vincent's School. (CoC.)

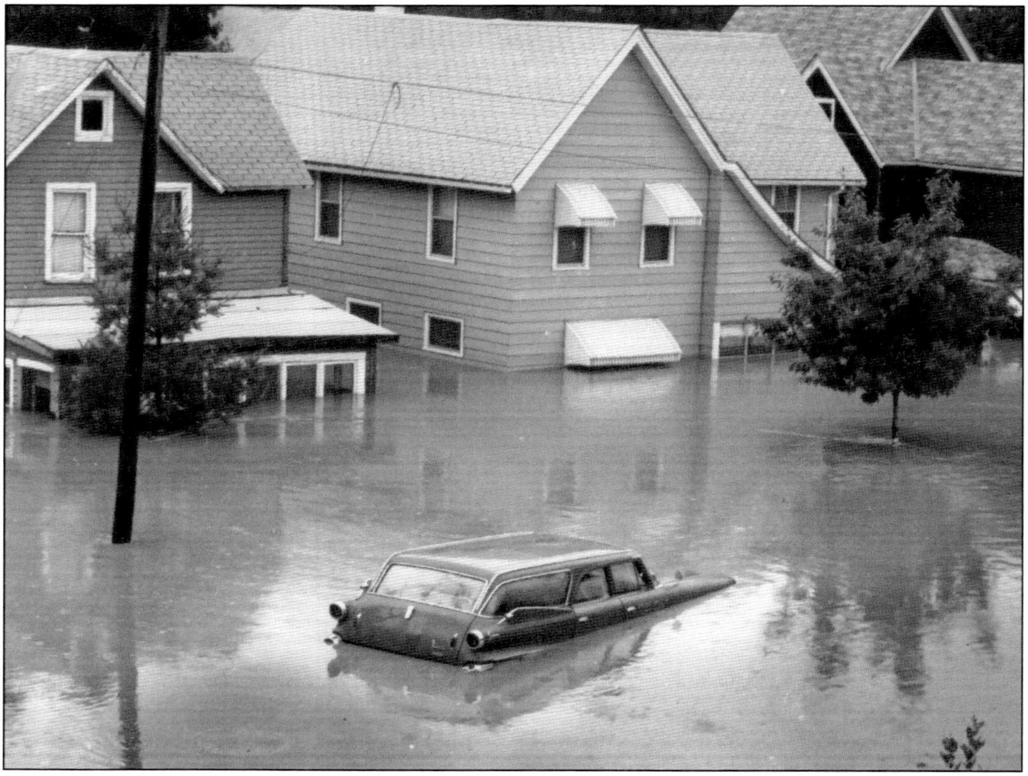

Either this station wagon on Bridge Street (near the Erie station) was flooded before the owners realized, or they got caught in the flood and had to abandon it. Notice how deeply the houses are inundated. Notice also that the wagon has fins, though they are much more understated than they would have been a decade earlier. (CPP.)

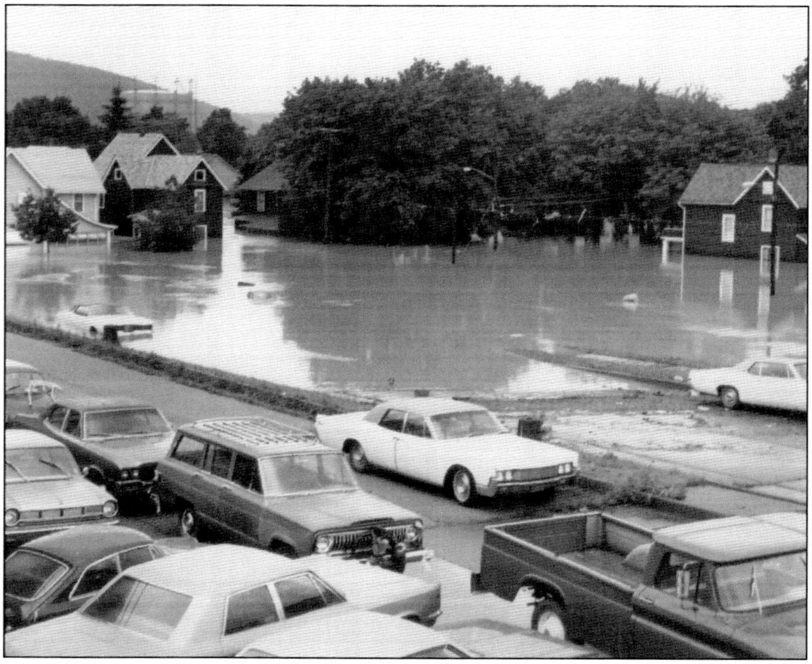

Many worried residents started moving their vehicles to higher ground during the night—though one sedan was not moved far enough. About 1,200 vehicles were damaged or destroyed. This scene is near the Erie station. (CPP.)

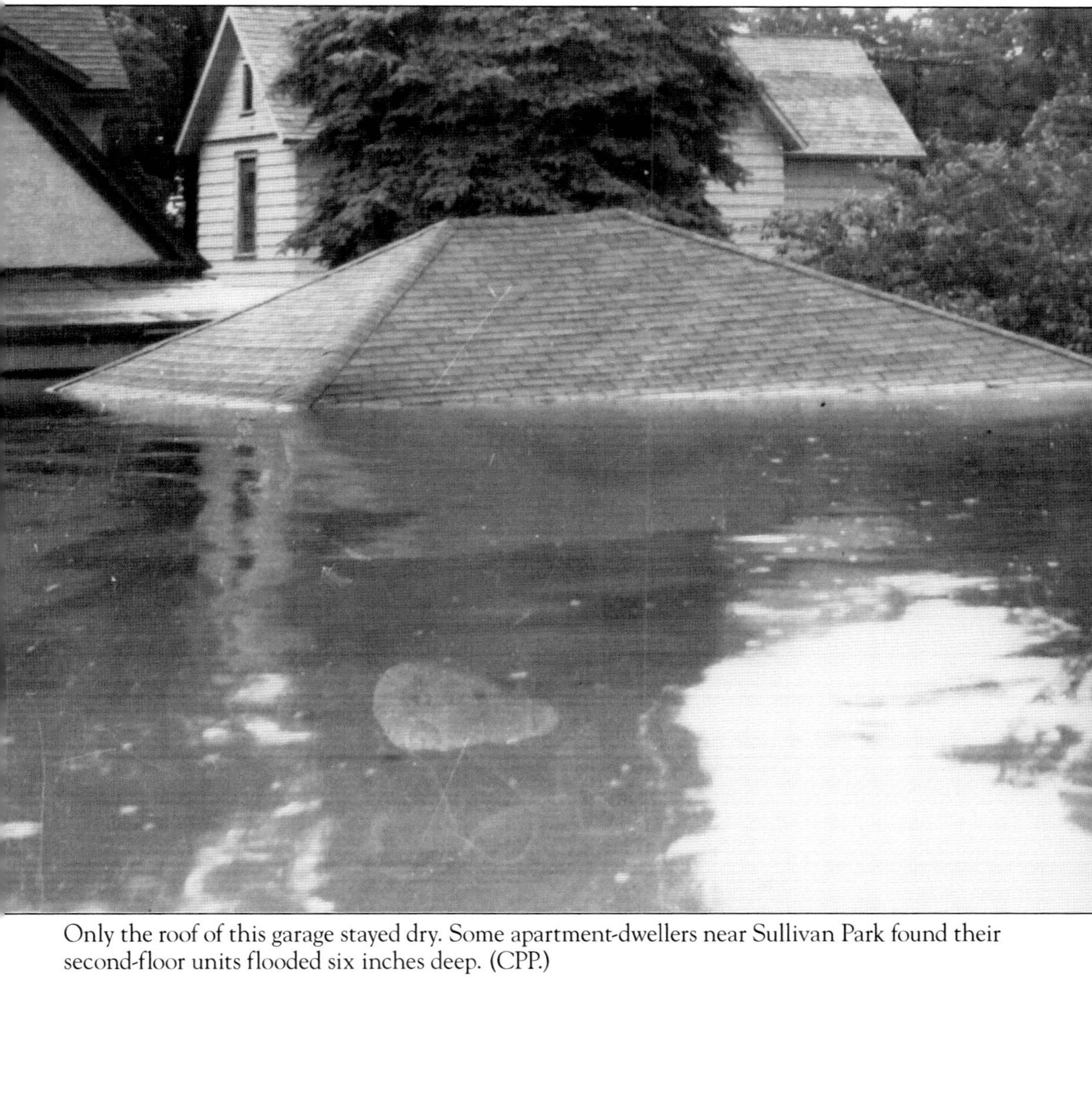

Only the roof of this garage stayed dry. Some apartment-dwellers near Sullivan Park found their second-floor units flooded six inches deep. (CPP.)

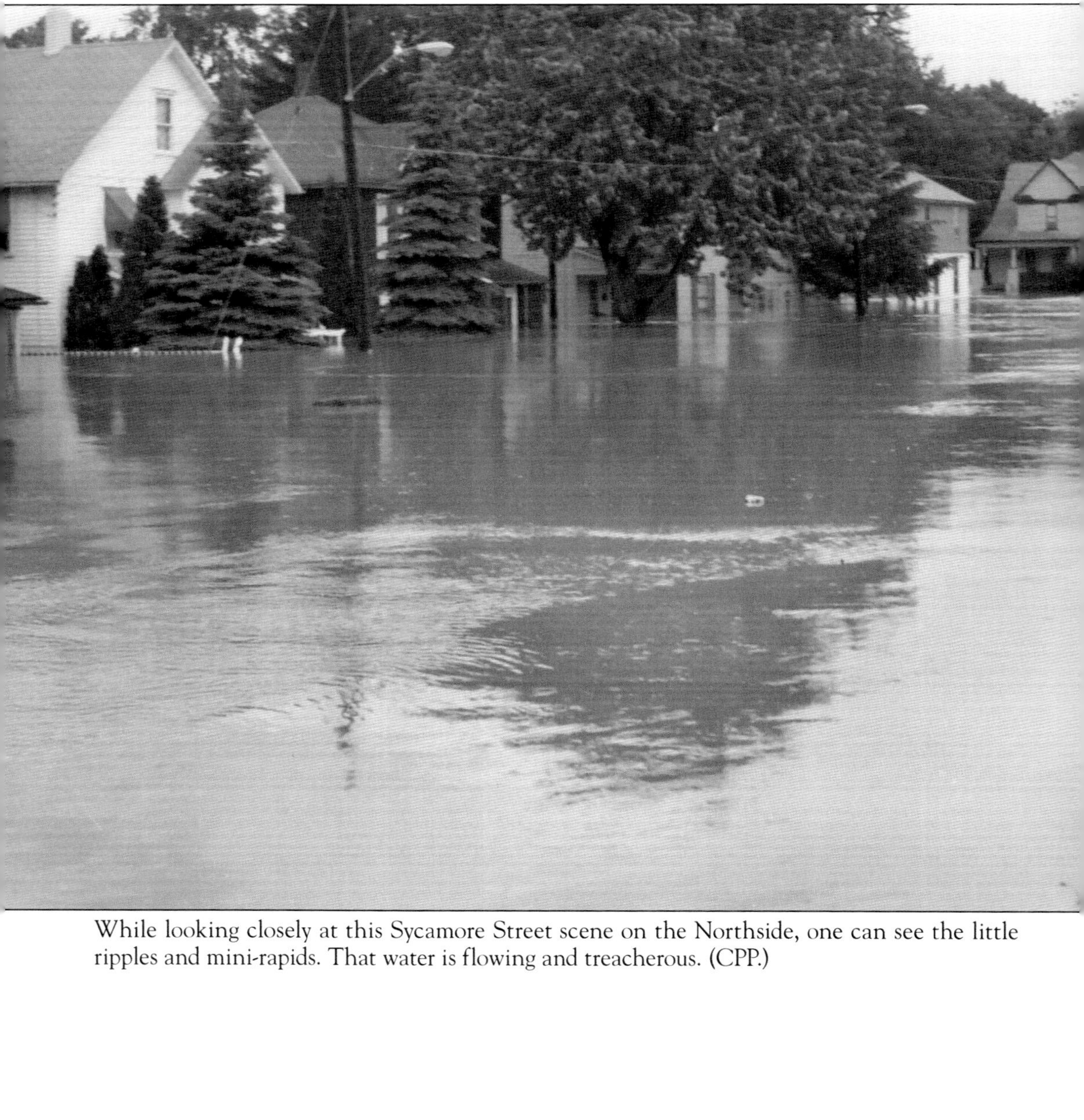

While looking closely at this Sycamore Street scene on the Northside, one can see the little ripples and mini-rapids. That water is flowing and treacherous. (CPP.)

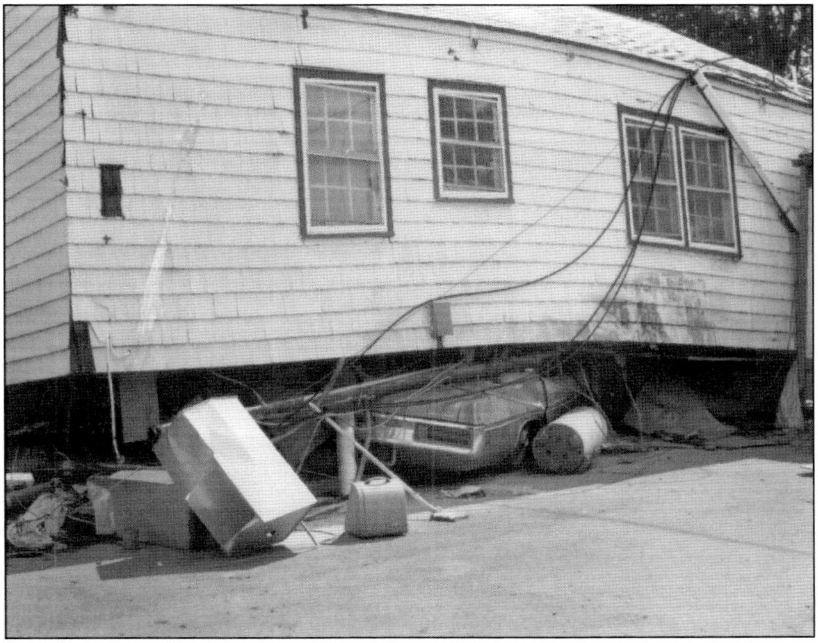

This house in the Houghton Plat (essentially a peninsula with the Chemung on one side and Post Creek on the other) drifted far enough to crush a car. (CPP.)

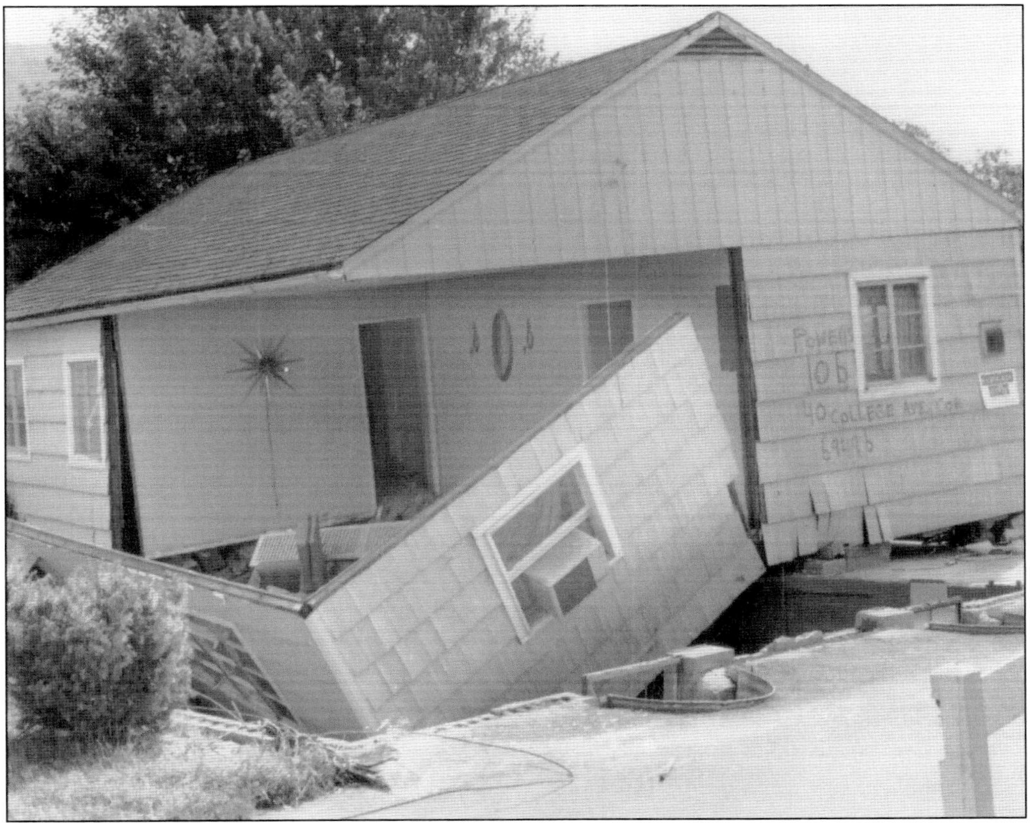

"Condemned Unsafe" (notice the small placard on the right) seems a sad-but-solid evaluation. About 1,500 homes met a similar fate. College Avenue in the unincorporated settlement of Gibson is near the Narrows Creek. The wall clock reflects 1960s design and tastes. (CPP.)

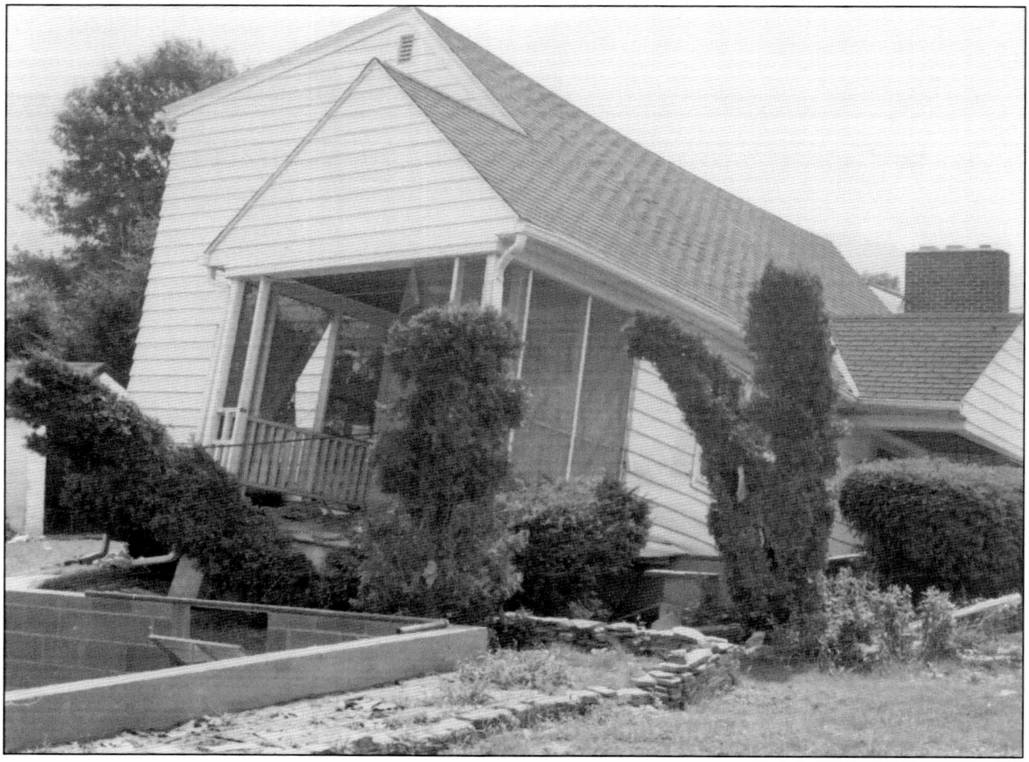

Has this house in the Houghton Plat come off its moorings from the foundation on the left or did that once anchor an entirely different dwelling? Over 400 homes in the Corning area were demolished or floated off, including a few that just vanished altogether. (CPP.)

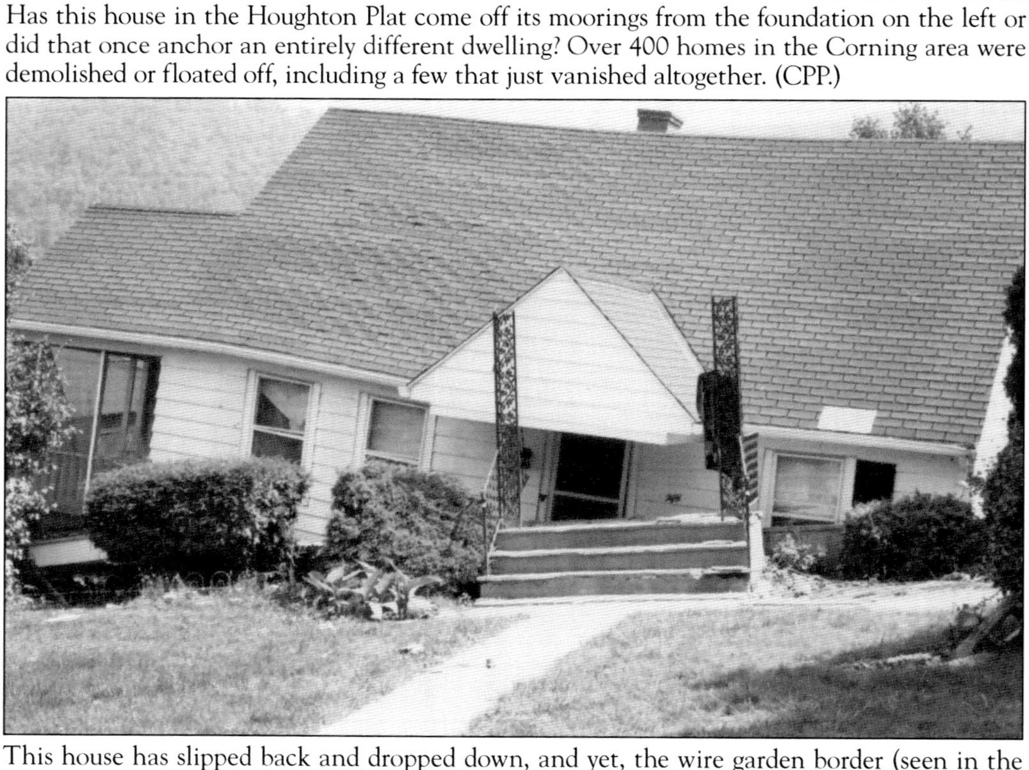

This house has slipped back and dropped down, and yet, the wire garden border (seen in the lower-left corner) has survived it all and is still in place. (CPP.)

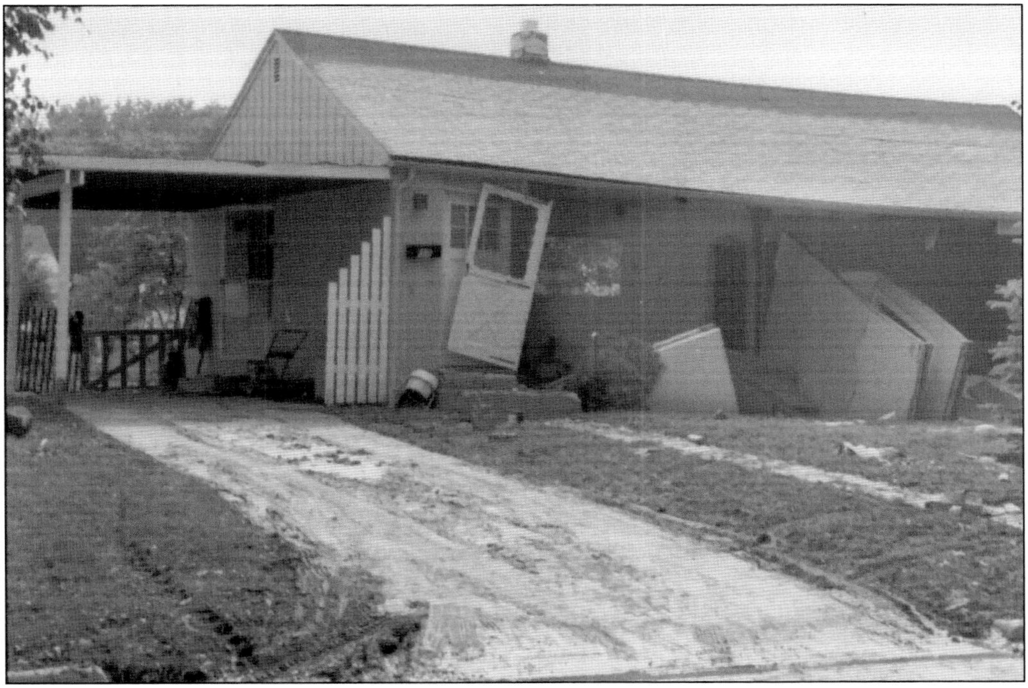

Cleanup work seems to have already begun at this Houghton Plat home; notice the gas can on the lawn and the lawn mower under the carport. Just around Corning, some 2,500 homes that survived were damaged. Many would take a year or more of hard work to make them habitable again. (CPP.)

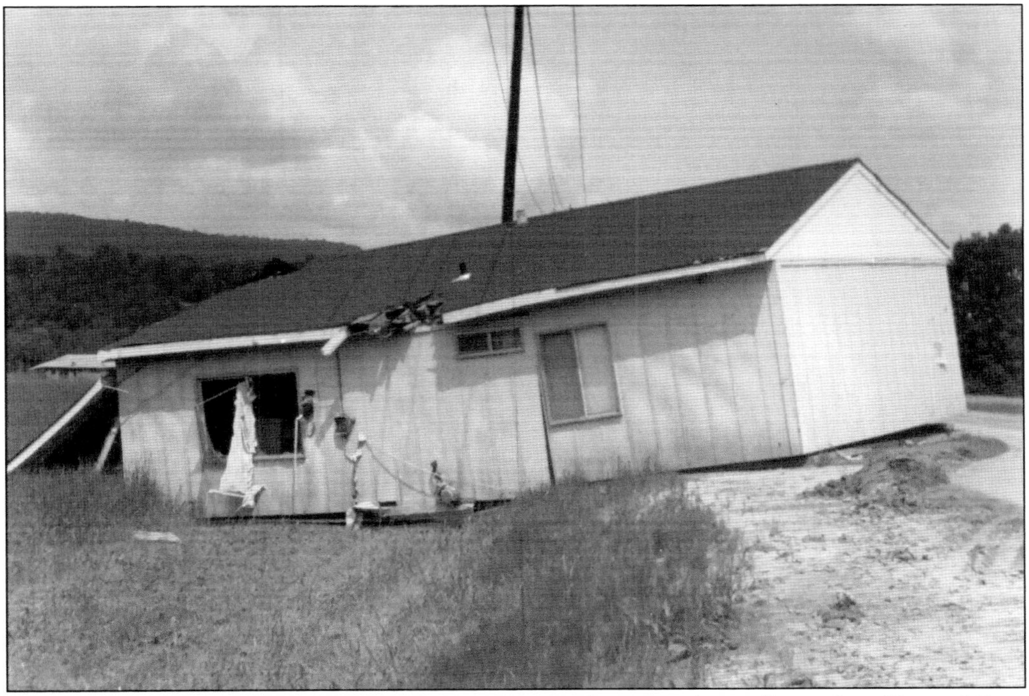

Wherever this structure began its wanderings, it wound up near the traffic circle in Painted Post. It looks as though the utility pole brought it to a halt. (CPP.)

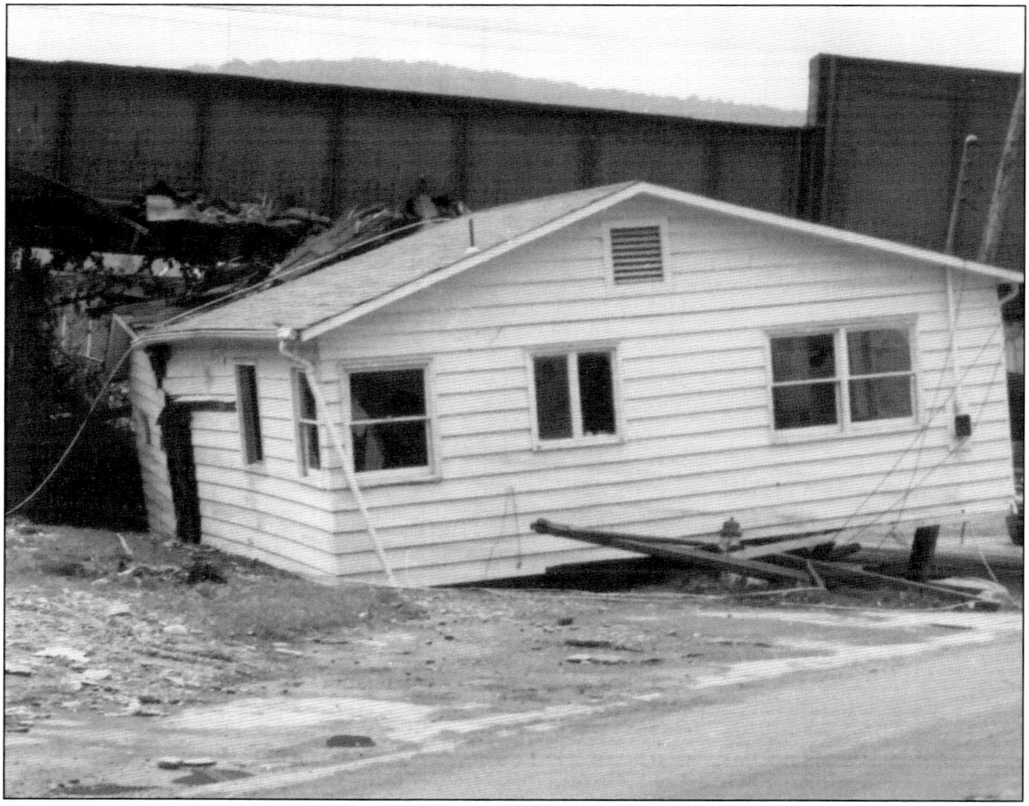

This Riverside house jammed itself into and under the railroad overpass. (CPP.)

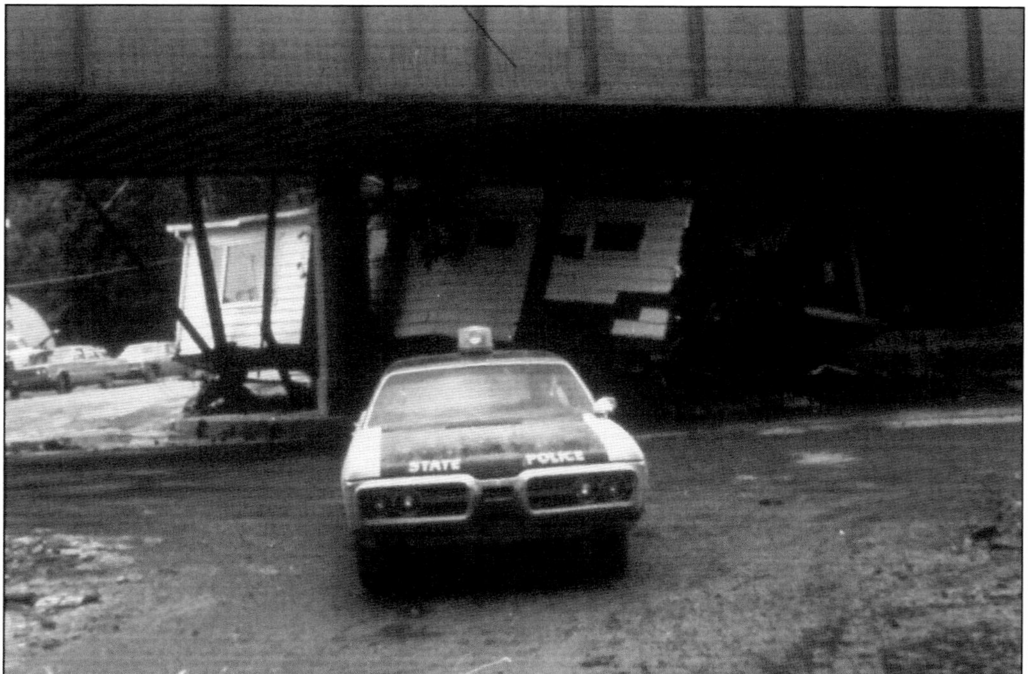

Neither the house nor the bridge benefited from this new arrangement. (RET.)

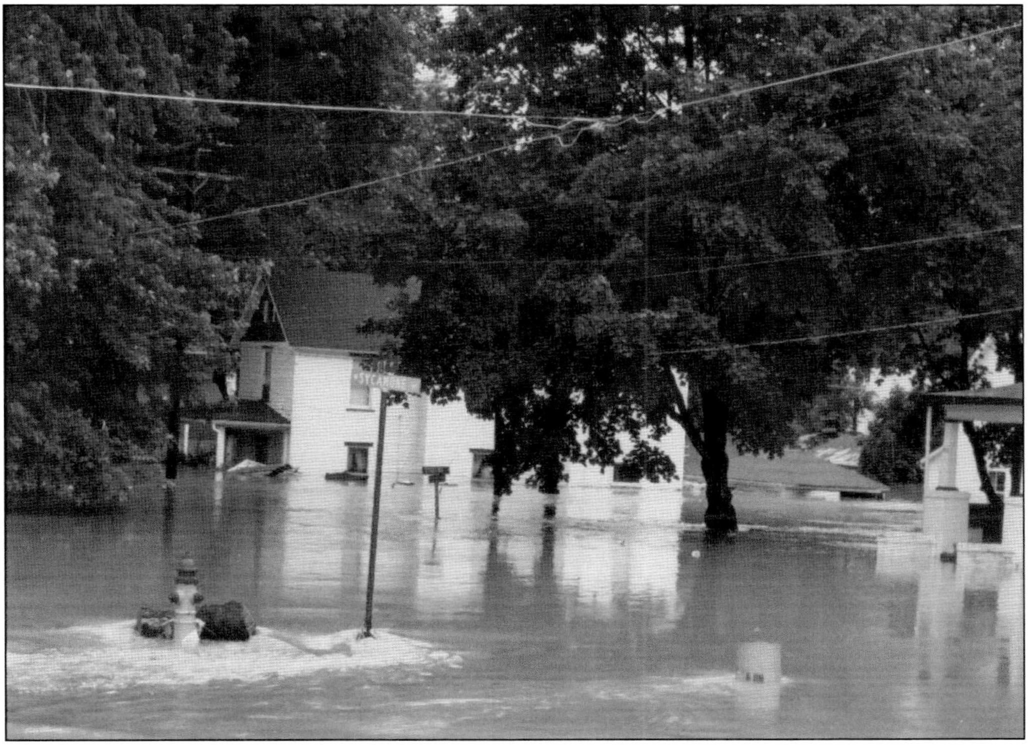

These houses at Sly and Sycamore Streets in the city of Corning are three-quarters of a mile away from the river—well past the Glass Works headquarters, Glass Center, several schools, what is now the Patterson Inn Museum, and hundreds of other homes. (CPP.)

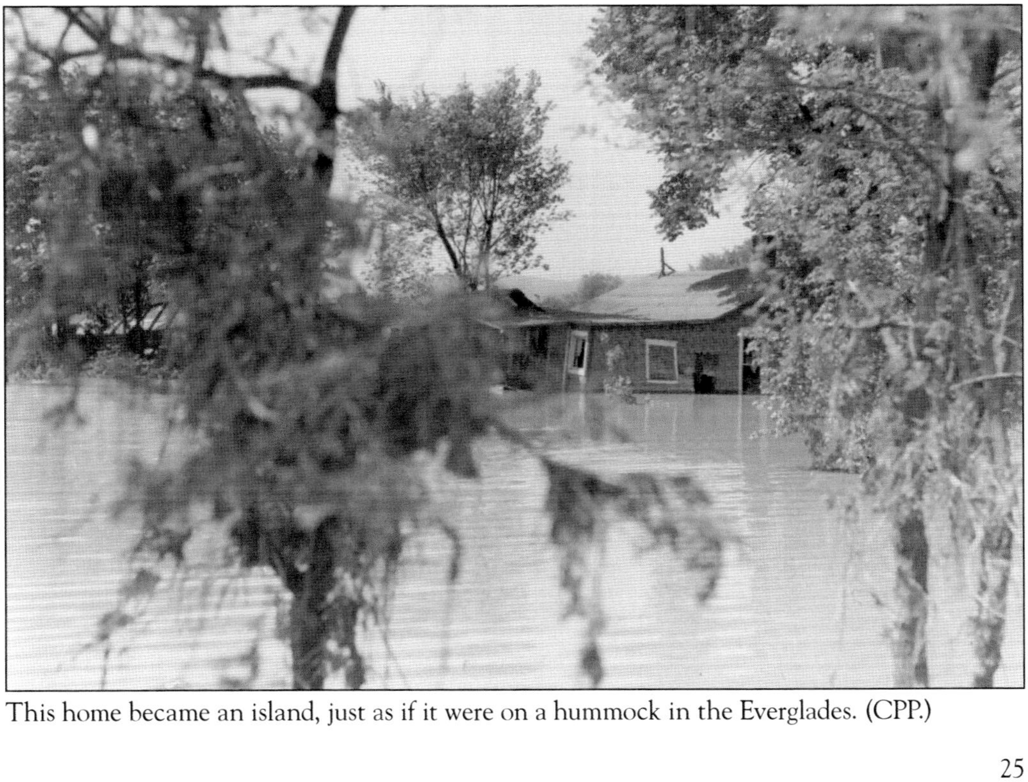

This home became an island, just as if it were on a hummock in the Everglades. (CPP.)

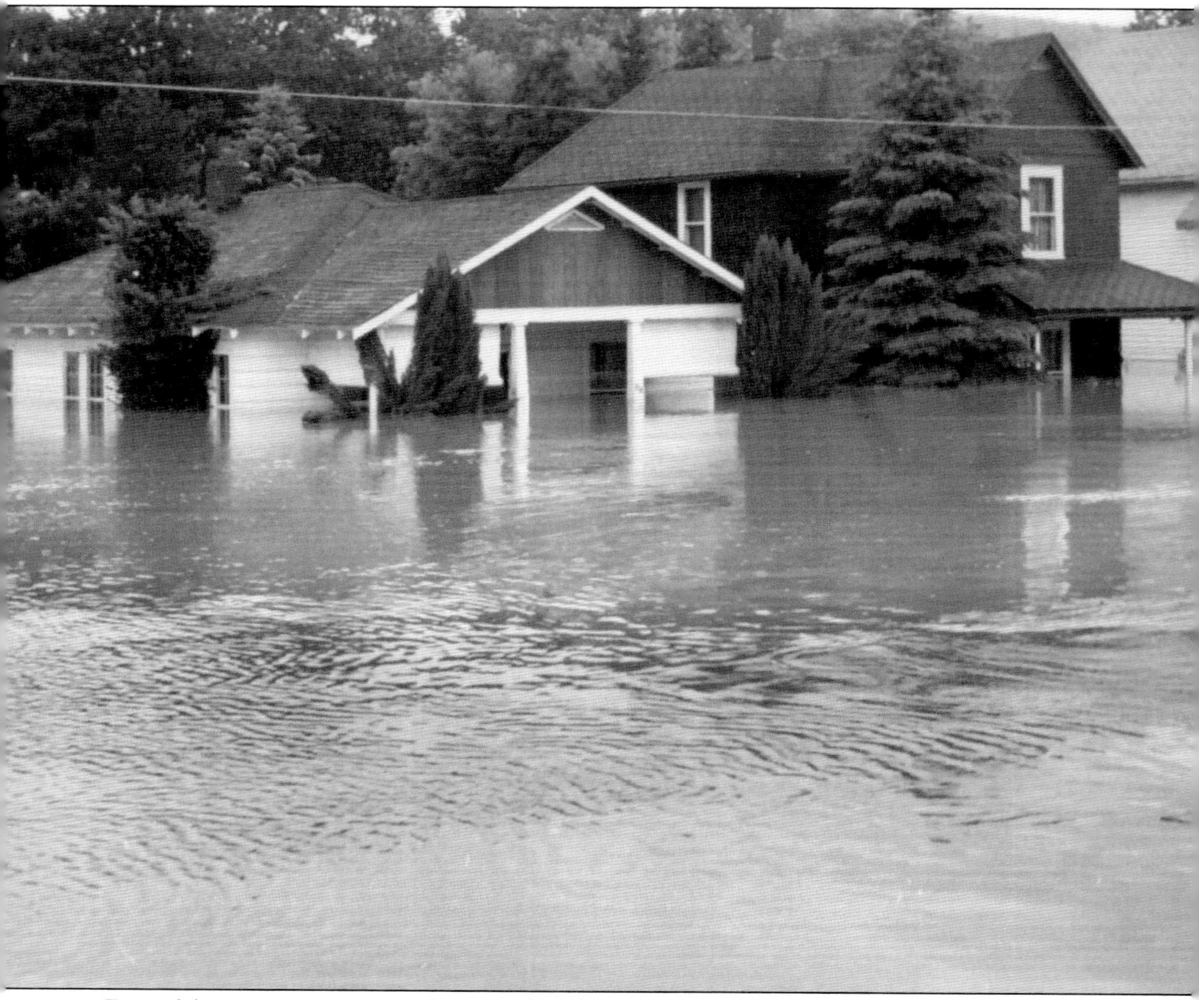

Even if the structures remained sound, these homeowners and occupants were going to lose most or all of their possessions. Some scrubbed and boiled compulsively, but homeowners and antique dealers around Corning all testify that "flood mud" has a unique consistency, color, and smell. Some people are still finding it in the oddest places.

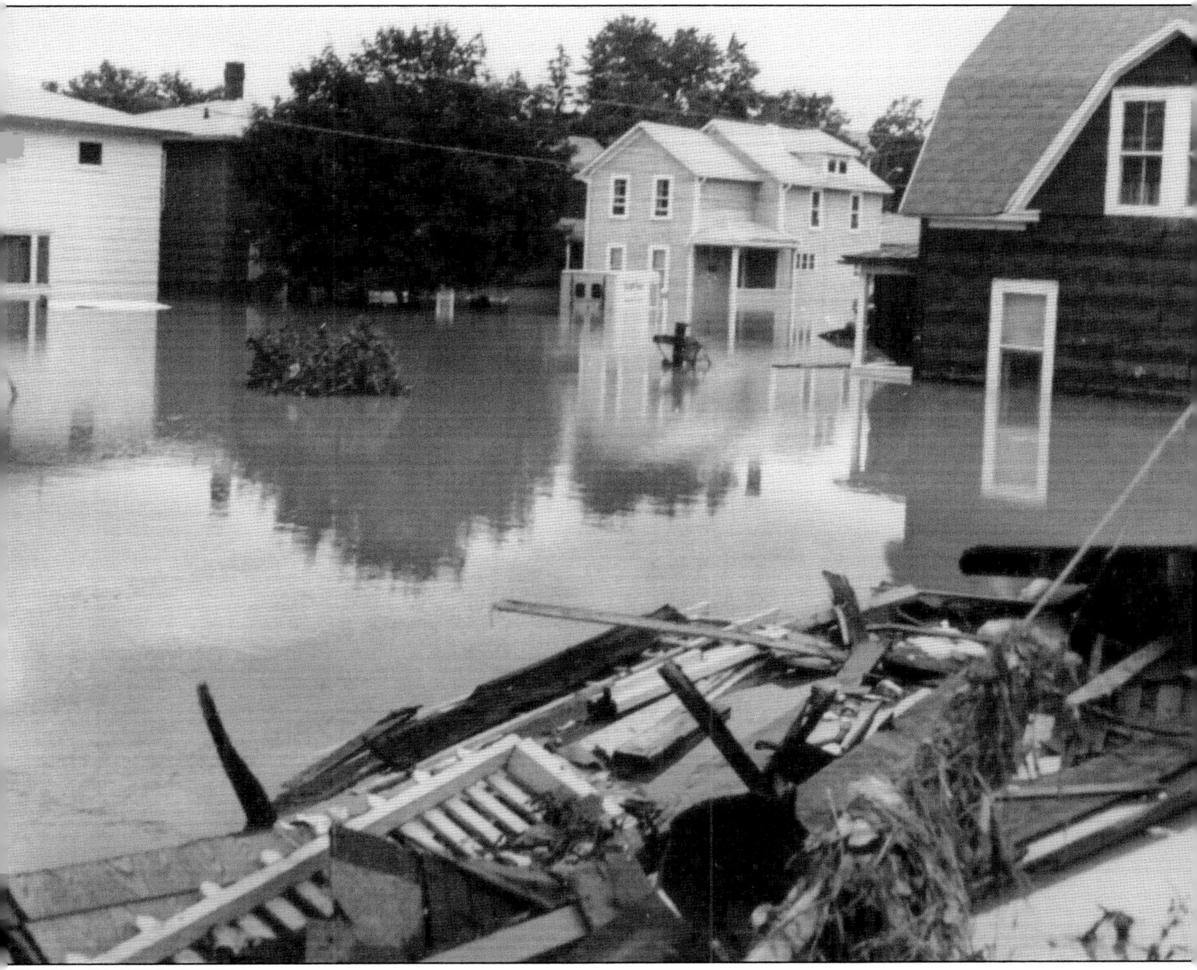

This view is near the old Centerway Motel, not far from Corning's business and shopping district. Notice the half-submerged commercial van in the background. (CPP.)

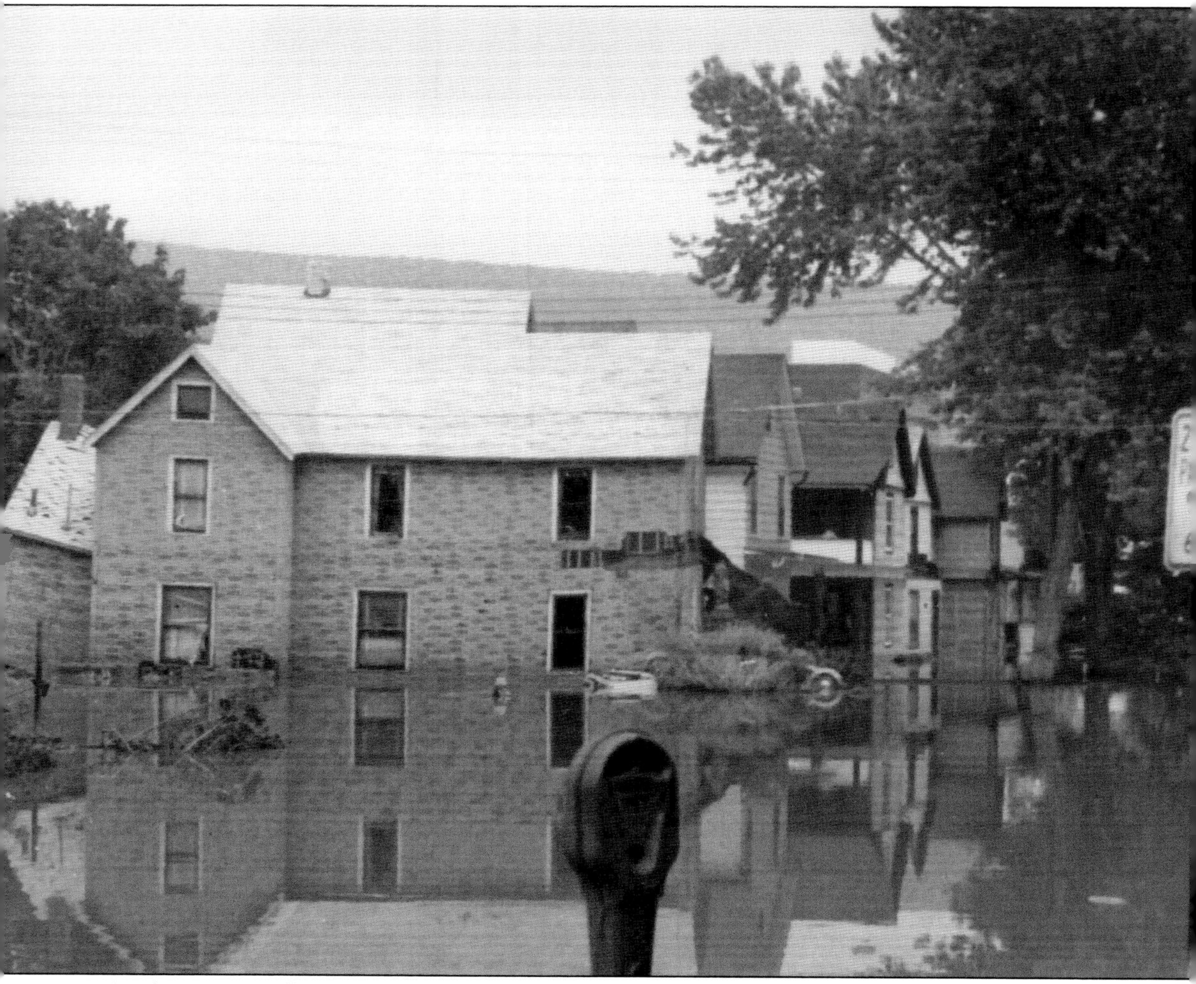

As the water stills, this scene near East William and Ferris Streets in Corning's Northside looks peaceful, almost beautiful. The impression is deceptive, though. That water is still dangerous. (CPP.)

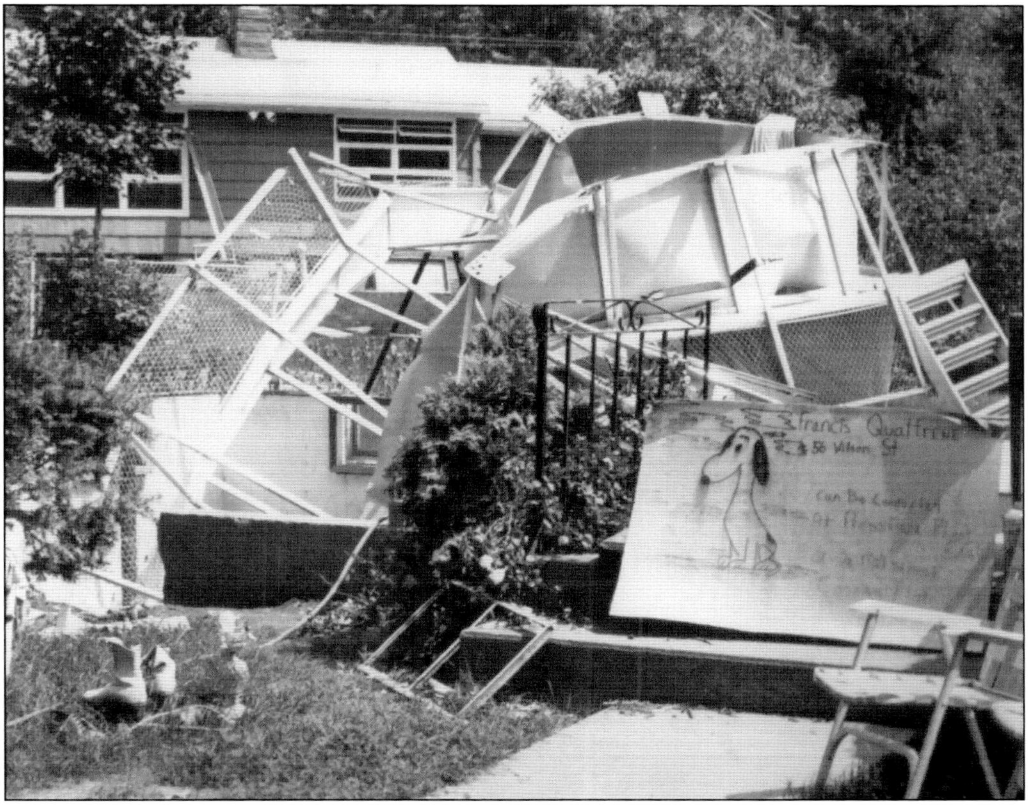

Snoopy had become outstandingly popular by 1972; it is no surprise that people turned to the world-famous beagle for comfort. Eerily imitating war refugees, this Wilson Street family has posted contact points at the Glass Works pressware plant and in Coopers Plains on the town line with Campbell, which was spared the worst of the flooding. Notice the boots and the lawn chair. With grim irony, the wreckage may be from an aboveground pool. (CPP.)

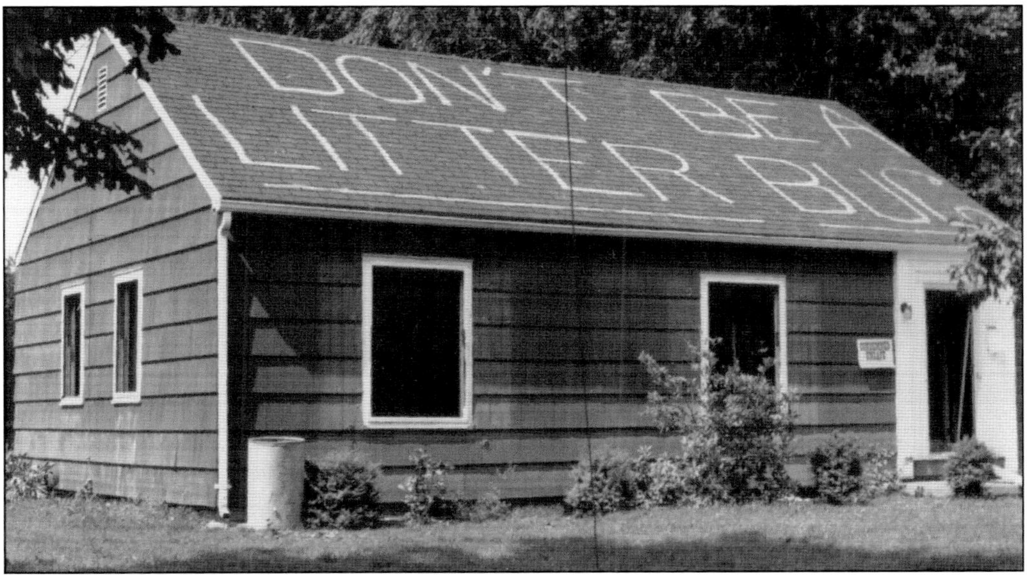

This owner in the Houghton Plat also permitted himself an indulgence of whimsy. (CPP.)

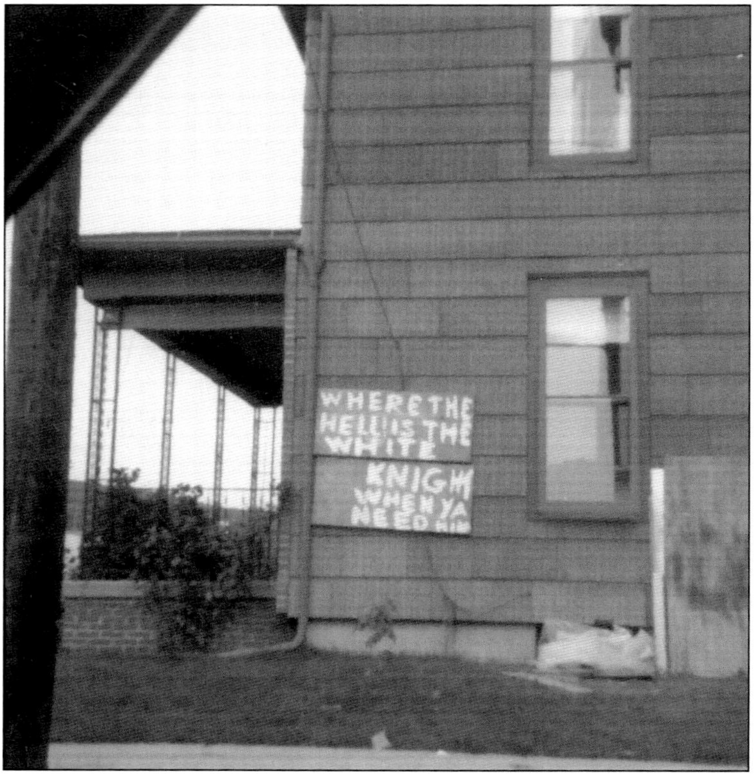

This Southside resident is calling on the White Knight, an Ajax laundry detergent television commercial character who galloped through towns cleaning things up ("Stronger than dirt!") with his magical jousting lance. (AB.)

It looks as though this Ferris Street home will be saved, but the owners have pitched out their possessions—some, no doubt, prized treasures—relentlessly. The garage also looks like a total loss. (CPP.)

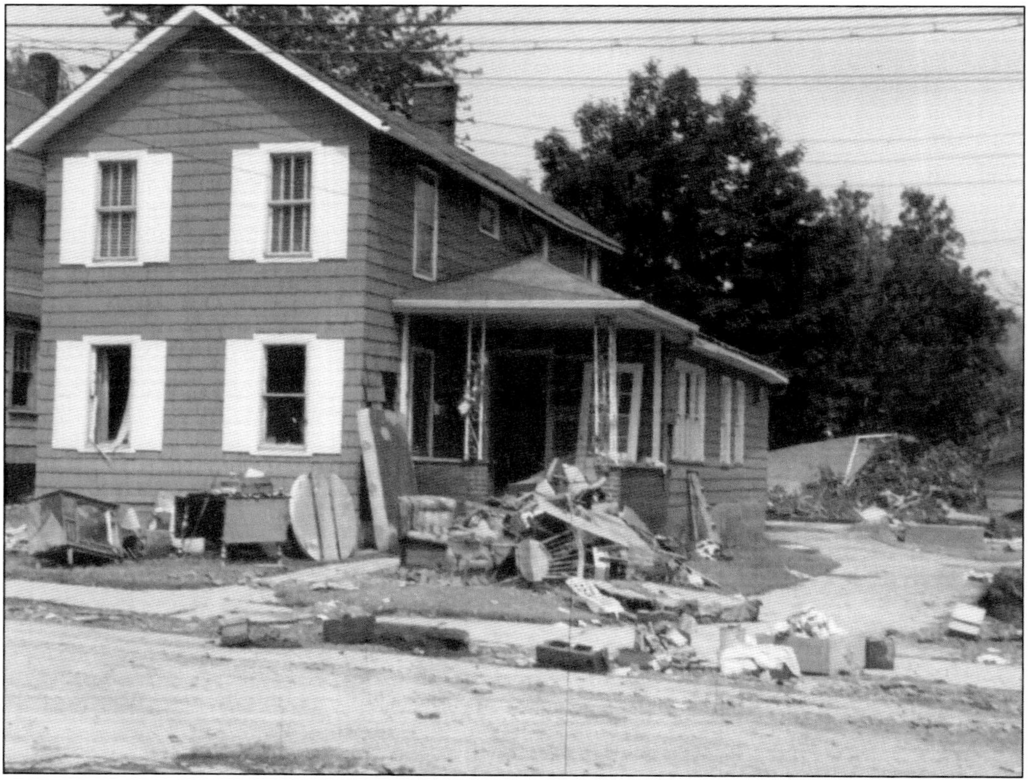

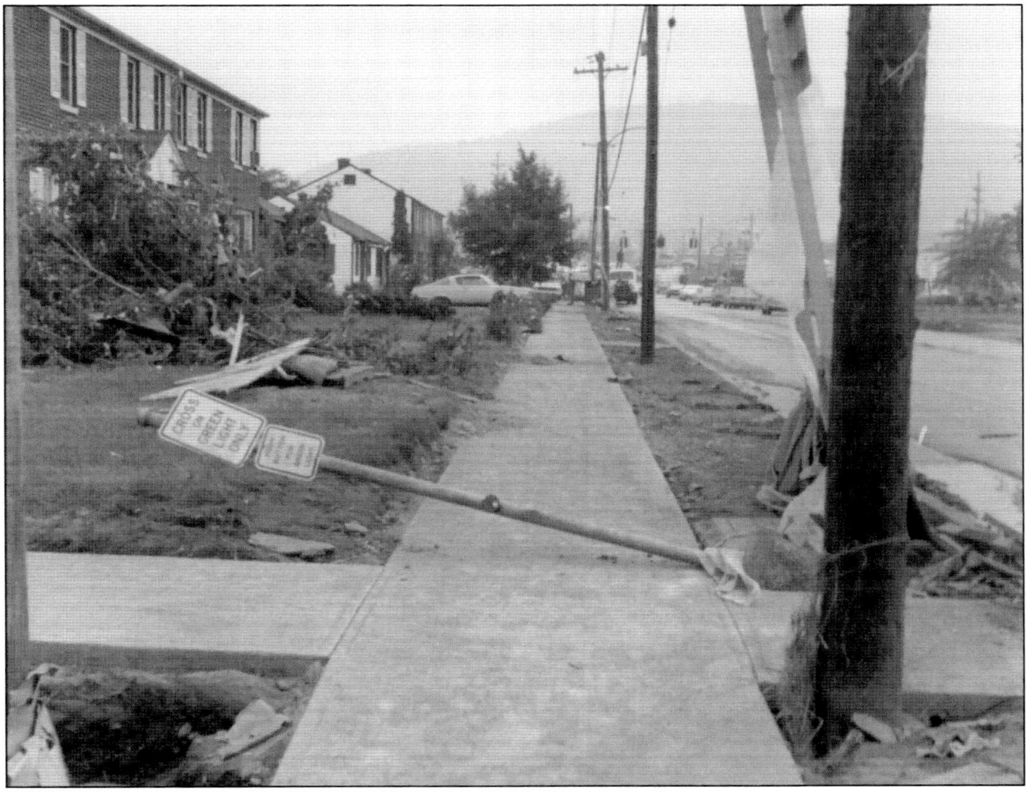

These town houses along the Centerway are still standing, and the street is starting to flow with traffic instead of water; however, plenty of work still lies ahead. (CPP.)

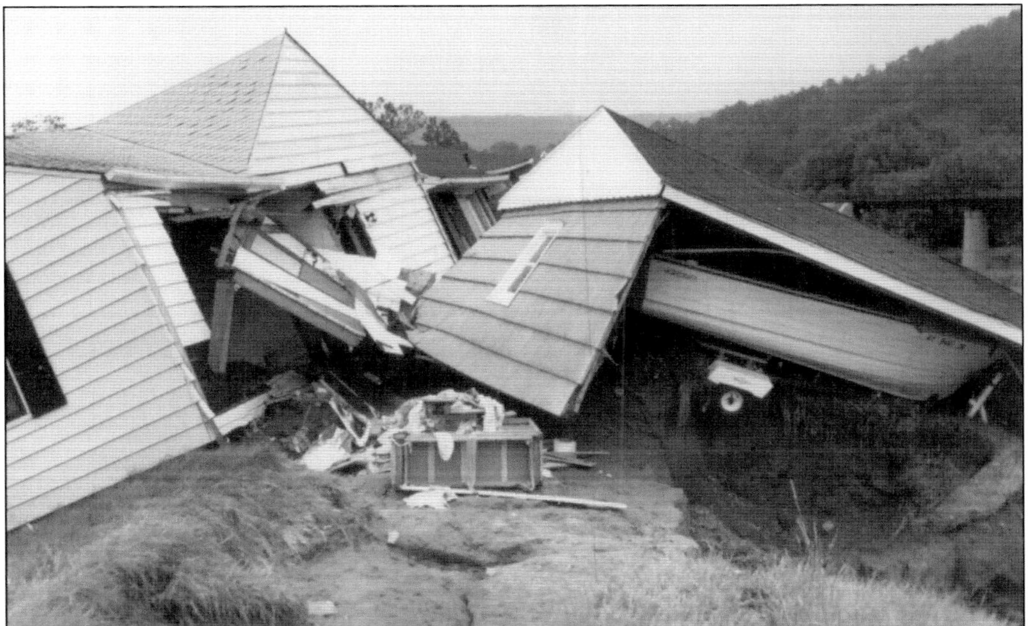

With a little bit more warning, that boat could have come in handy. Notice the Gibson Bridge in the background. (CPP.)

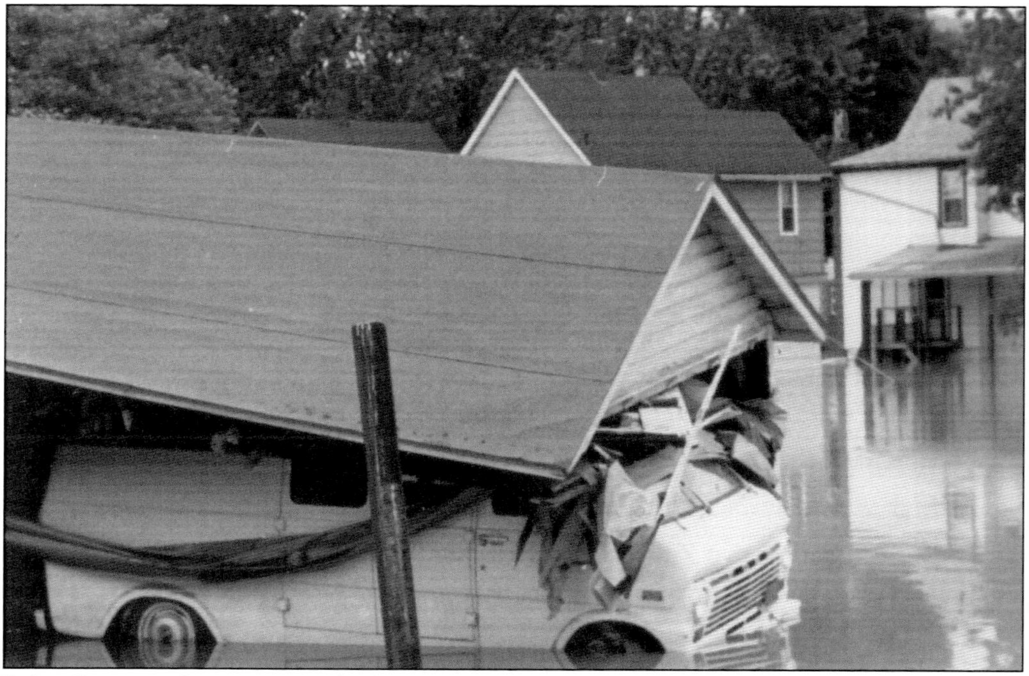

Baker Street in Corning's Northside was another inundated neighborhood. (CPP.)

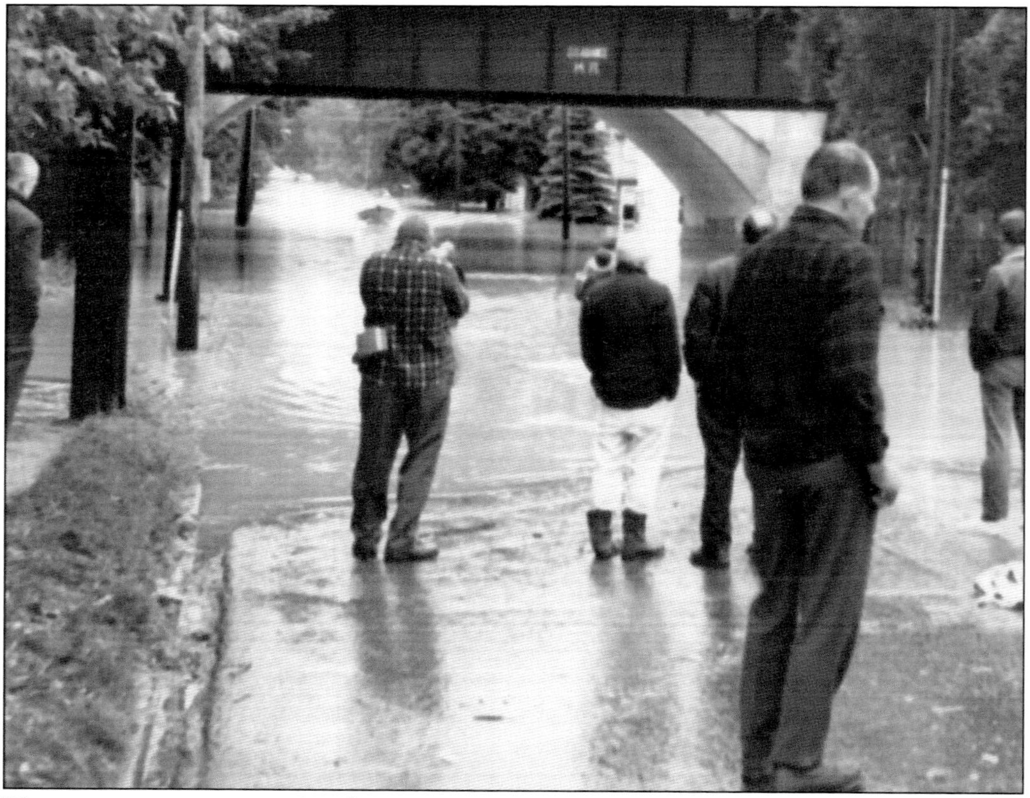

These men are waiting neither for a car nor a train (on the overhead viaduct) but for the boat speeding up Baker Street. (CPP.)

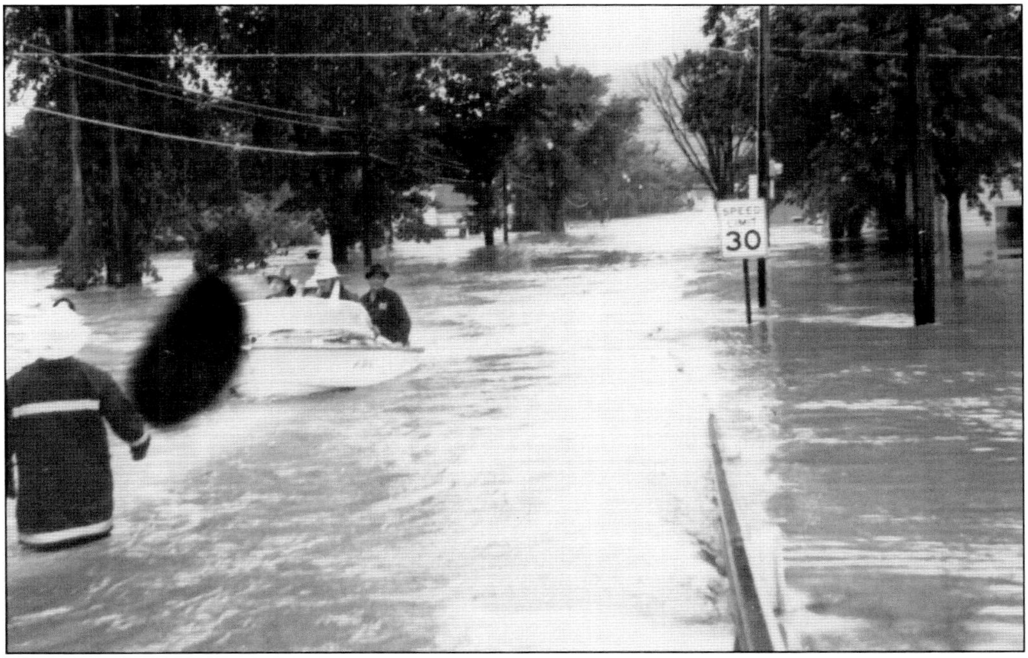

As ever, emergency workers risked their necks to save their neighbors. (CPP.)

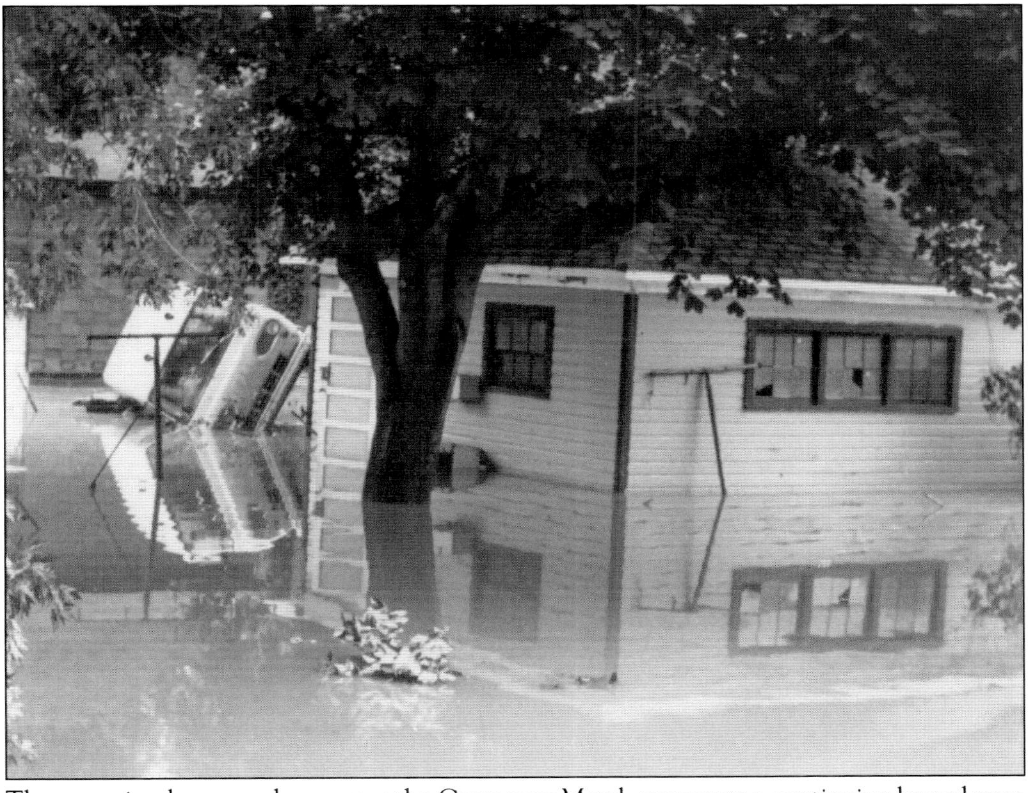

The precariously propped van, near the Centerway Motel, represents a continuing hazard even after the waters drop. For hundreds of miles, the flooded strip is filled with booby traps. Notice the clothesline poles. (CPP.)

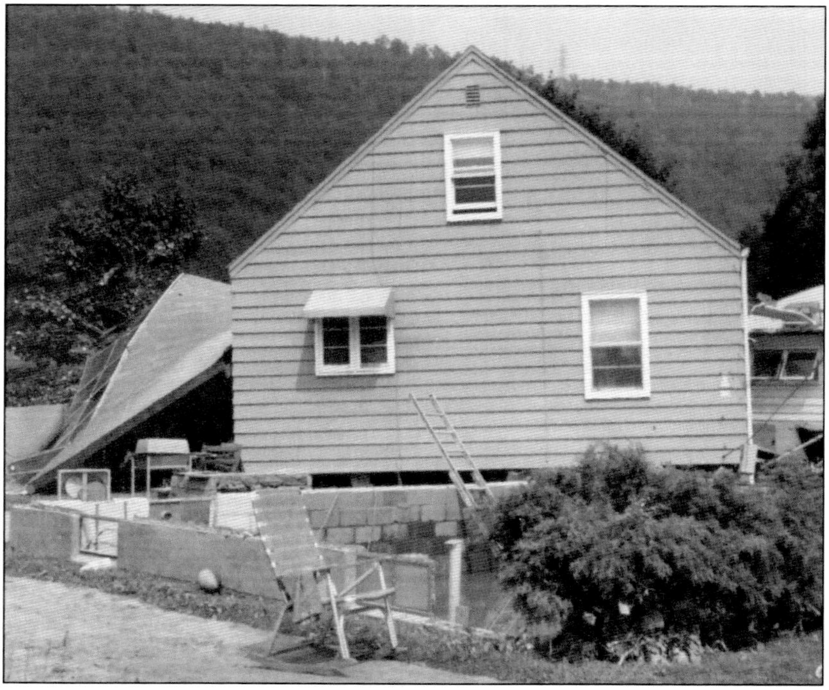

These folks in the Houghton Plat have managed to rescue a grill, a box fan, and a ladder, not to mention the ubiquitous lawn chair. (CPP.)

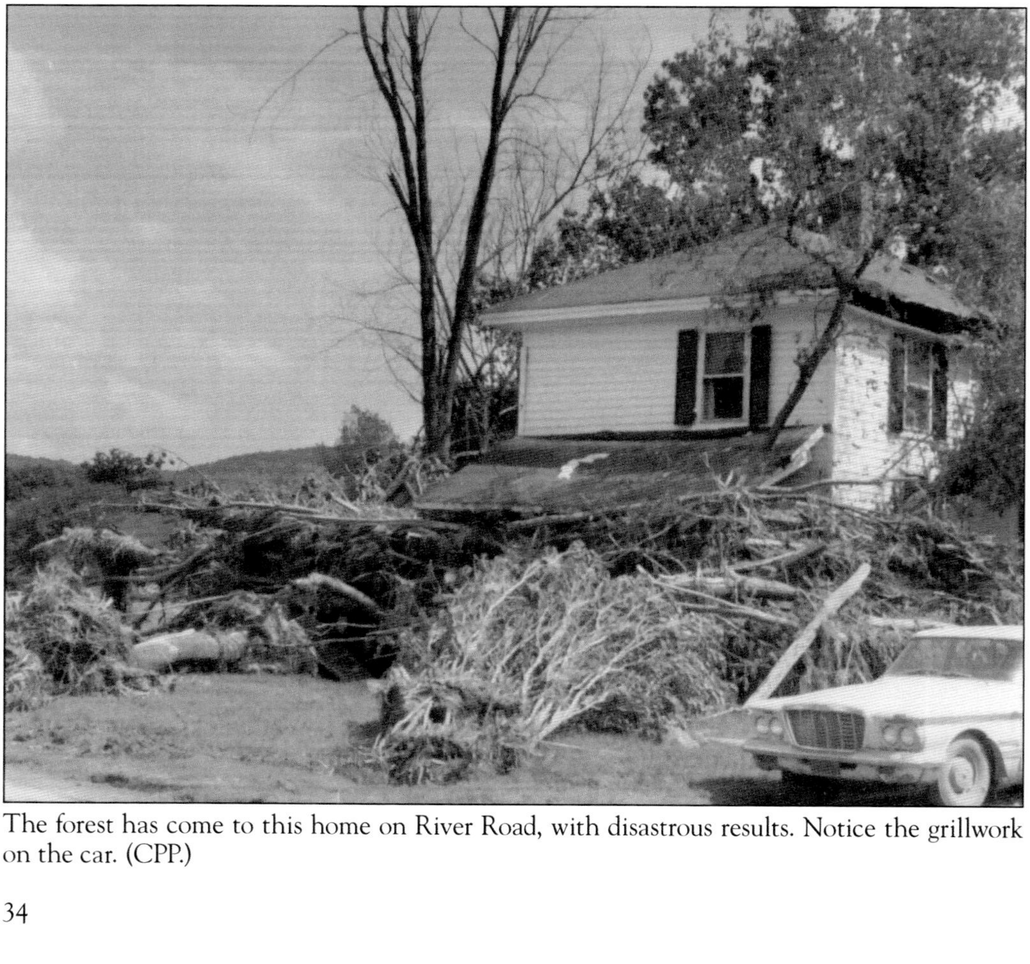

The forest has come to this home on River Road, with disastrous results. Notice the grillwork on the car. (CPP.)

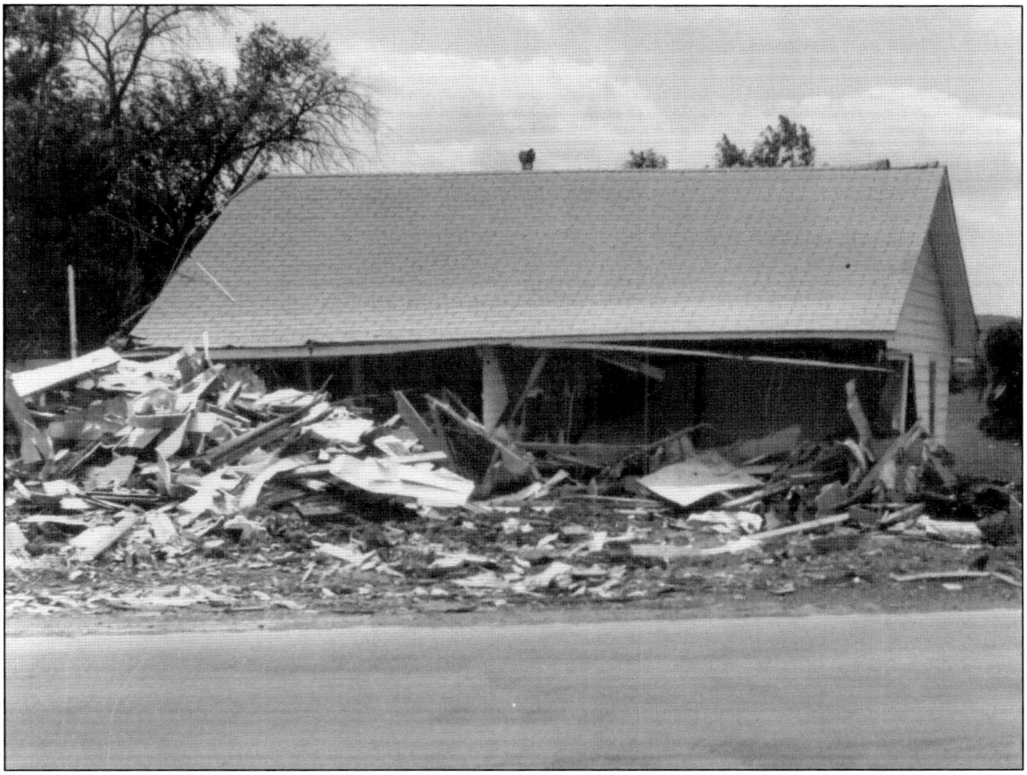

This place, also on River Road in the South Corning area, was left little more than a lean-to. (CPP.)

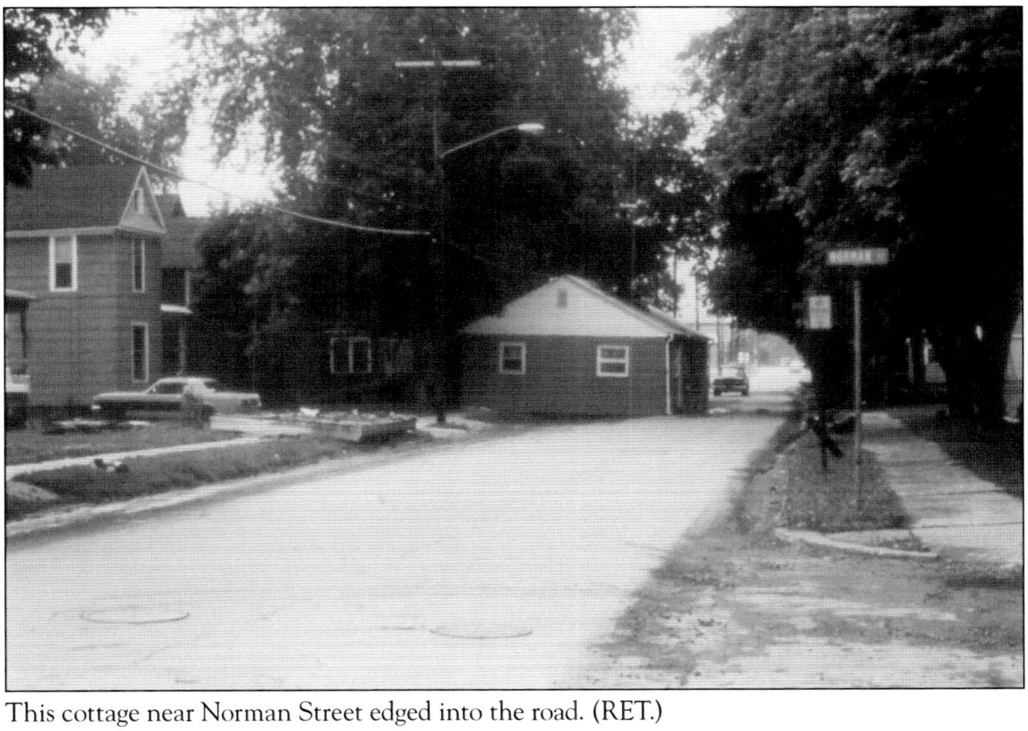

This cottage near Norman Street edged into the road. (RET.)

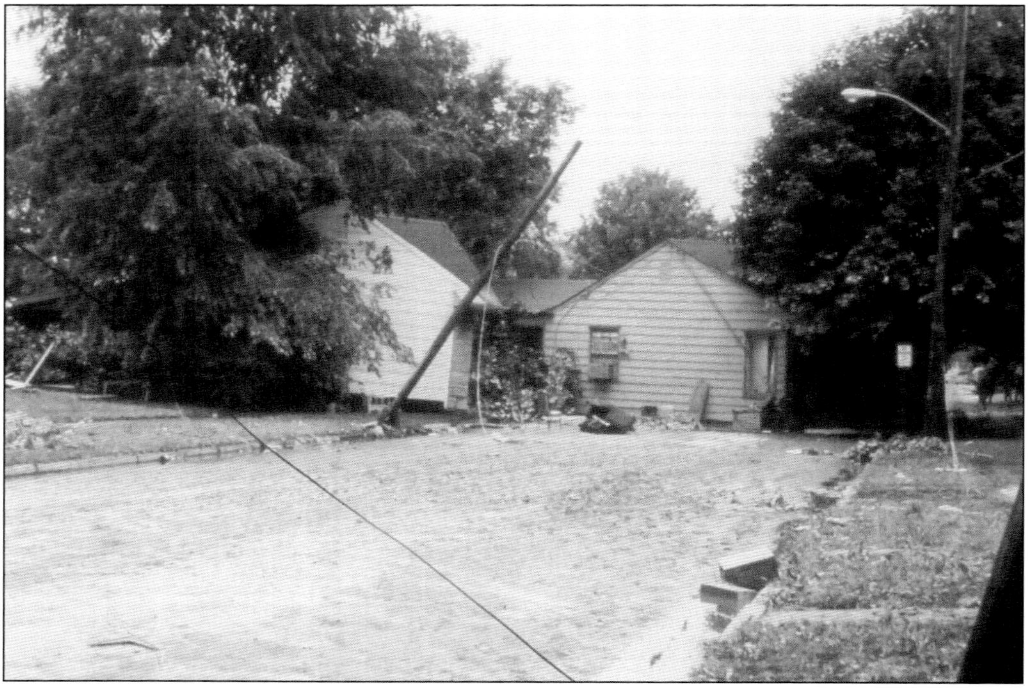

This even larger home also slid into the road. (RET.)

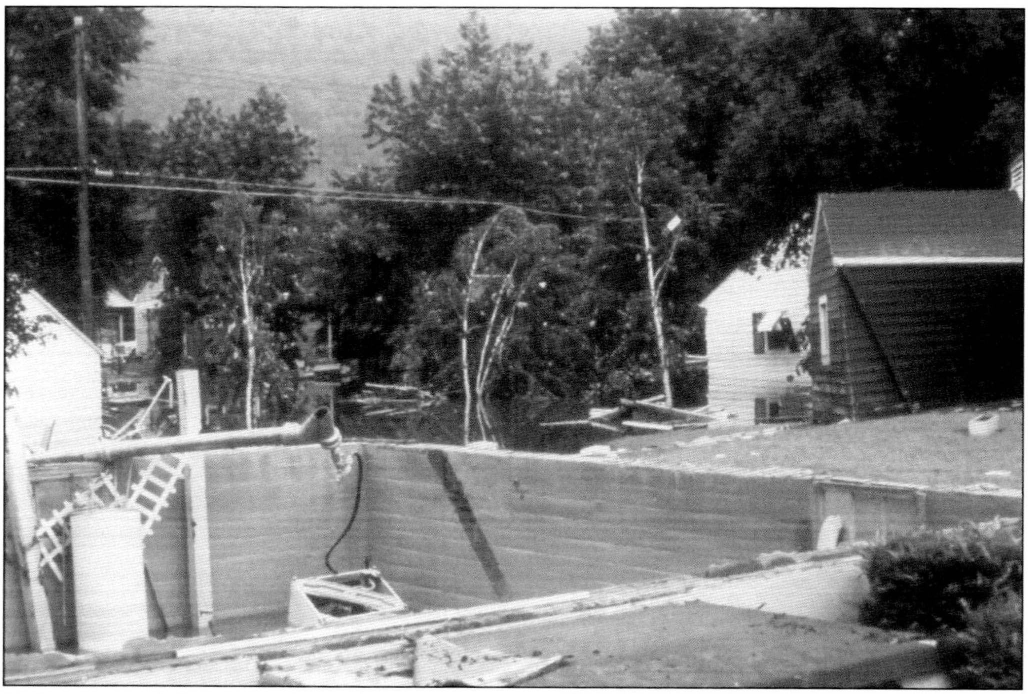

Perhaps one of those wandering homes went astray from this foundation. Notice that water is still standing in the yard. (RET.)

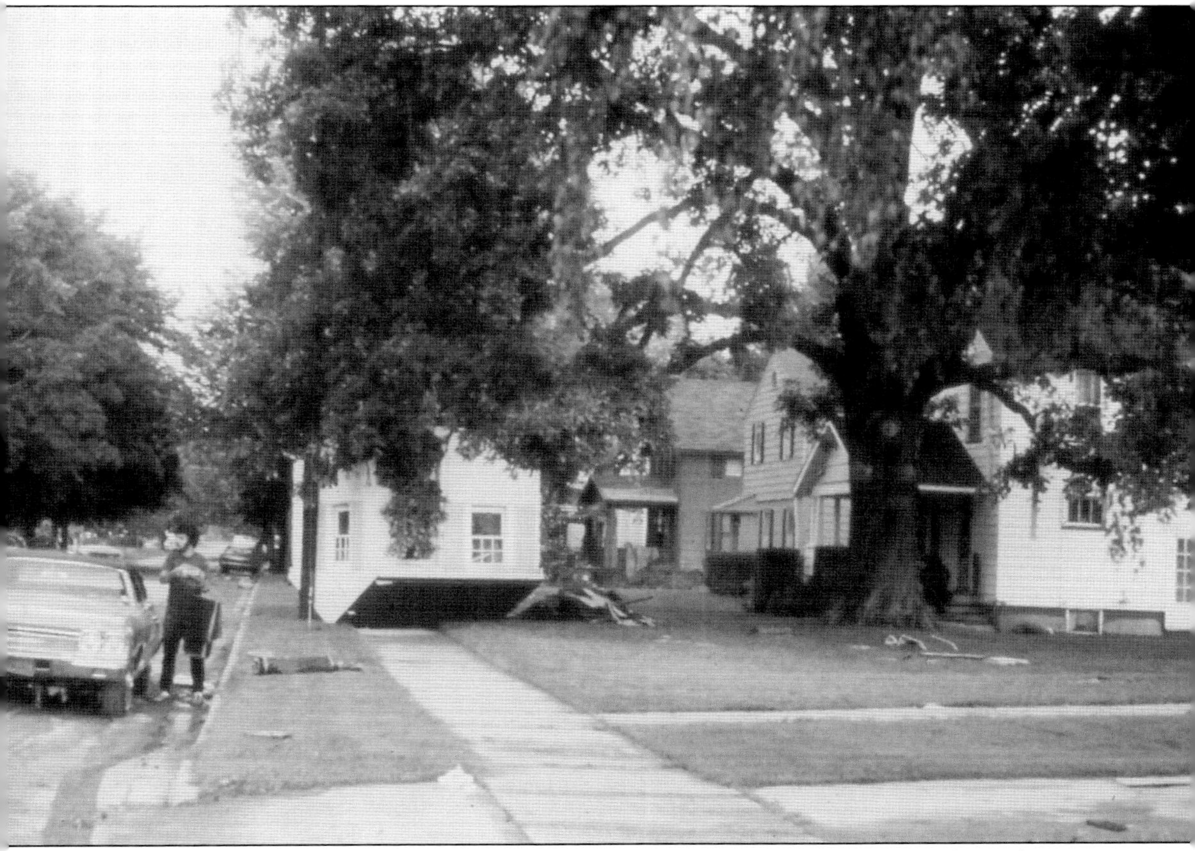

This small two-story building wound up standing on its head. Several photographers, despite severe demands on their time, took the trouble to immortalize this peculiar scene. (RET.)

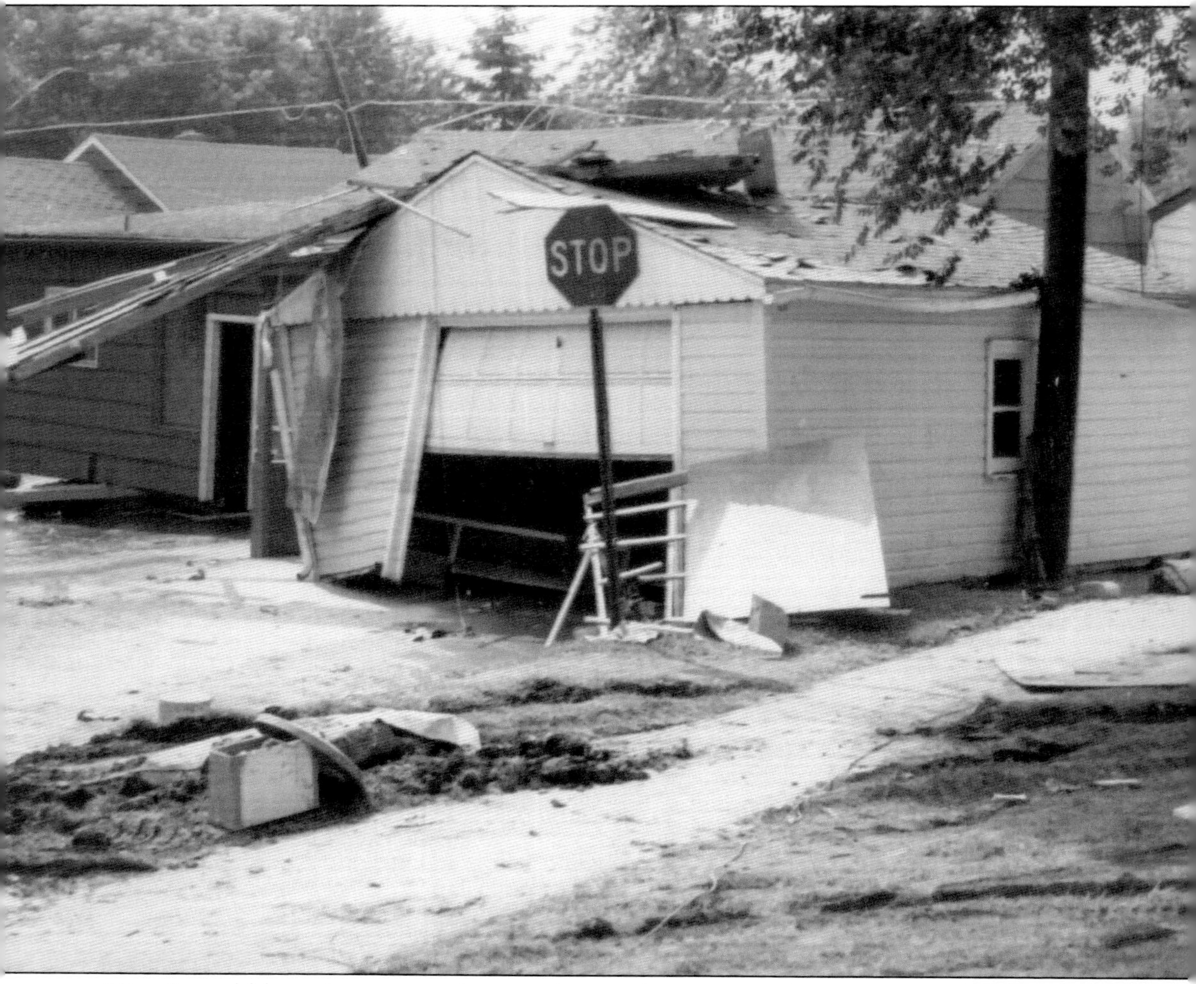

"Stop" would have been a good motto, but nothing on earth was going to hold back this onslaught. (CPP.)

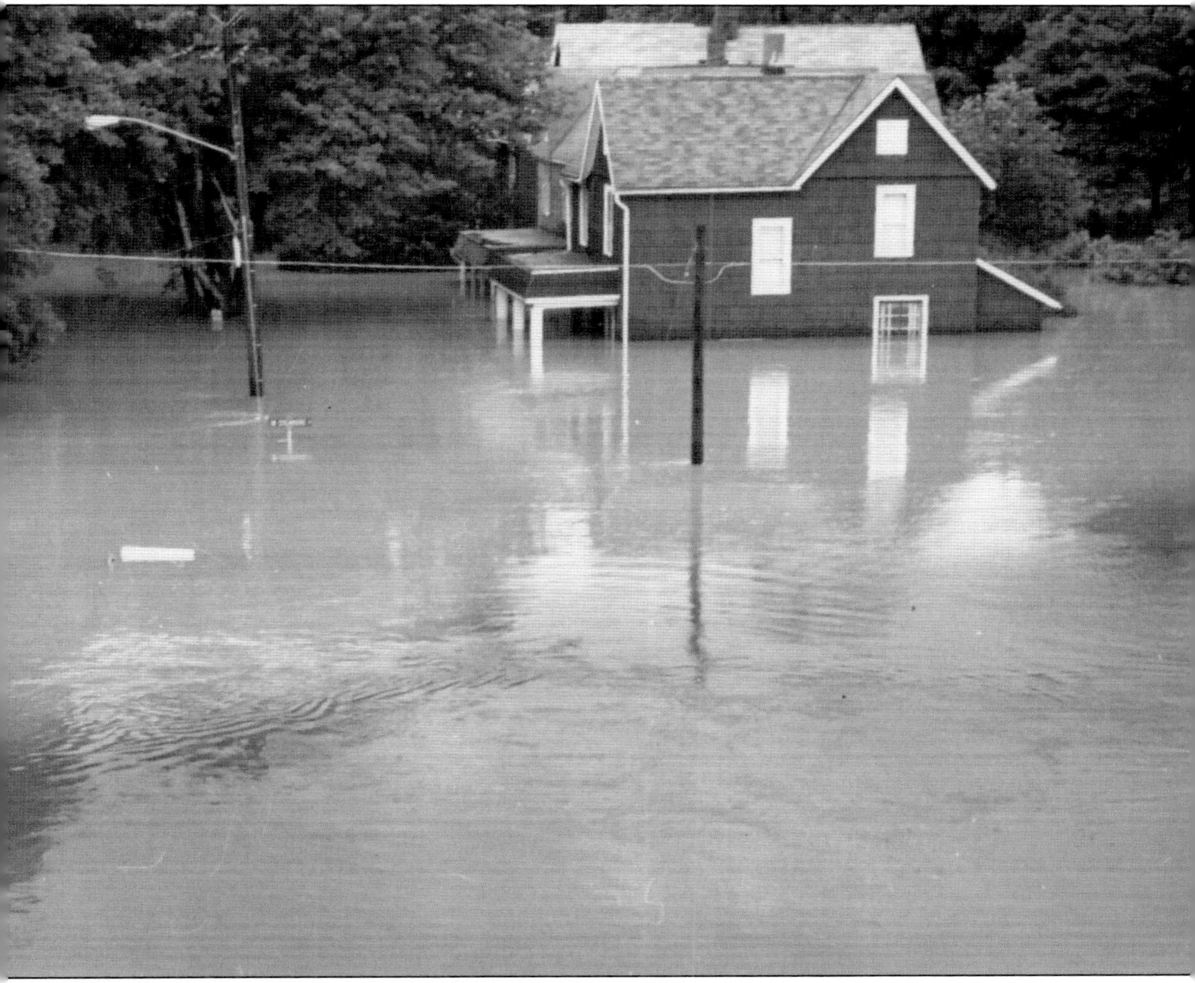

The flooding is still deep far back from the river at Bridge and Sycamore Streets. Notice that the street sign (in front of the utility pole on the left) is just barely keeping its head above water. (CPP.)

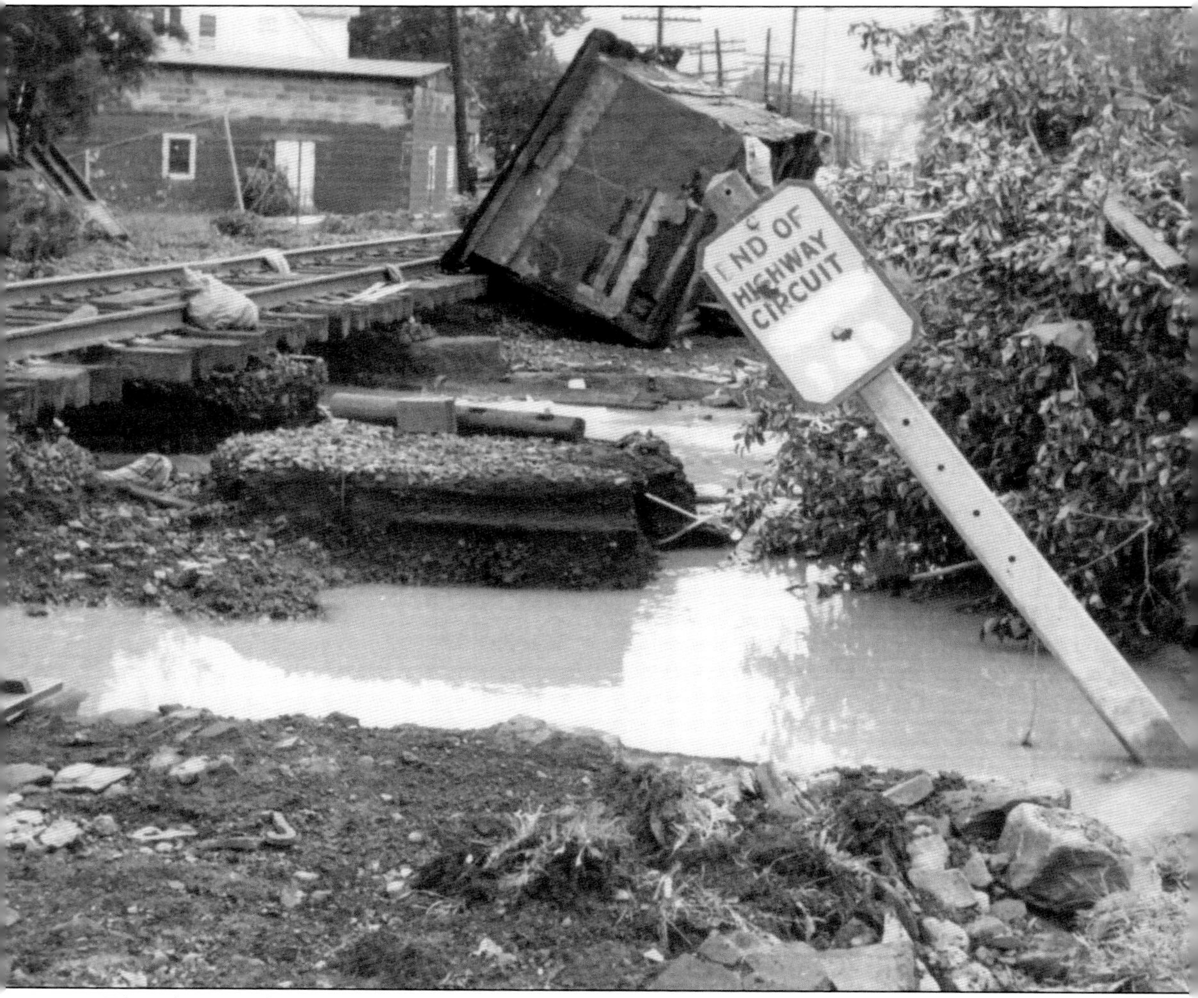

This photographer could not resist a bit of irony. The scene is on Baker Street in Corning, between the Post Creek and the Chemung River. (CPP.)

The Carroll family at Hamilton Circle captured this image between 2:00 p.m. and 3:00 p.m. on June 23. They noted that the water had started receding about 11:00 a.m. that day. (CPP.)

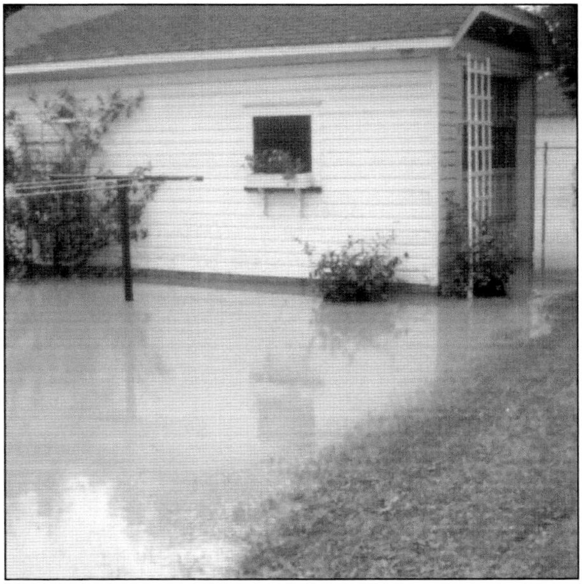

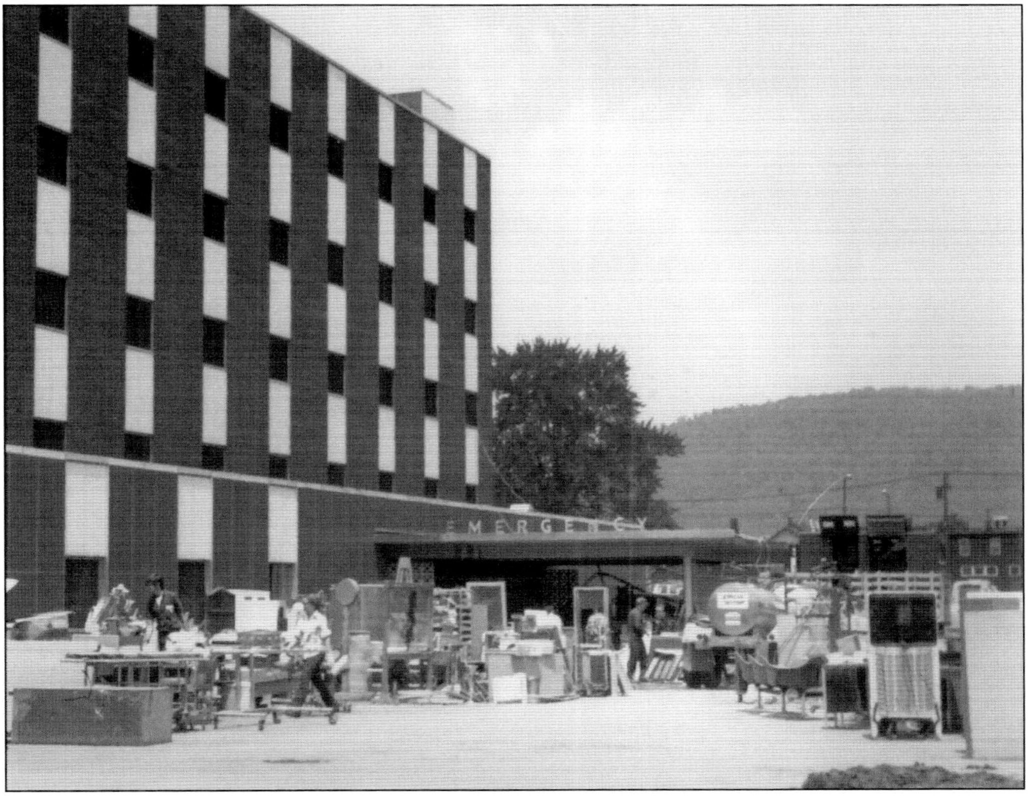

At Corning Hospital, Dr. Jack D. O'Neil stood knee-deep in water and finished an emergency operation by flashlight. Owners of station wagons were begged to come in to have a patient laid out in the back beds of their cars in order to drive them to the Schuyler County Hospital in Montour Falls. It was nerve-wracking, but they got through. Then, Corning Hospital faced a long hard slog of cleaning, repairing, refurbishing, and reopening. Workers used fire hoses to clean the mud out of the ground floor. (CPP.)

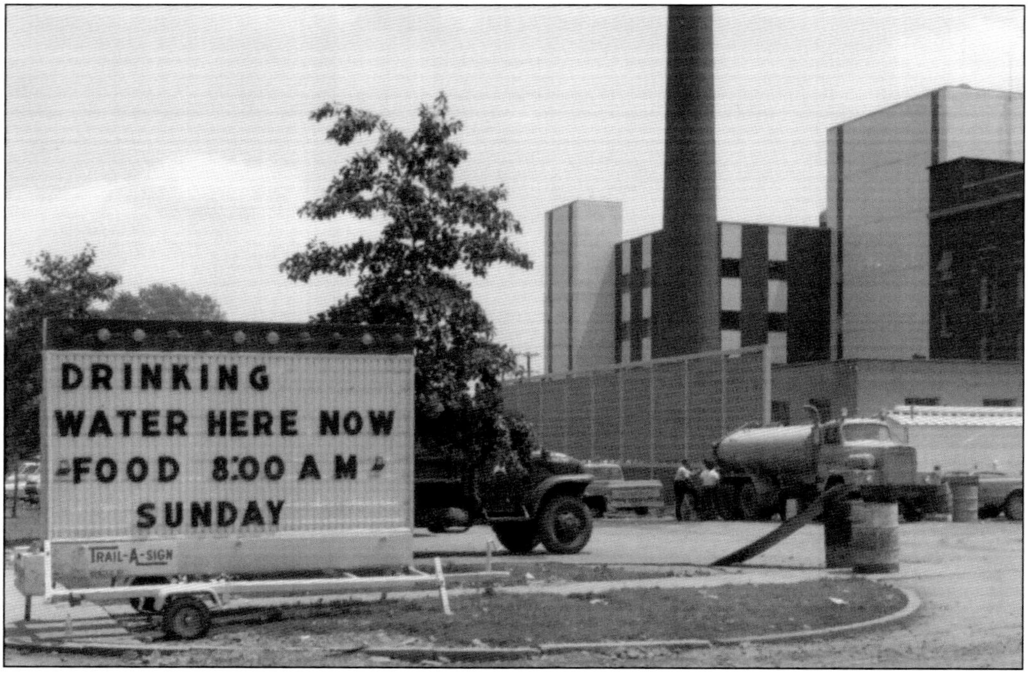

Water now, food Sunday—this scene at Corning Hospital on Denison Parkway was grimly familiar to many residents. (CPP.)

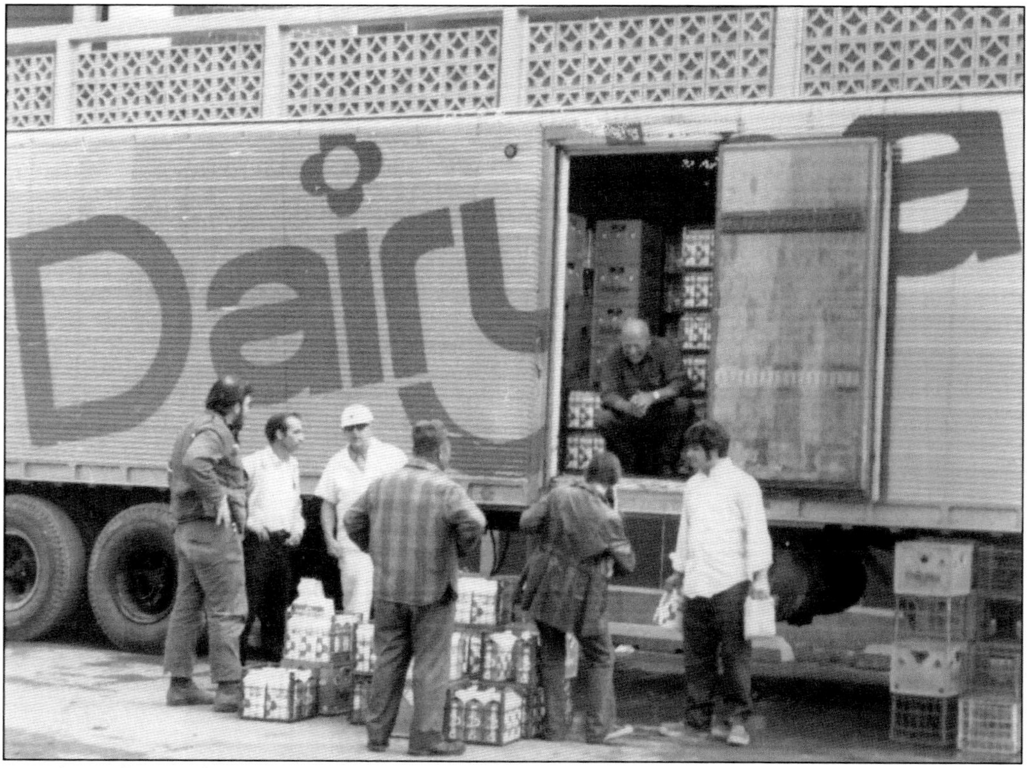

Suppliers all over the Northeast rushed goods to Corning. Whatever arrived (in this case, at the hospital) was welcome. (CPP.)

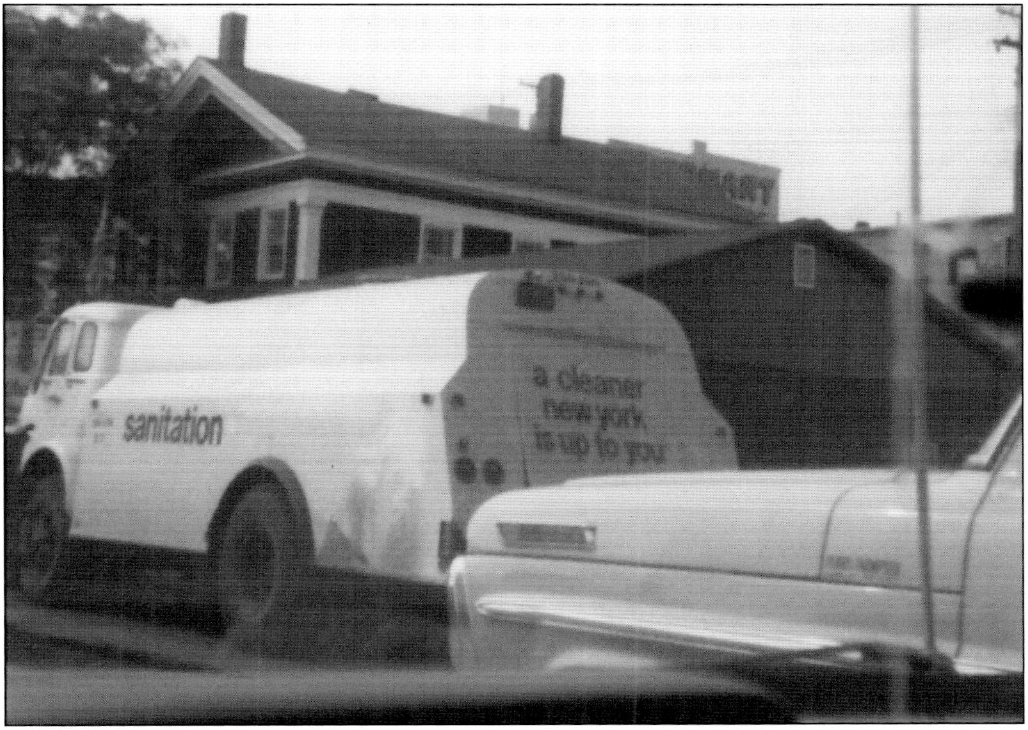

A sanitation truck from New York City helped deliver water. (AB.)

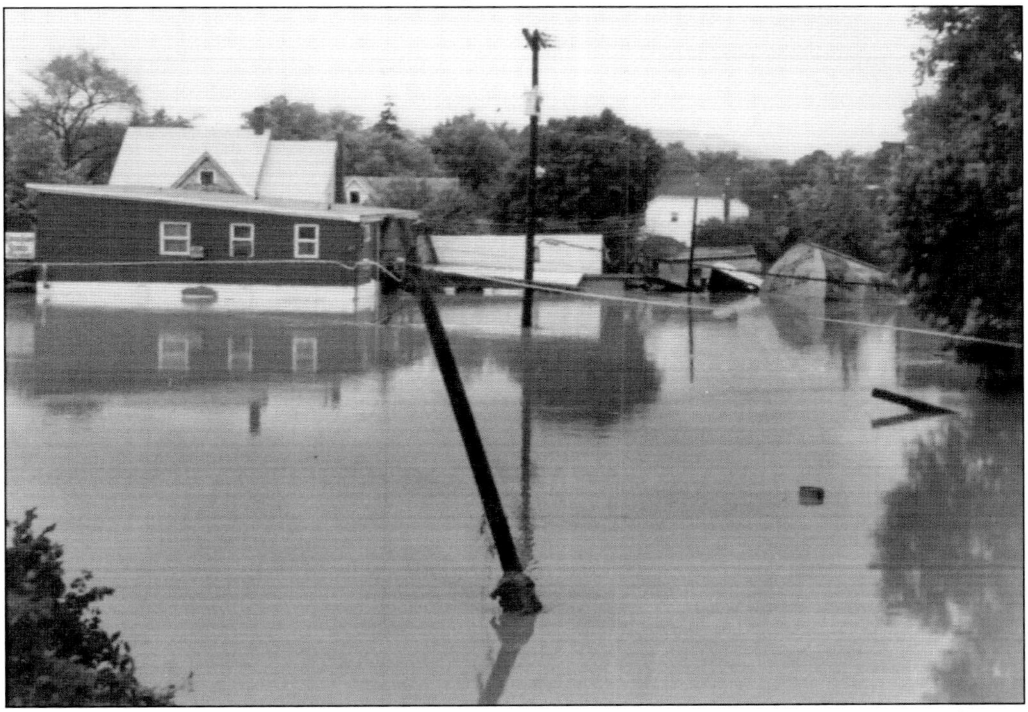

Snyder's Store in the village of Riverside (aptly named, but unfortunately situated) was one of many local businesses devastated by the flood. Notice the listing utility pole, the wrecked buildings in the rear, and what seems to be a floating cask in the middle right. (CPP.)

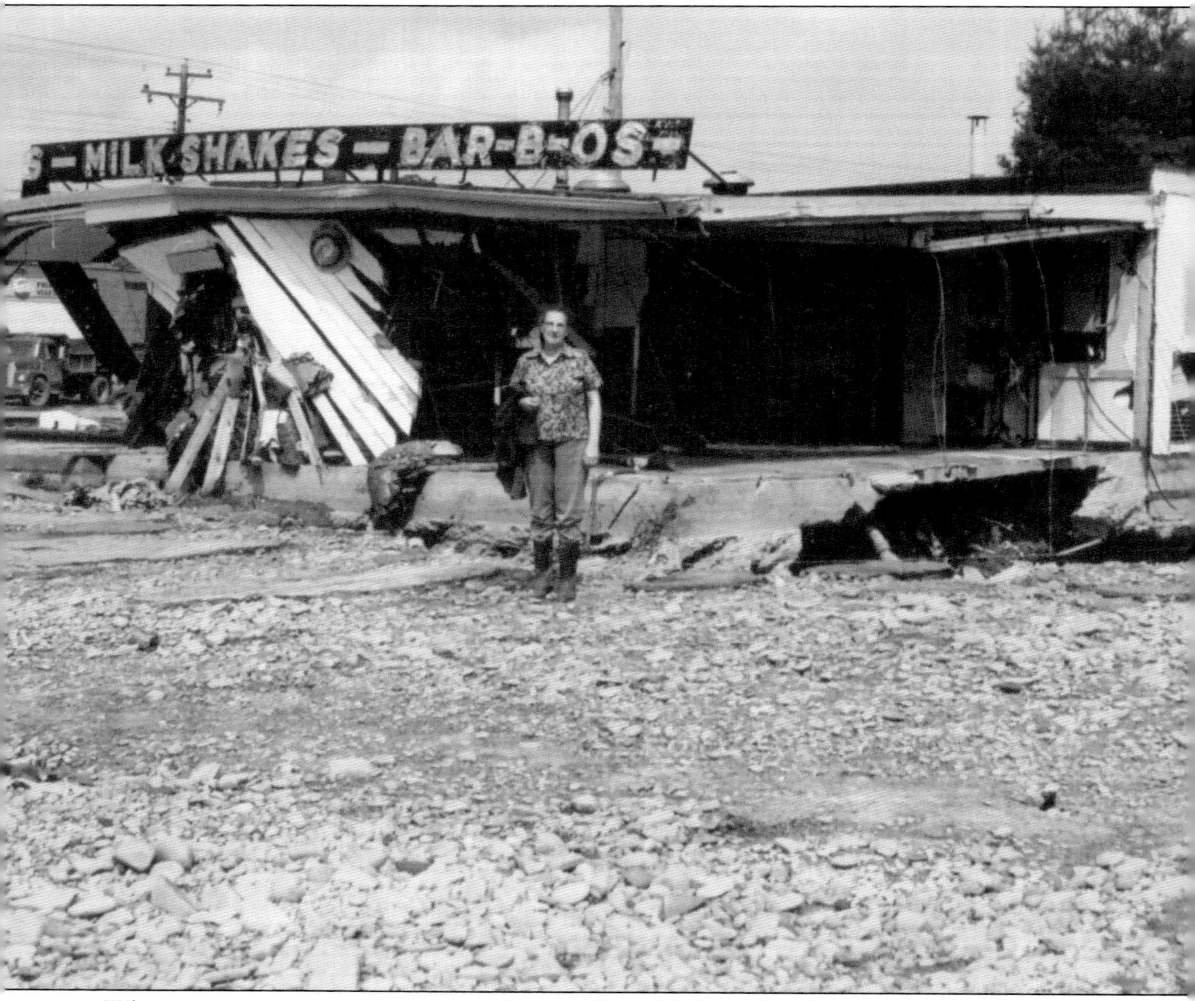

When a major corporation like the Corning Glass Works suffered, it was clearly a catastrophe, but the Glass Works had other resources from which to draw. Family-owned businesses, such as King's Dairy, often had nothing to fall back on, and many disappeared altogether. Notice the high boots and see how even the paving of roads and parking lots has been scoured away. Bonady's Produce Market is in the left background. (CPP.)

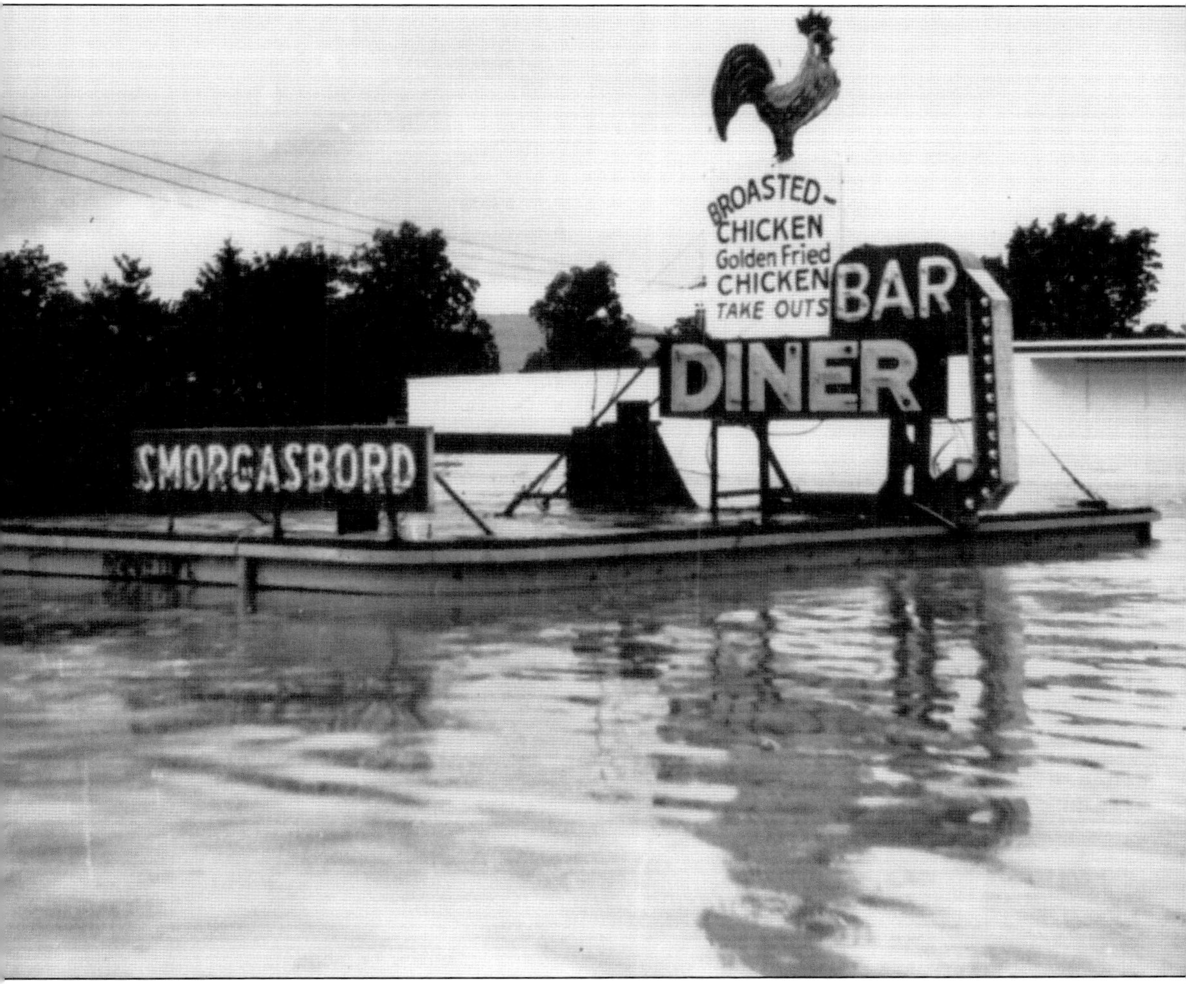

Al Hall's Diner, located on Hamilton Street in Painted Post, appeared to be floating off like Huck Finn's raft. (CPP.)

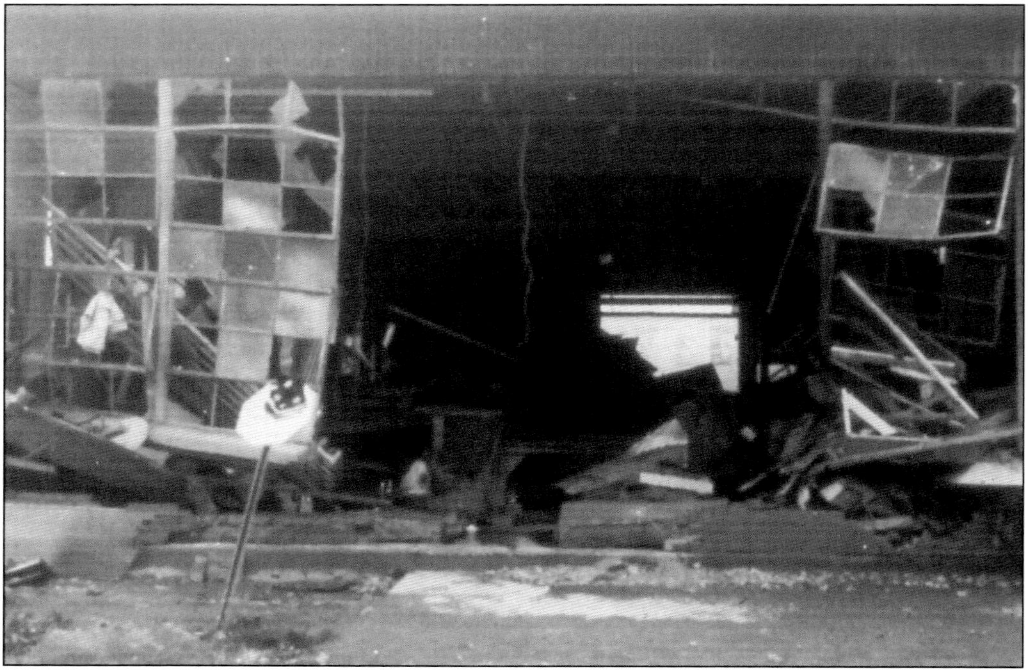

Water poured straight through this garage. (RET.)

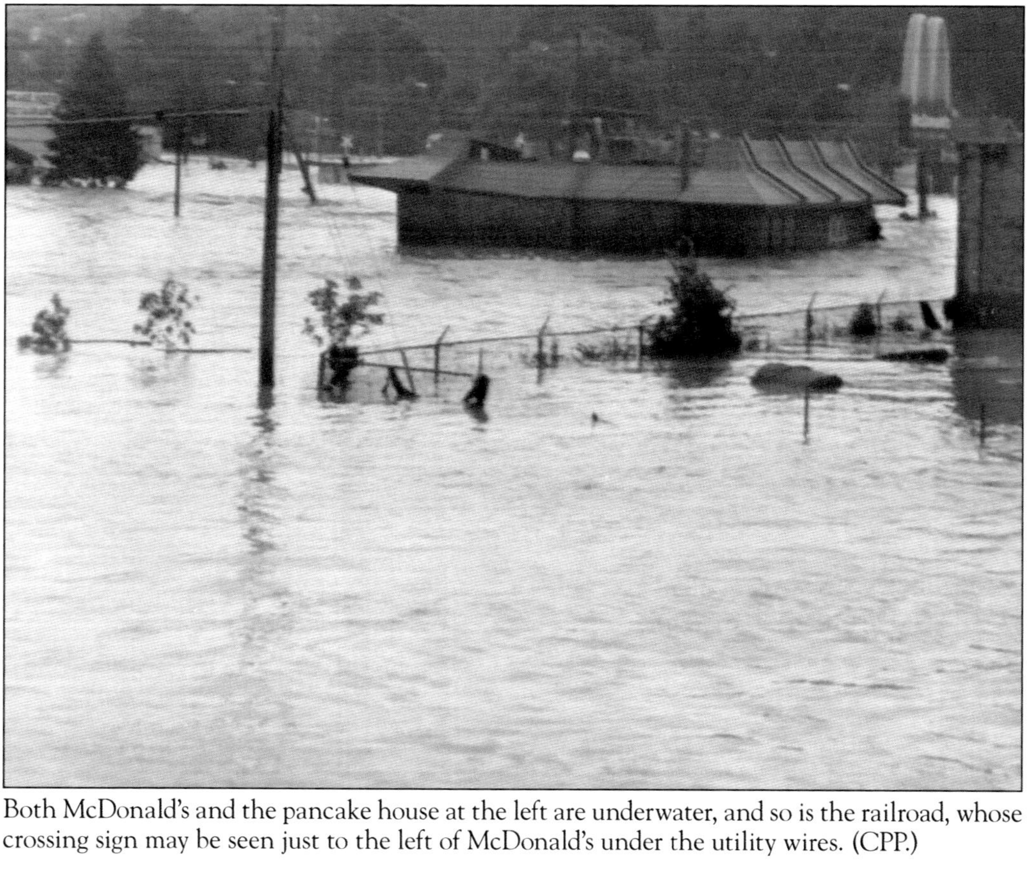

Both McDonald's and the pancake house at the left are underwater, and so is the railroad, whose crossing sign may be seen just to the left of McDonald's under the utility wires. (CPP.)

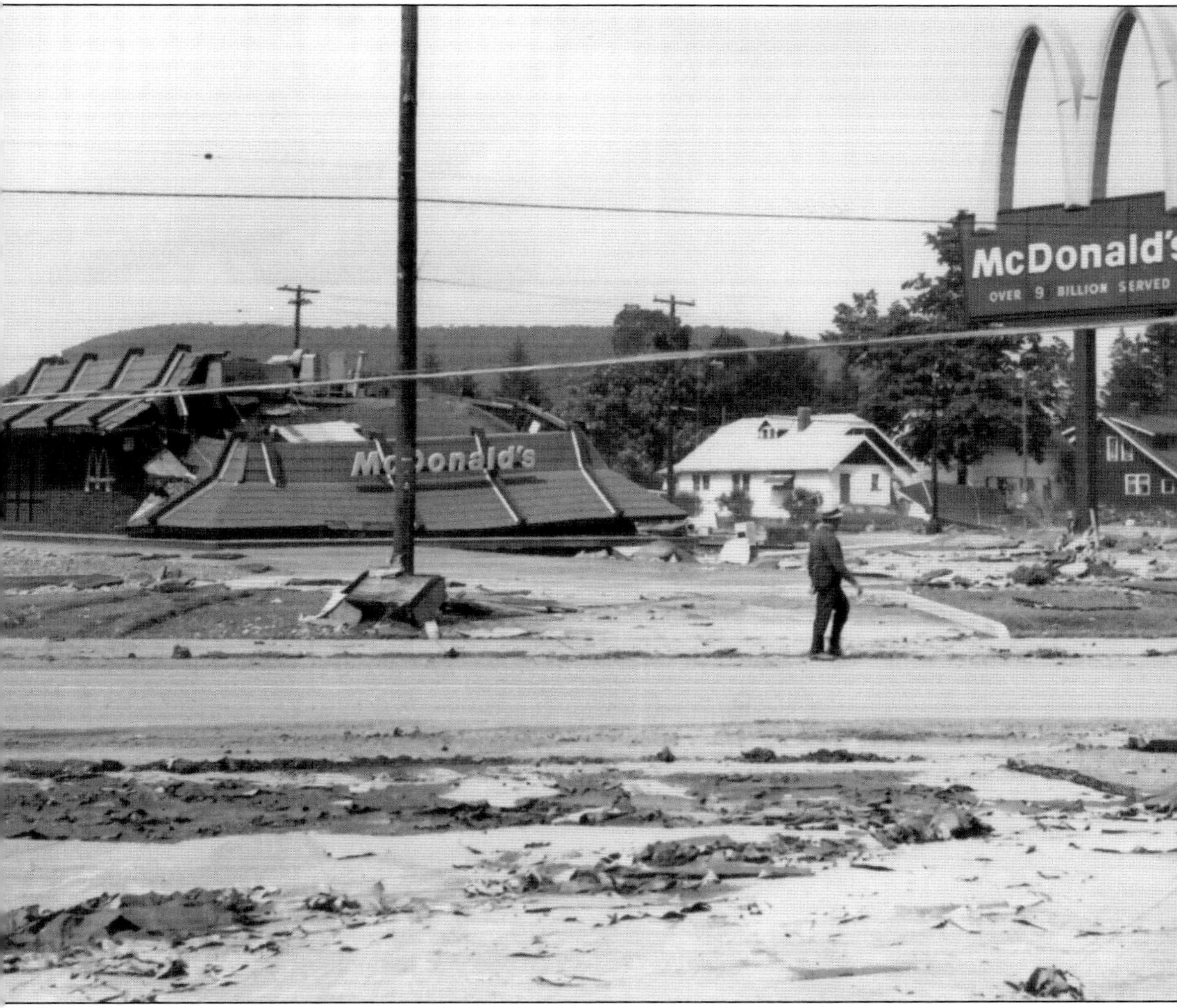

McDonald's may have served 9 billion hamburgers by 1972, but this particular unit (then on West Pulteney in Riverside) was not going to be boosting that total for a while. (CPP.)

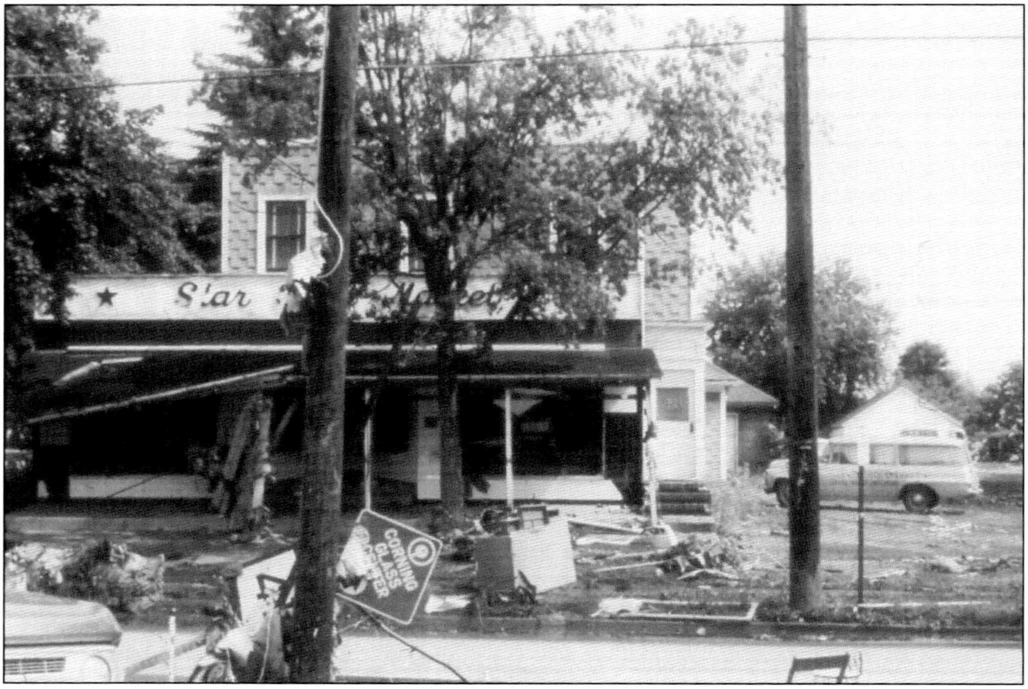

Star Market and its West Pulteney Street neighborhood were hammered by the storm. (RET.)

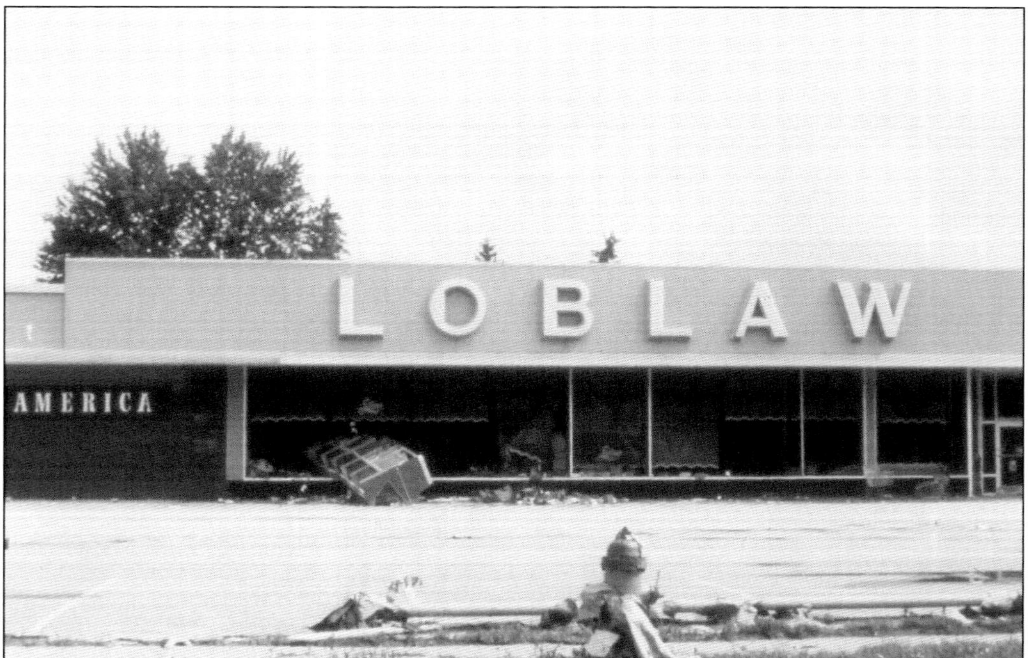

Floods washed in through, and then back out of, the front of Loblaw's supermarket on West Pulteney. Loblaw's reopened for business in a tent. (RET.)

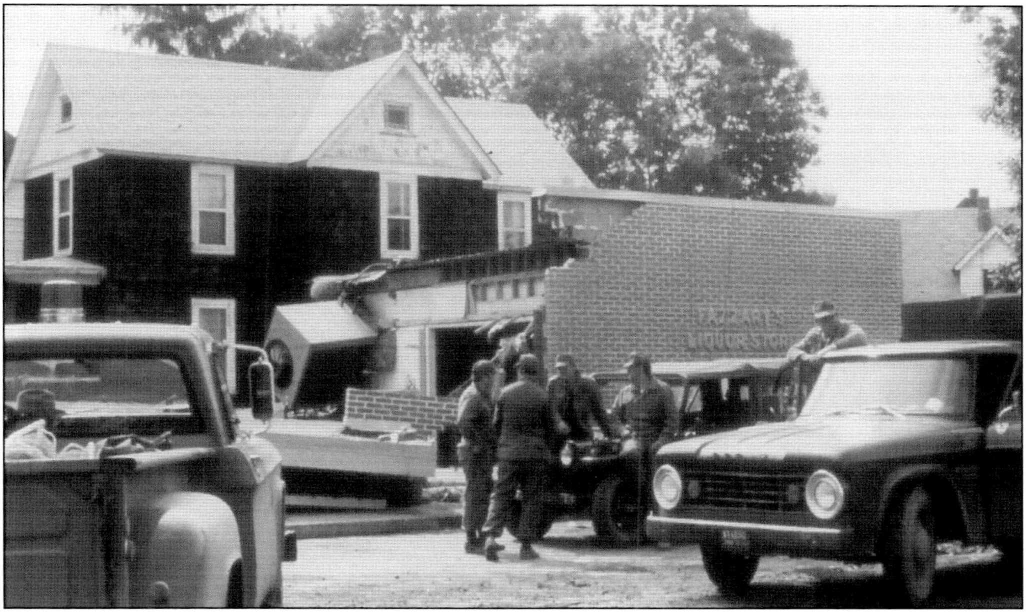

National Guardsmen gather outside Fazzary's Liquor. Some local residents were startled to spot armed guardsmen toting beer bottles. It turned out that the Genesee Brewery in Rochester had rushed thousands of gallons of distilled water into production for the emergency, using the containers they had on hand. (RET.)

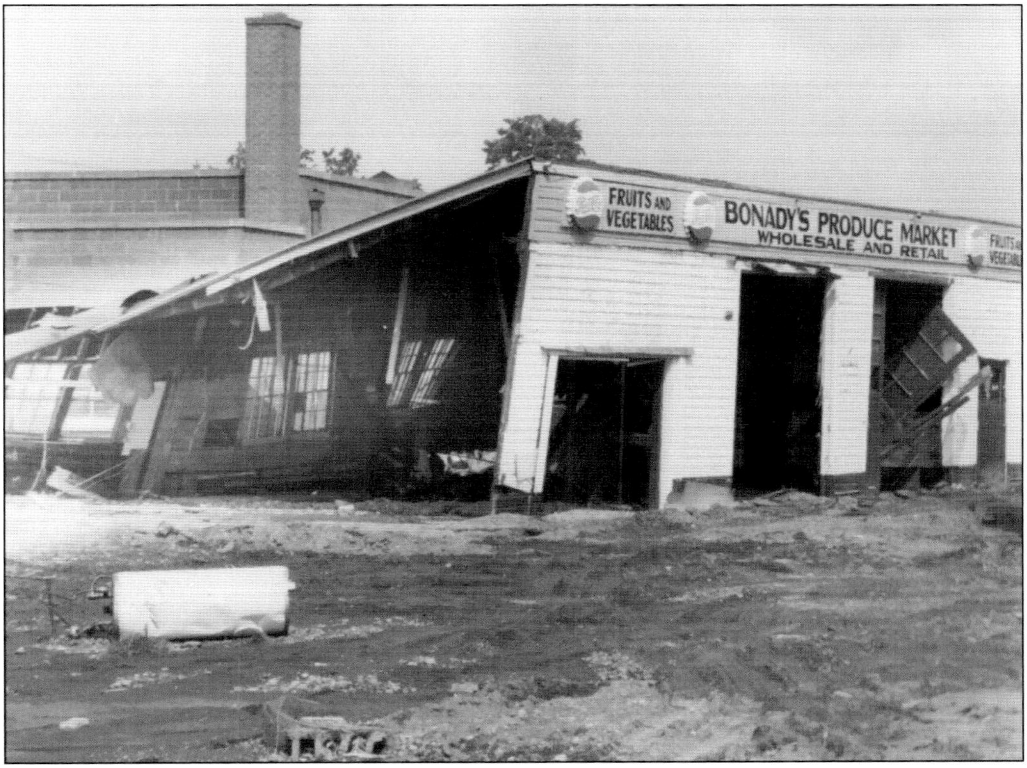

Besides having its interior wiped out, Bonady's Market saw its building folded up on itself. Somebody's hot-water heater is in the foreground. (CPP.)

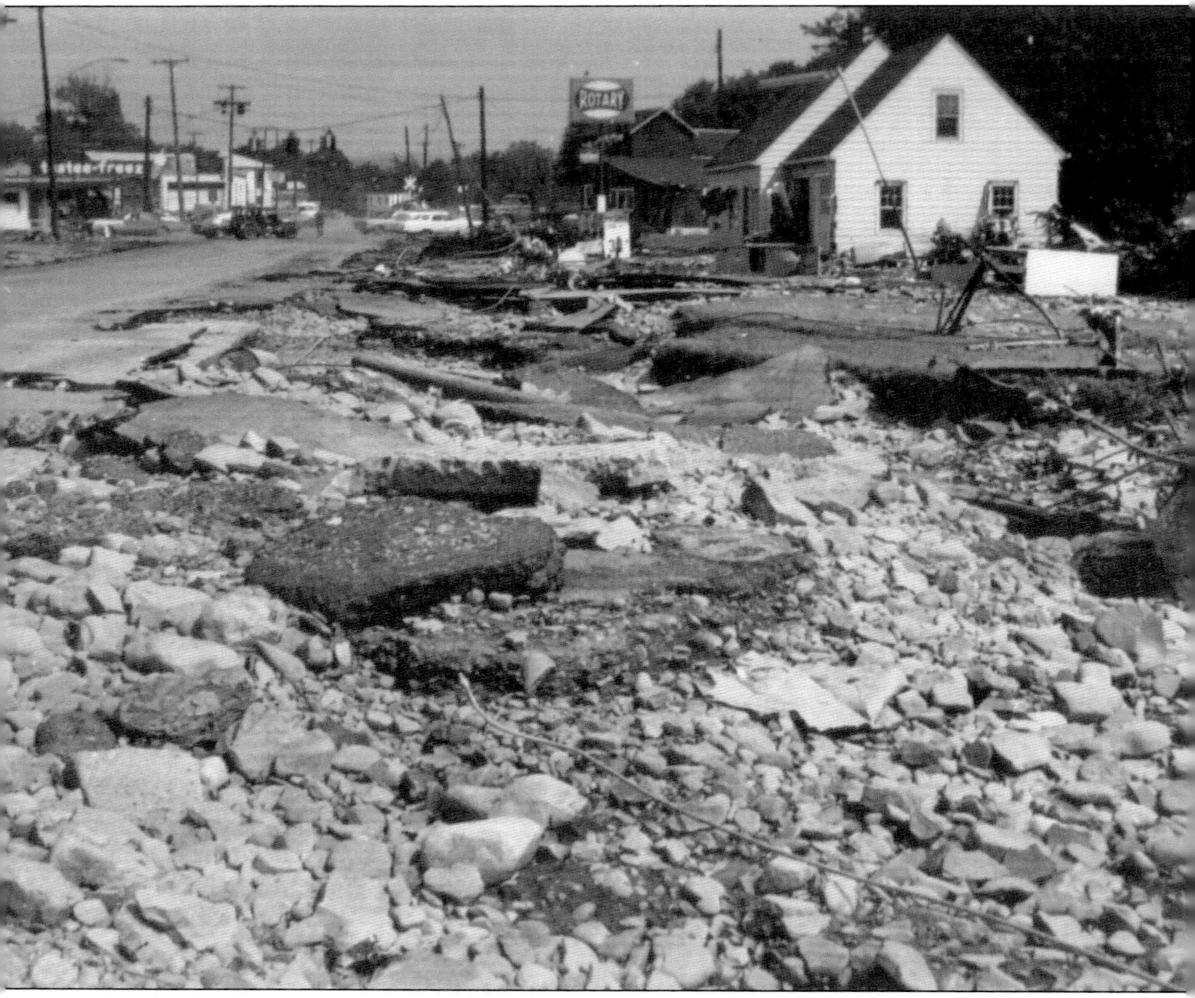

Besides the damage to structures, contents, road, and railroads, public utilities—such as electricity, natural gas, sewage, telephones, and water—were also cut off. Those who remember 1972 may enjoy a moment of nostalgia for the sign advertising 34¢ gasoline. (CPP.)

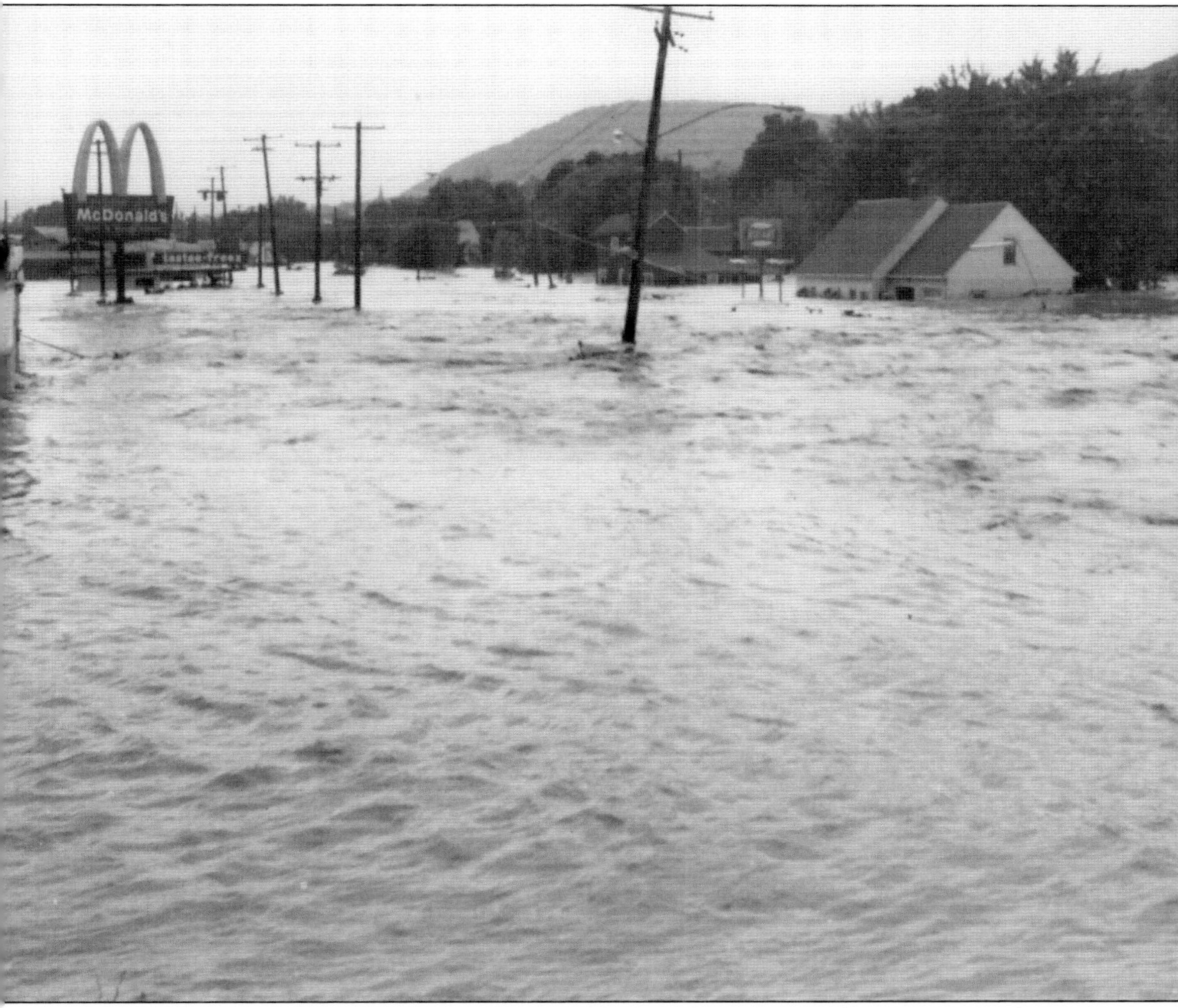

Corning area residents watched bricks and concrete blocks rushing along on the water at 25 miles per hour. Electricity was out for five days, then began slowly being returned to customers. (CPP.)

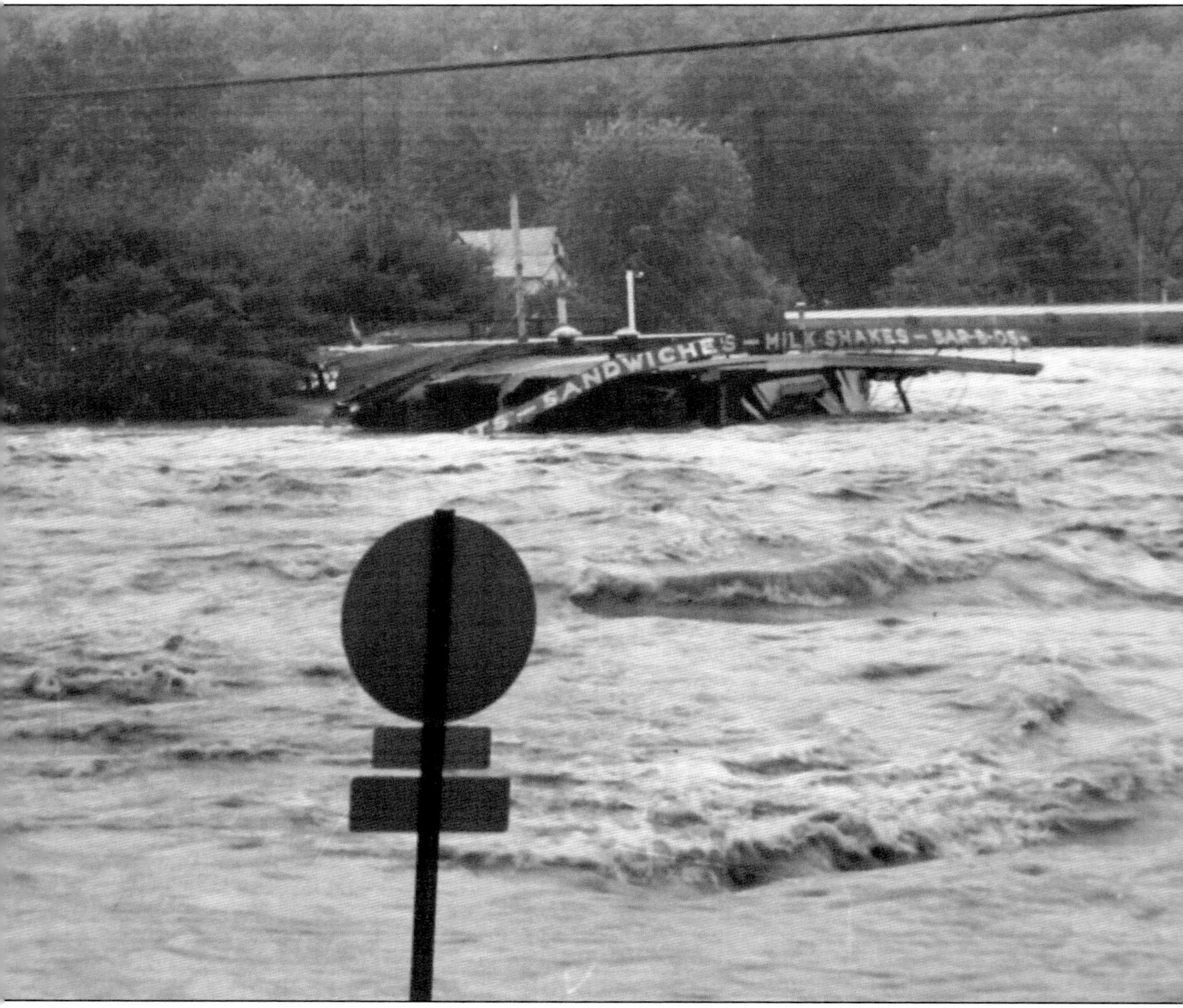

Damage came not just from the level and volume of the water but also from its force and speed. (CPP.)

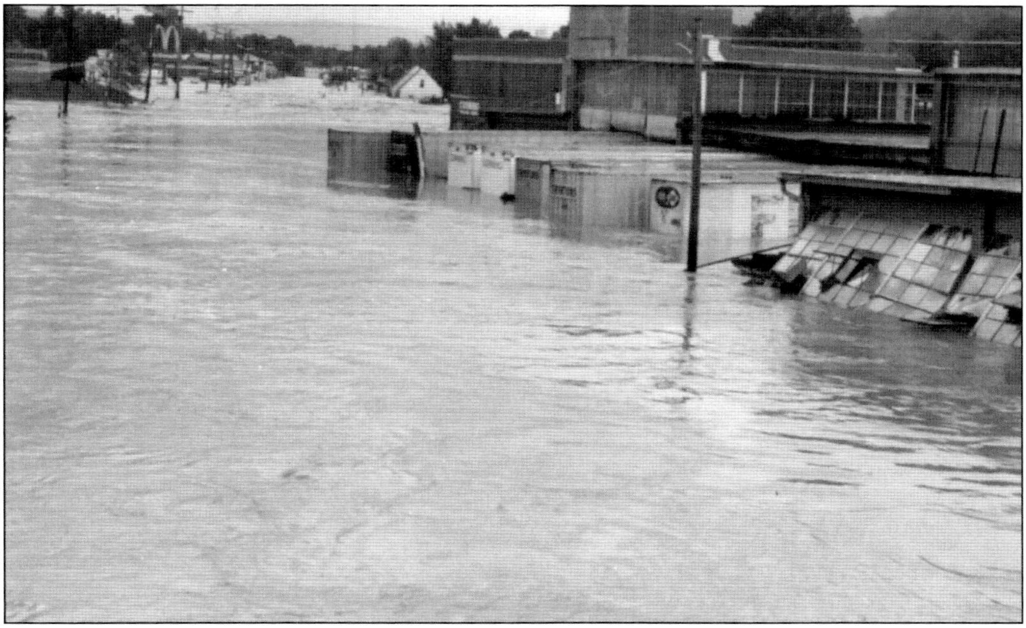

The Corning Box Factory, just down the road from the Rotary gas station, was not spared either. (CPP.)

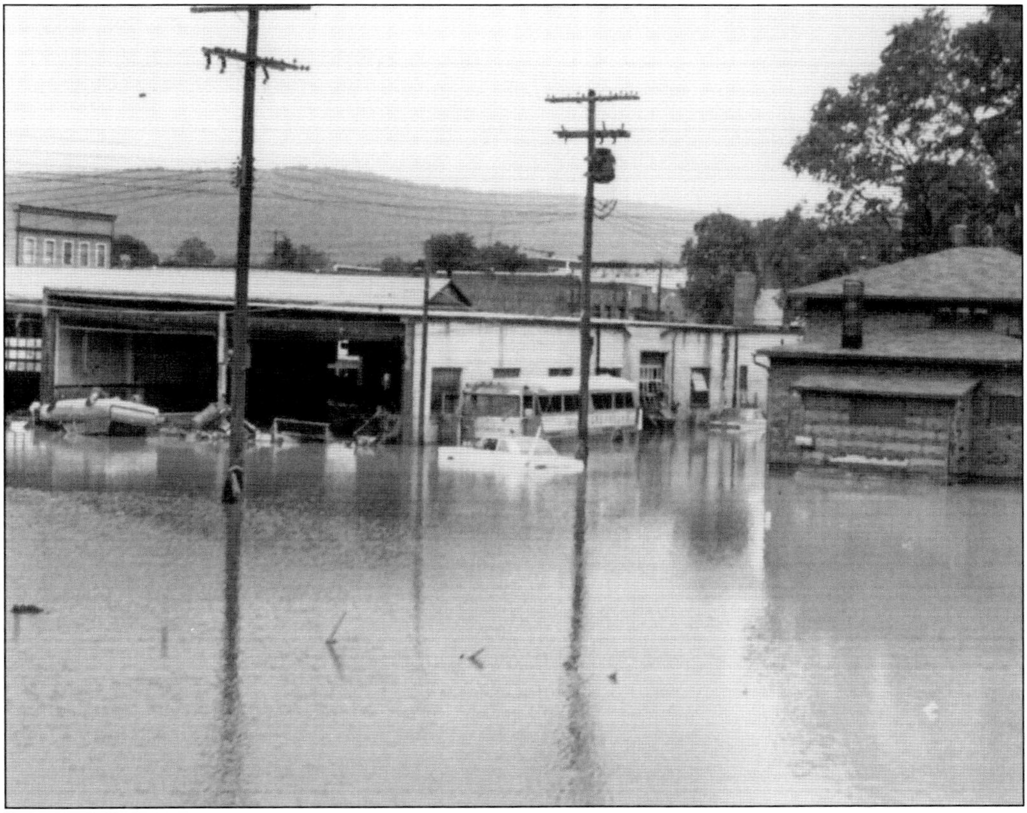

Two cars and a Greyhound bus are flooded at the Rambler Garage on Ferris Street. Flipped on its back, a third car (at the left) has floated off. (CPP.)

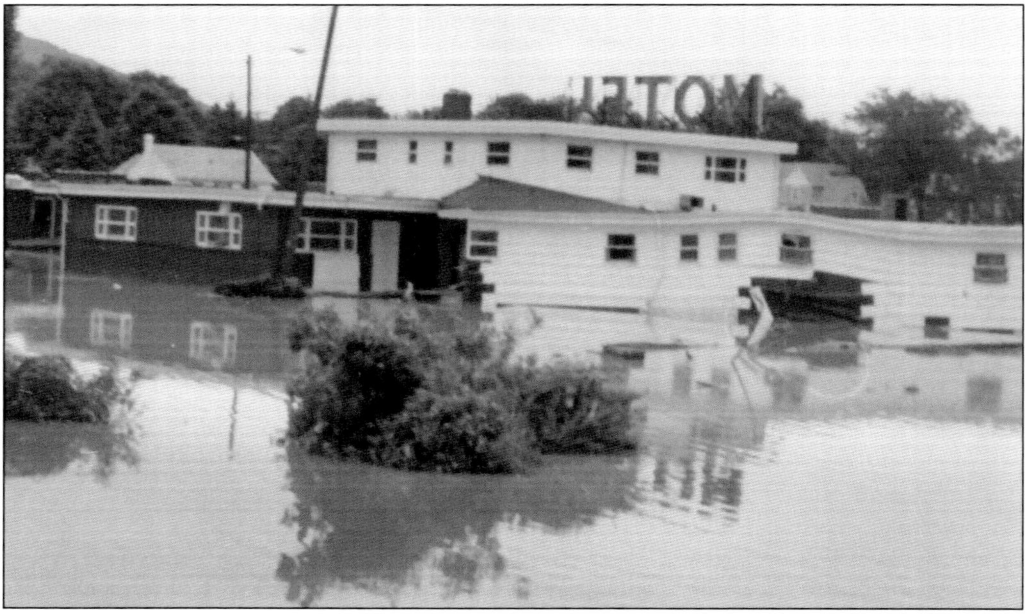

As evidenced in this image, the Centerway Motel, across from the Museum of Glass, fared badly. (CPP.)

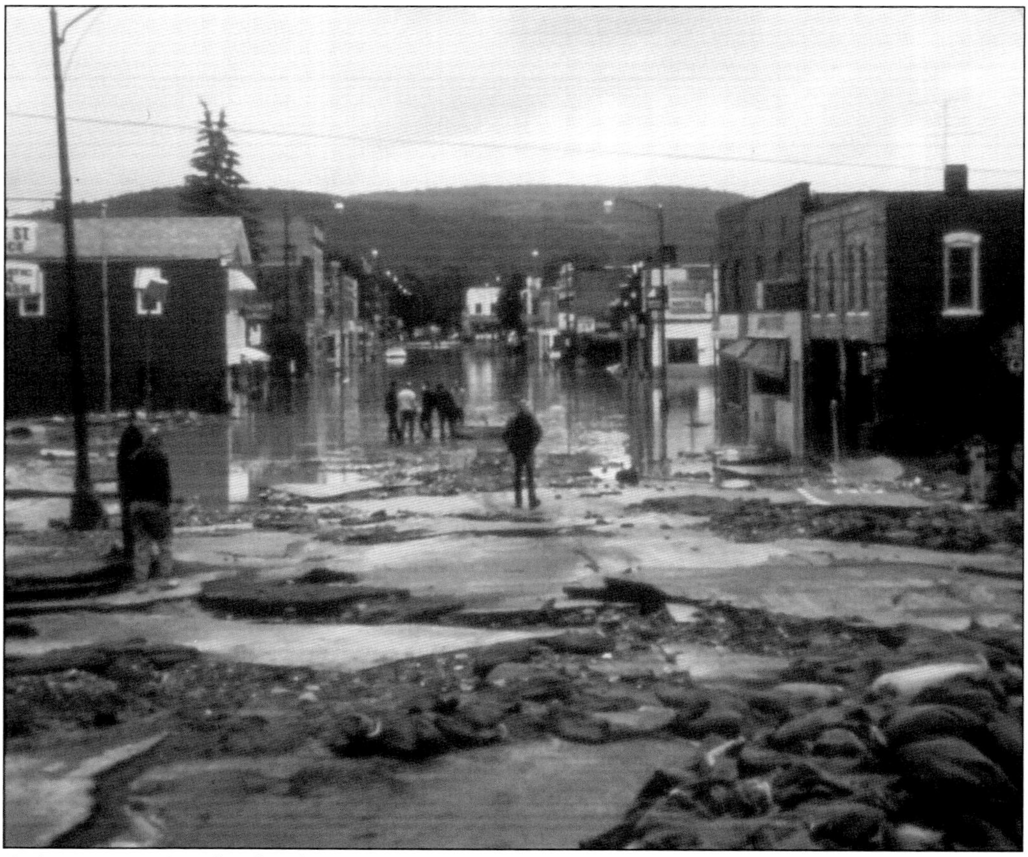

A day or two after the flood, water still stands on Bridge Street. (RET.)

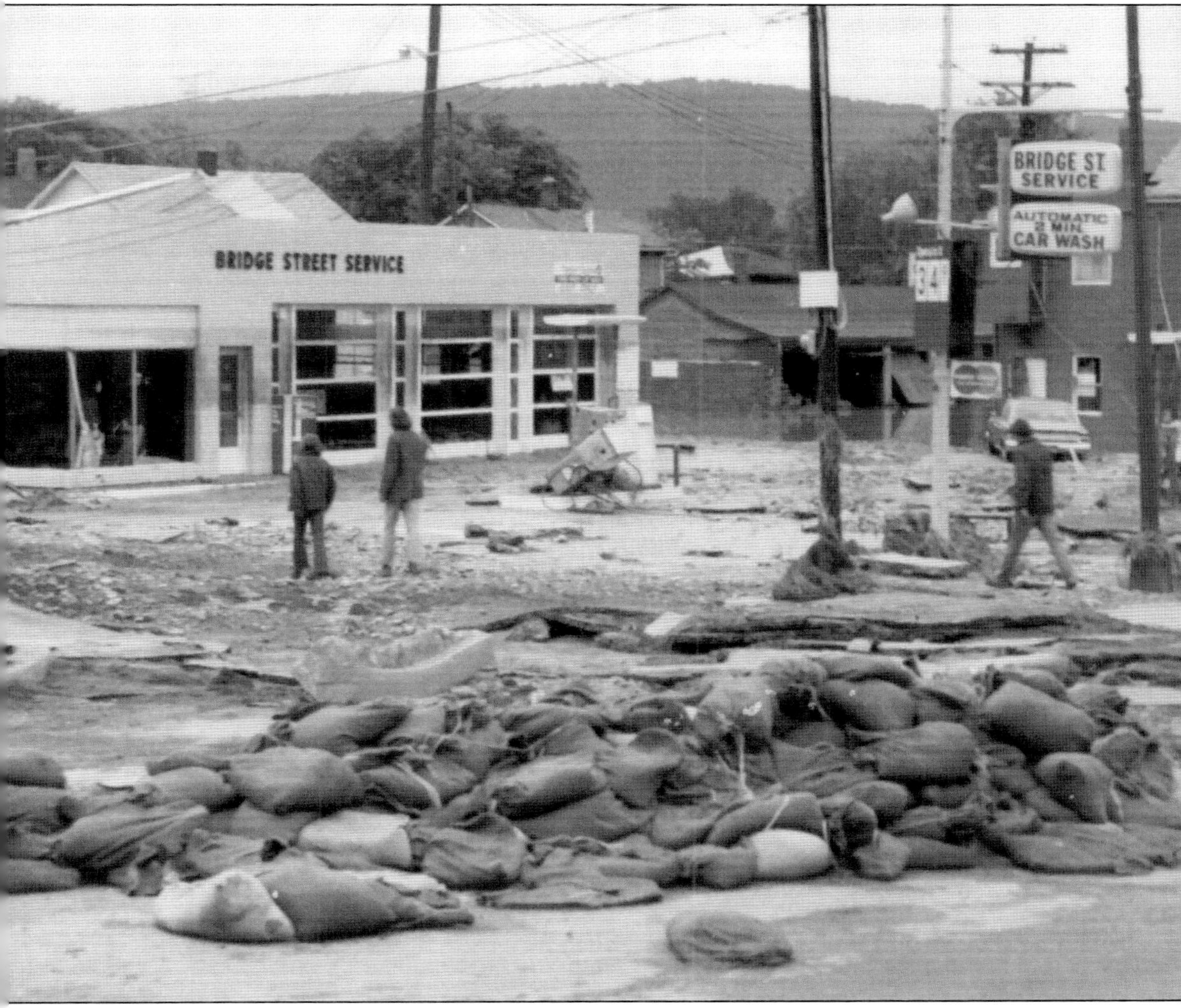

Someone did his or her best to protect the neighborhood, but sandbags were not enough to stop this monstrosity. Bridge Street in Corning, as the name suggests, crosses the Chemung, and it suffered accordingly. The glass has been knocked out of the service station's windows and doors, while one pump has been twisted off its moorings. This scene also reminds people that getting around in the flood zone continued to be very dangerous even after the waters receded. (CPP.)

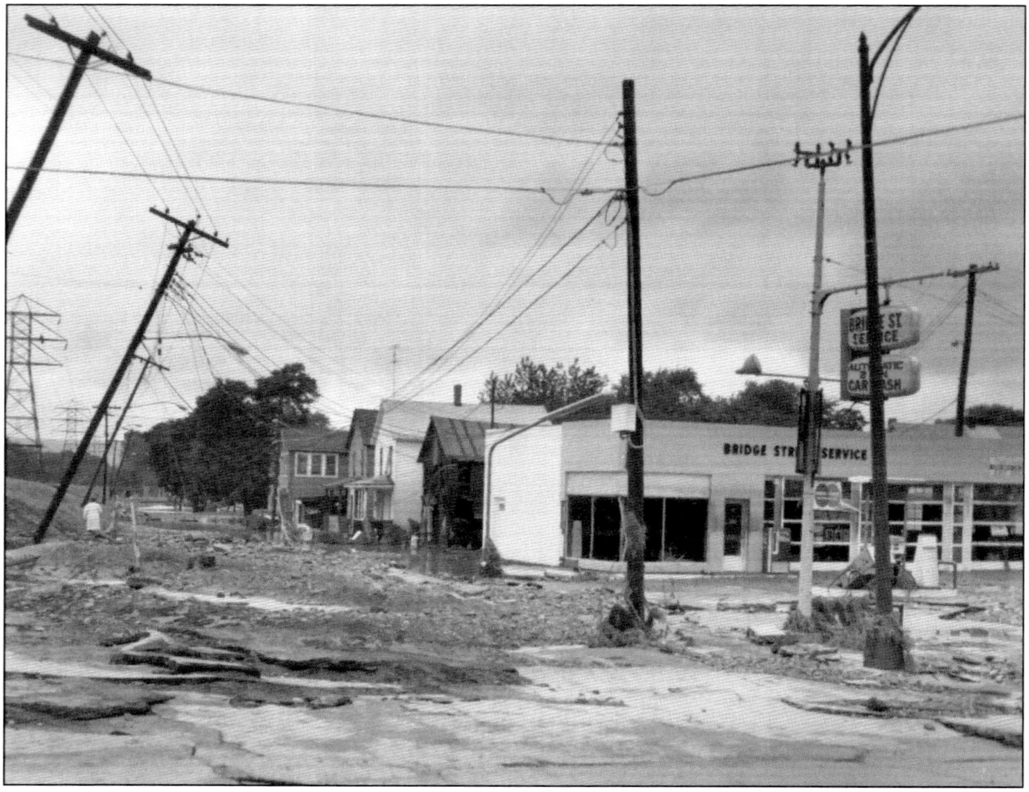

Nearby residences, streets, and utility systems fared no better than the service station had, despite the dike just visible on the left. Dikes broke in several places, beginning in Painted Post around 4:00 a.m. Even where the dikes held, the rivers often just flowed over them. (CPP.)

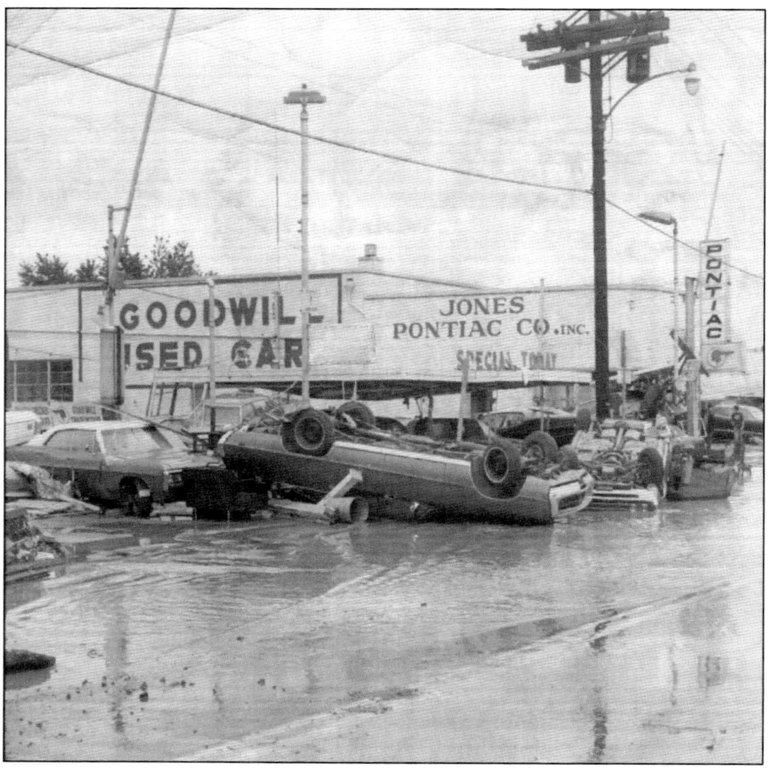

Think of the force and volume needed to toss these cars around and the financial loss it represented for the owners. (CPP.)

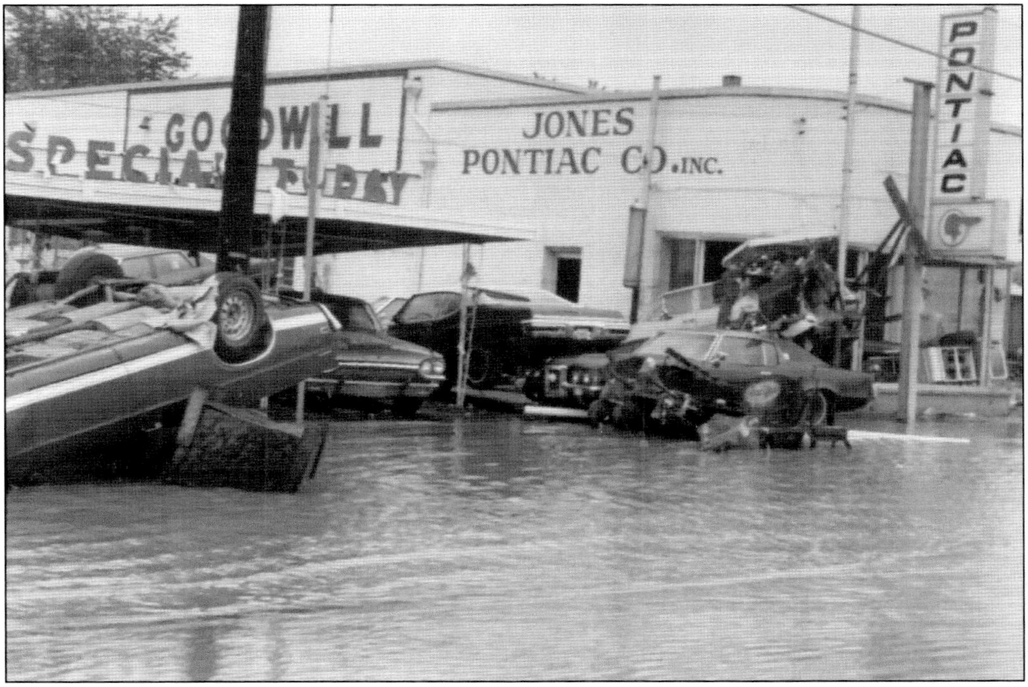

Jones Pontiac was on Centerway, near the Museum of Glass. (CPP.)

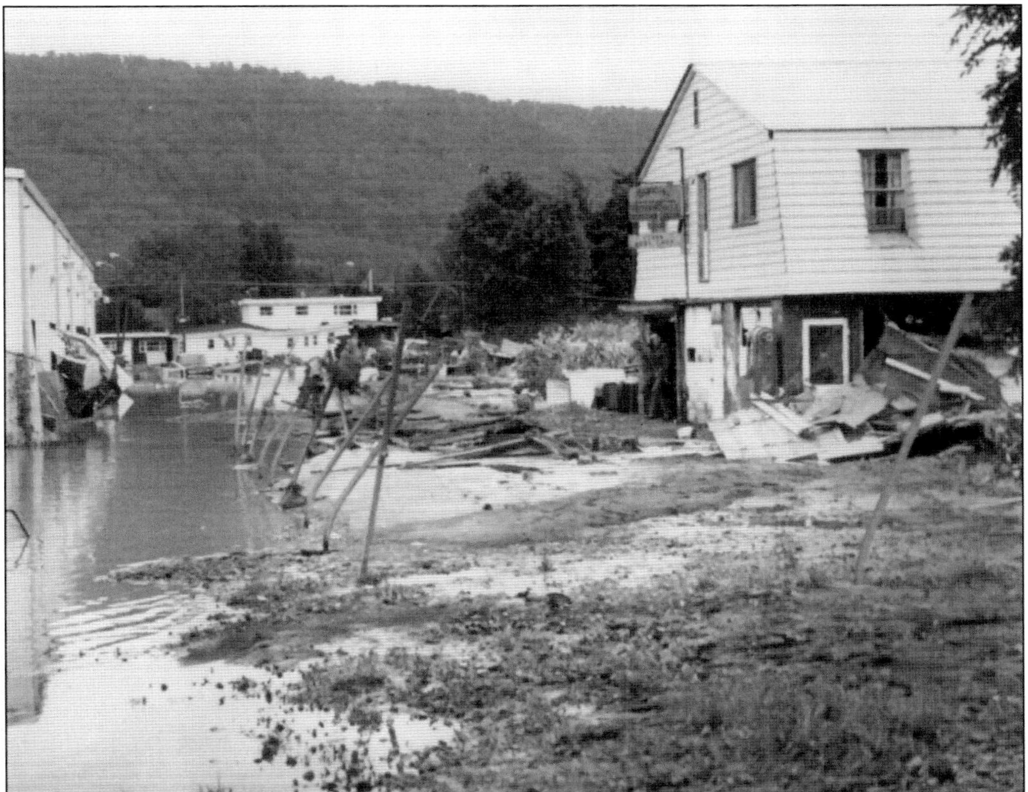

Clark's Body Shop was in the same neighborhood as Jones Pontiac. (CPP.)

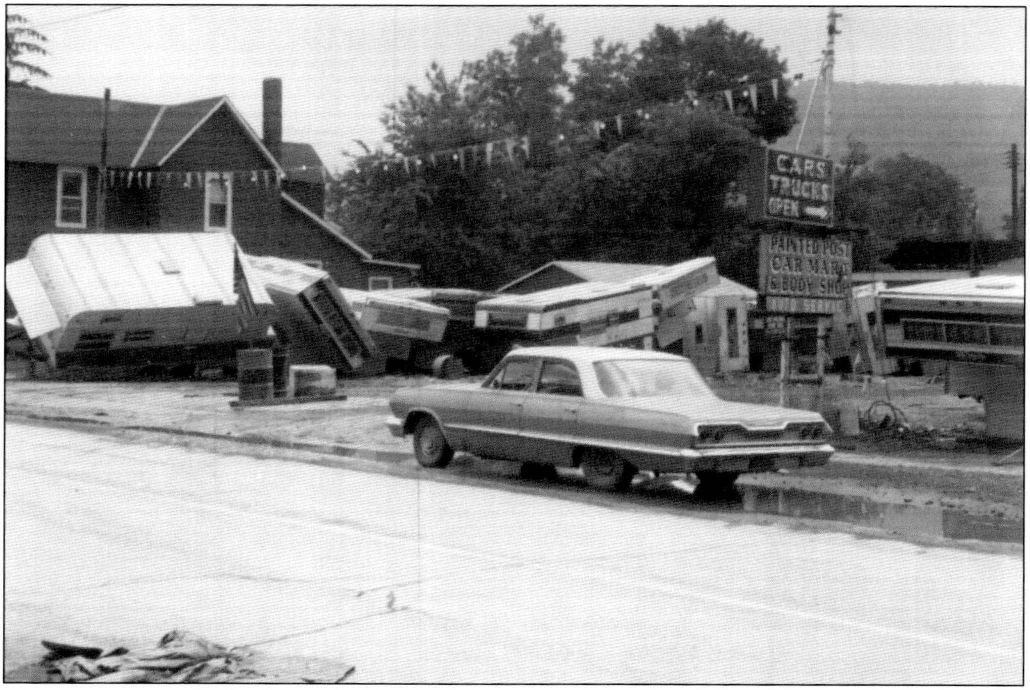

These recreational vehicles at the Painted Post Car Mart (East High Street) have also fared badly, but at least neatly. (CPP.)

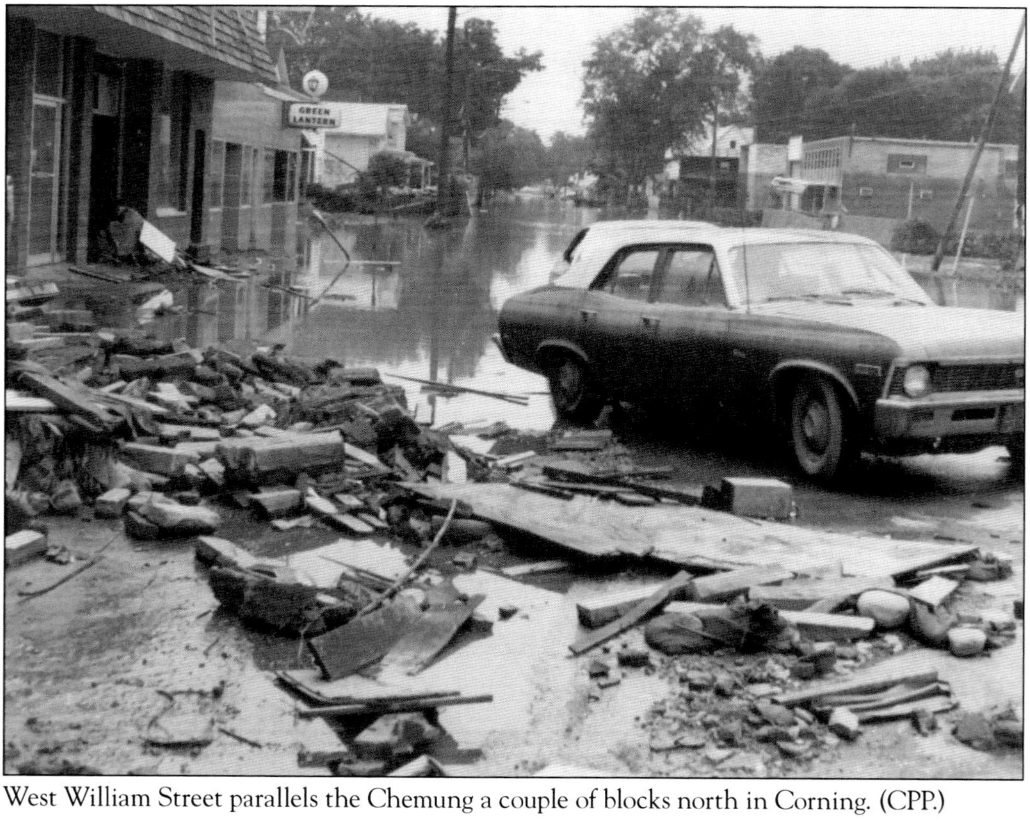

West William Street parallels the Chemung a couple of blocks north in Corning. (CPP.)

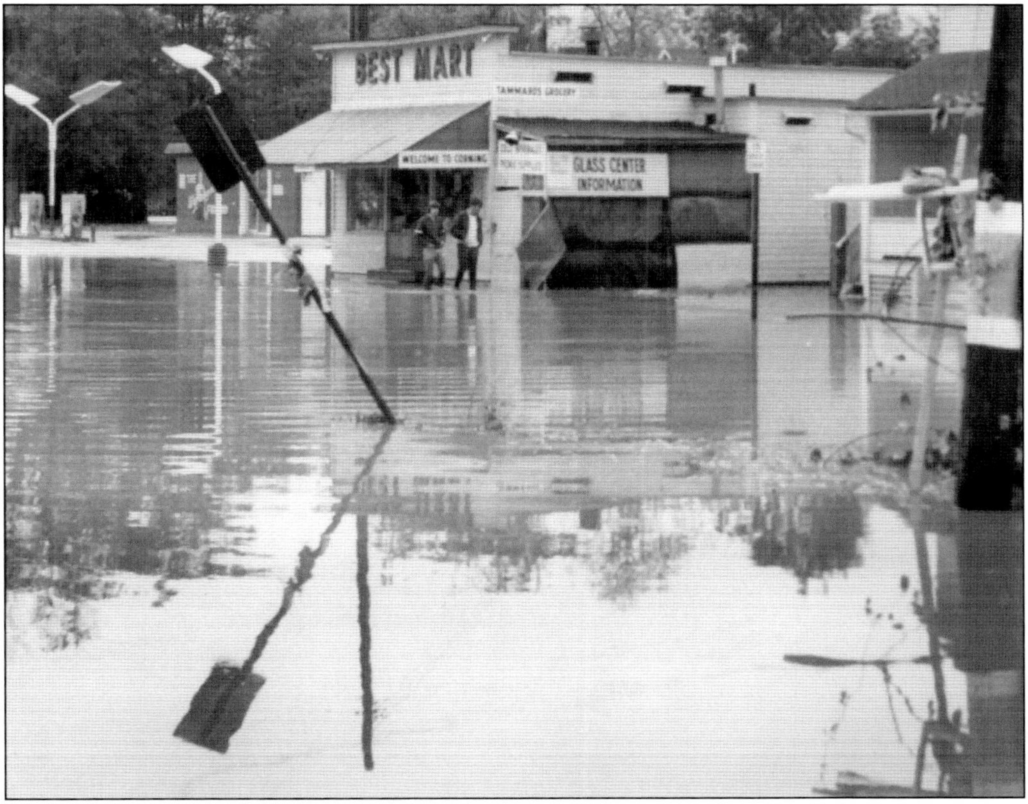

"Welcome to Corning," reads the sign on Tammaro's Best Buy Grocery in Baker Street. It also advertises "Cold beverages. Picnic Supplies. Glass Center Information." (CPP.)

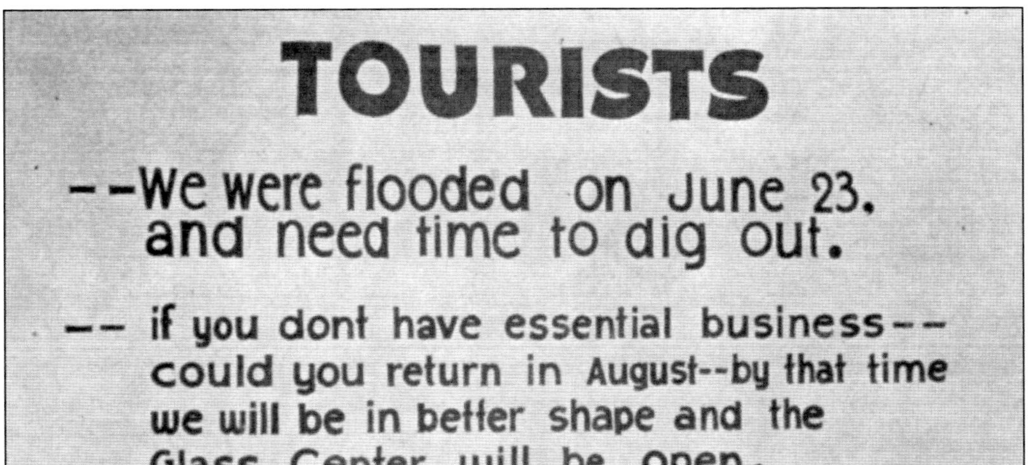

For months after the tragedy, makeshift road signs would beg tourists not to come to Corning. (CPP.)

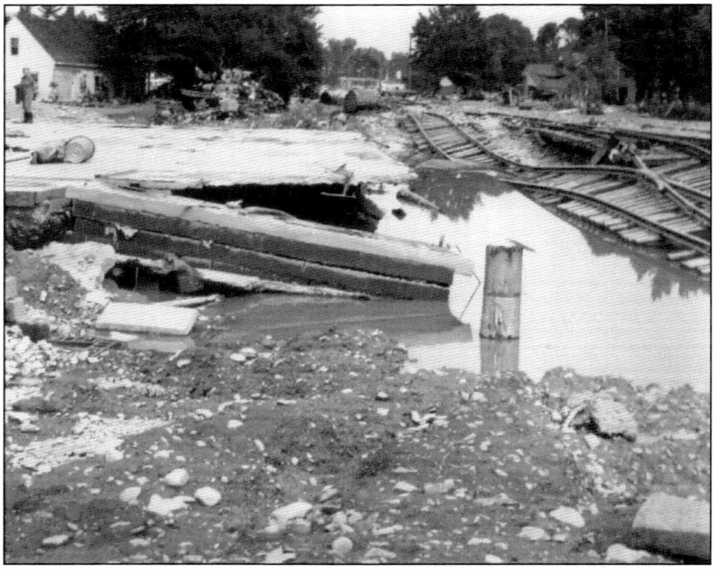

The Rotary Gas Station suffered badly, and the rail lines behind it fared perhaps even worse. Hurricane Agnes finally put the Erie Lackawanna Railroad—a major corporation, with roots stretching back more than a century—out of business. Even discounting the impending bankruptcy, the disruption of rail and road traffic would hurt the entire nation. (CPP.)

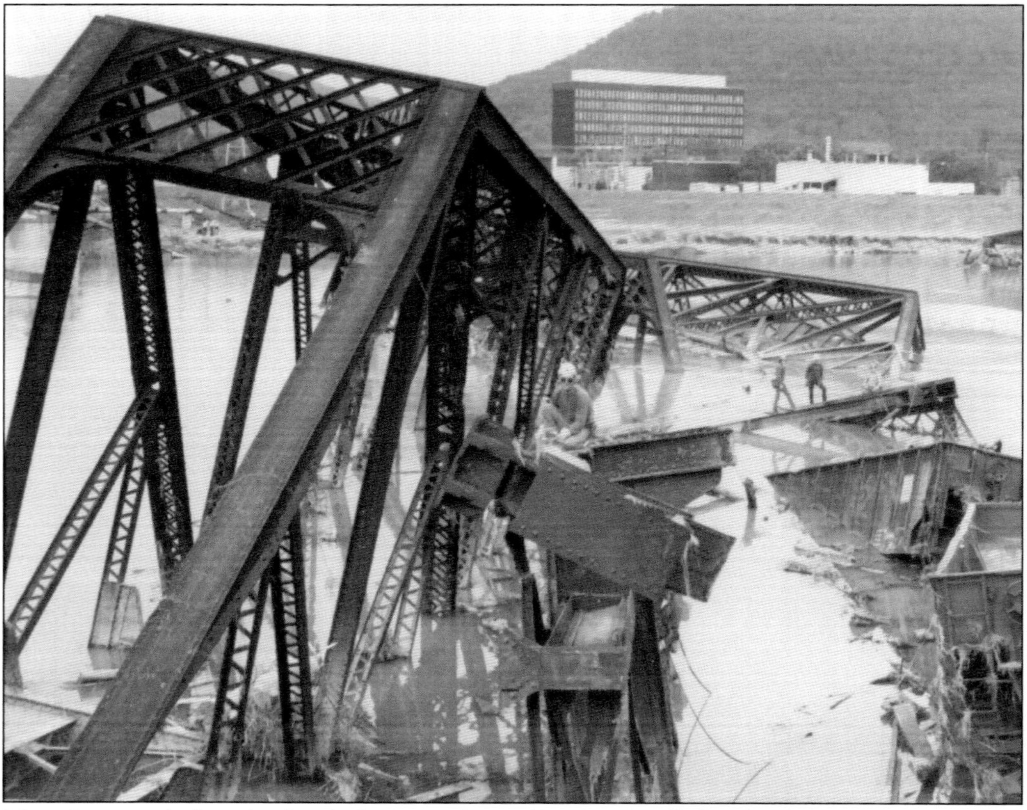

The afternoon before the flood, the Penn Central Railroad pulled 15 loaded coal gondolas onto its bridge over the Chemung in Corning, hoping to anchor it down. About 14 hours later, the bridge was lost anyway, inadvertently creating a dam that helped force water over both banks into the city. The Corning Glass Works world headquarters is in the background, with the Corning Glass Center/Corning Museum of Glass to the right. (CPP.)

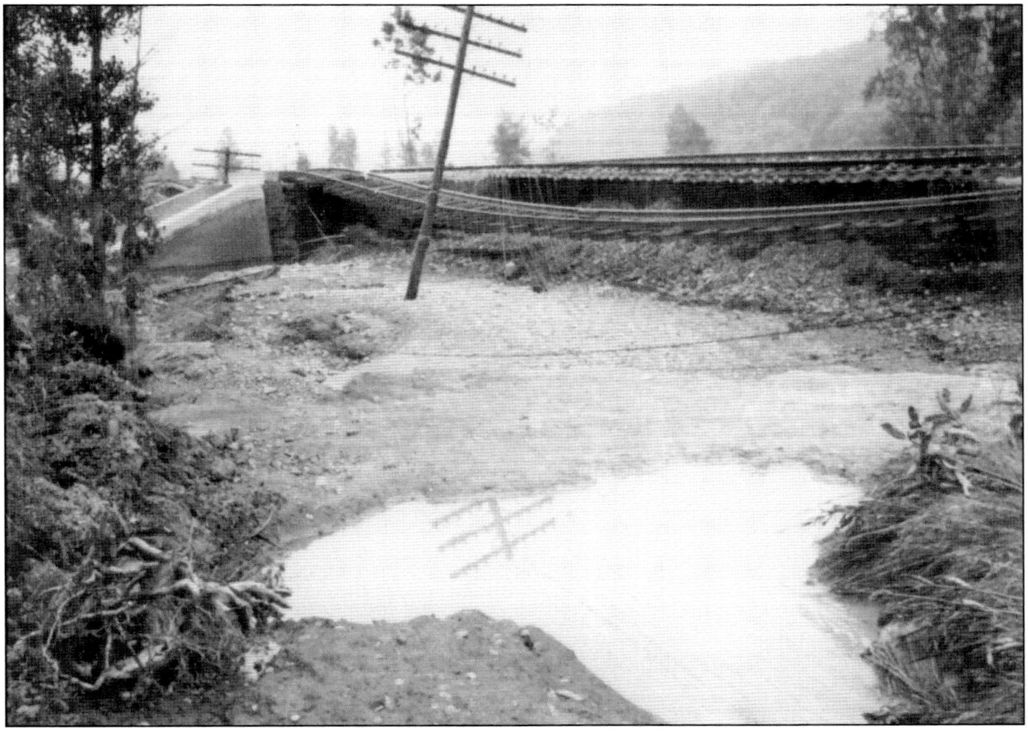

Gang Mills, located south of Corning in the town of Erwin, is the site of a significant rail yard, now operated by Norfolk Southern. Besides the damage to the rail bed, bridge, and tracks, notice the downed utility lines. Hurricane Agnes's catastrophic damage to railroads drove the creation of the federally sponsored Conrail freight line in 1976. (EL.)

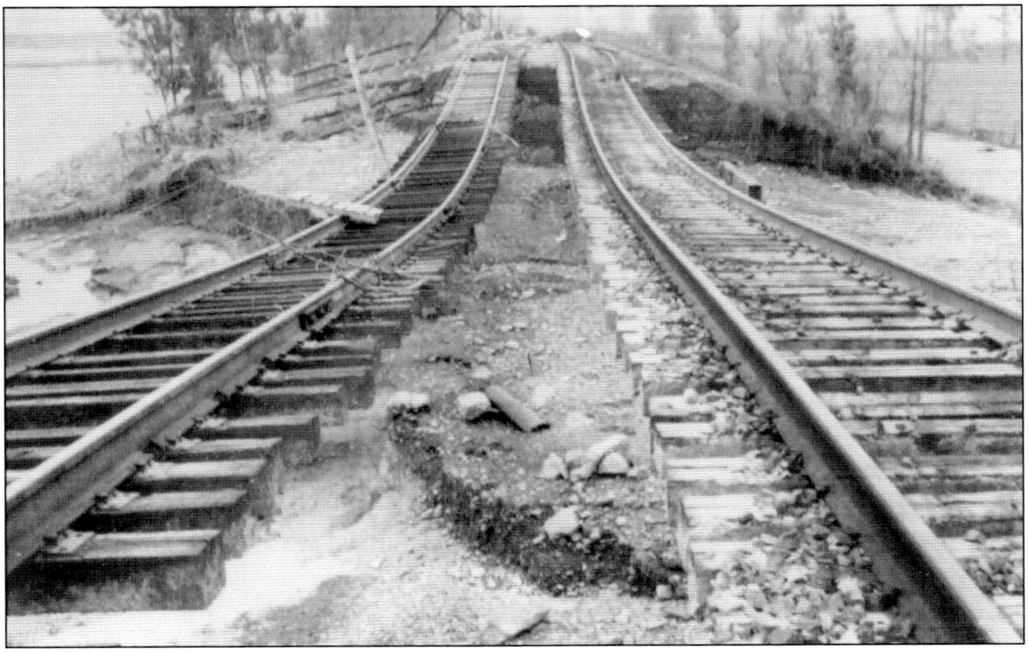

The earth itself would have to be restored before anything could be done with these tracks in Gang Mills. (EL.)

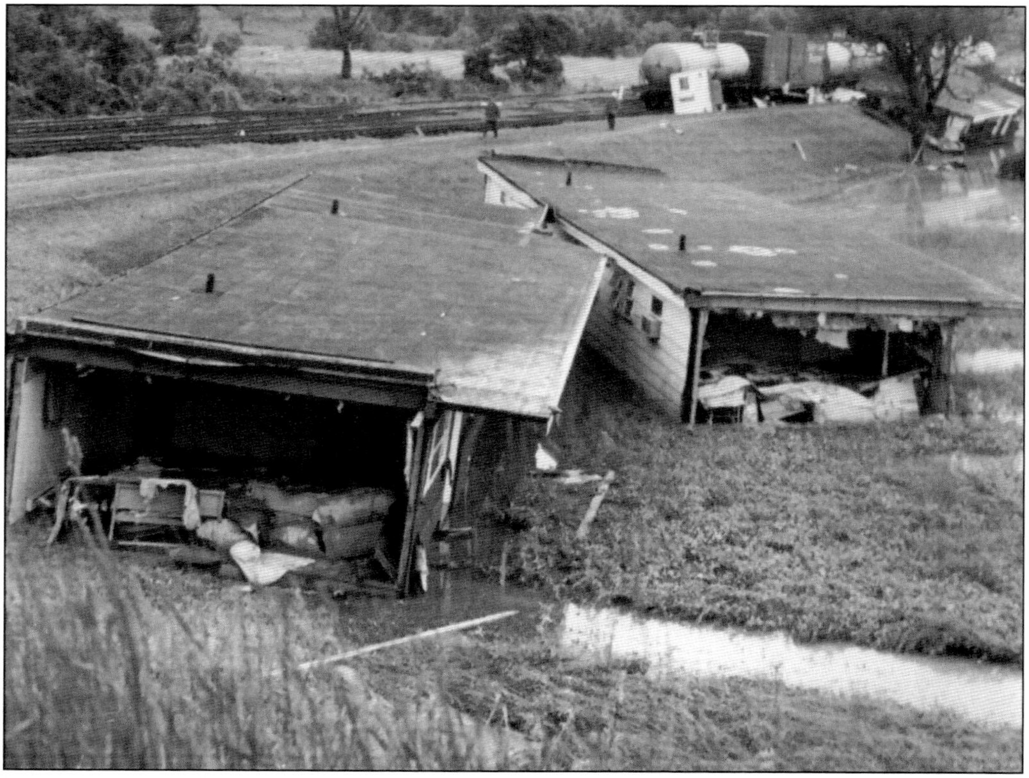

Some sections of the Centerway Motel sailed off to collide with the railroad. Neither side could claim to have won the encounter. (CPP.)

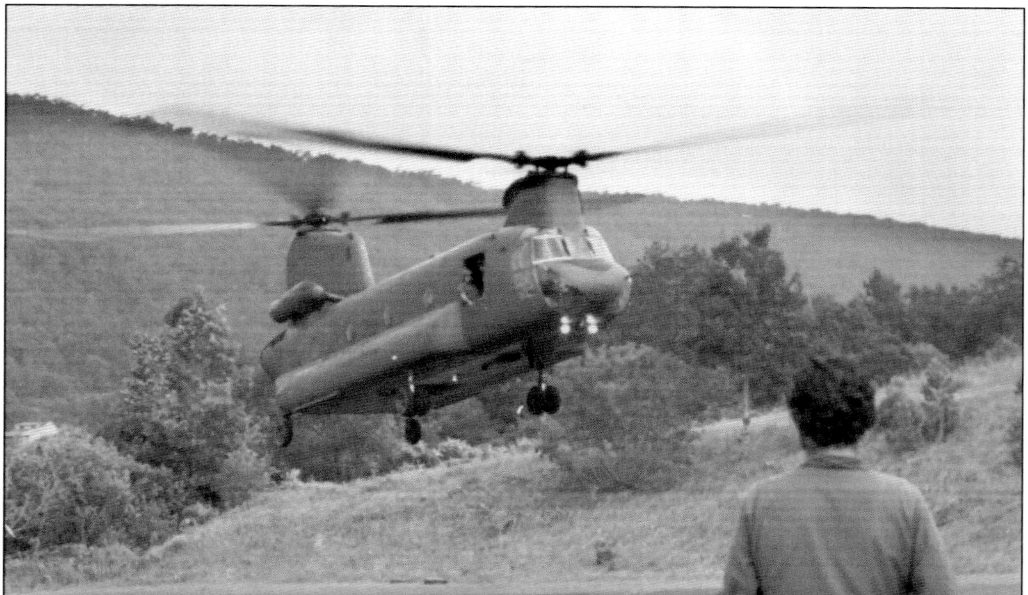

Helicopters and the armed forces became saviors in the Southern Tier and throughout the gash carved out by Agnes. Reserves and the National Guard turned out statewide. The Navy sent helicopters from as far away as Rhode Island. (CPP.)

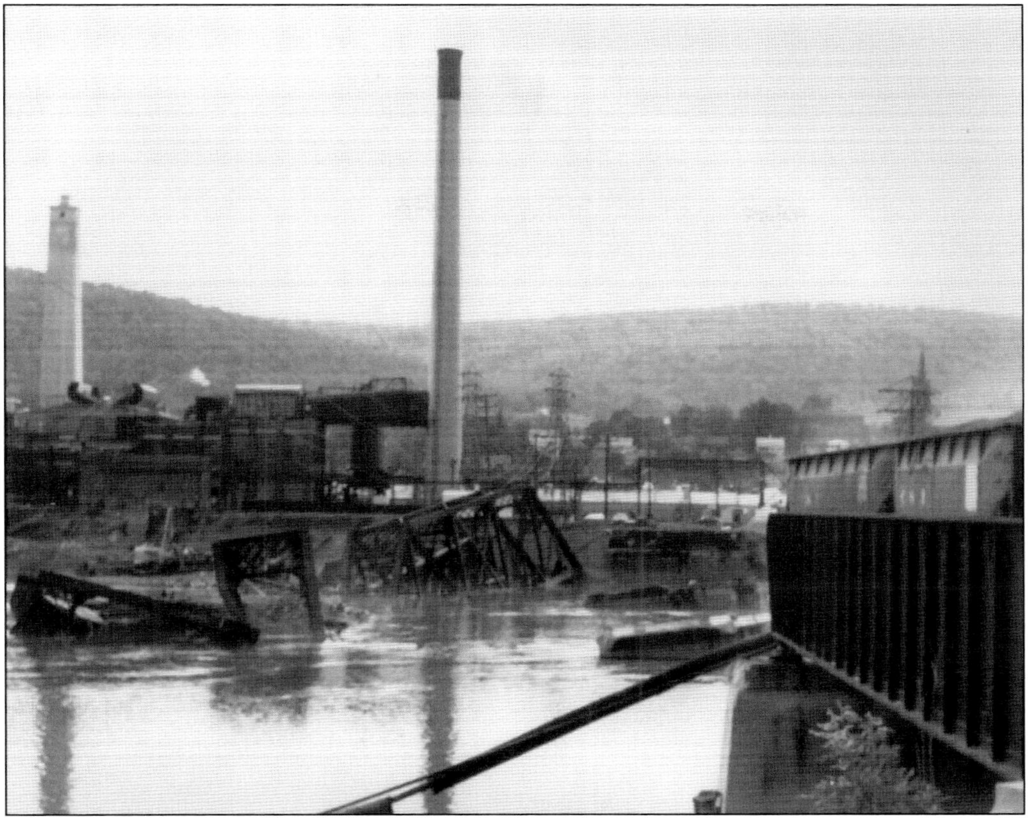

The bridges, the electrical system, and the Glass Works—all of which are visible here—were out of business for far too long. (CPP.)

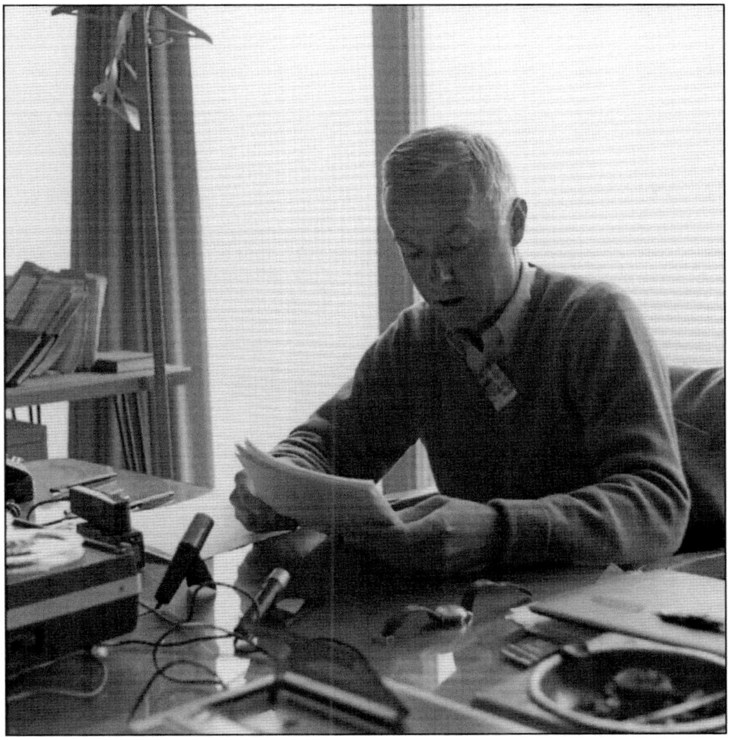

On June 27, Glass Works chairman Amory Houghton Jr. took to those airwaves and print columns that were still functioning to speak clearly and firmly: the Glass Works was staying in Corning, would rebuild in Corning, would help rebuild the city of Corning, and would lend money to its employees and their families. Perhaps no action in the city's history has been more significant. (CI.)

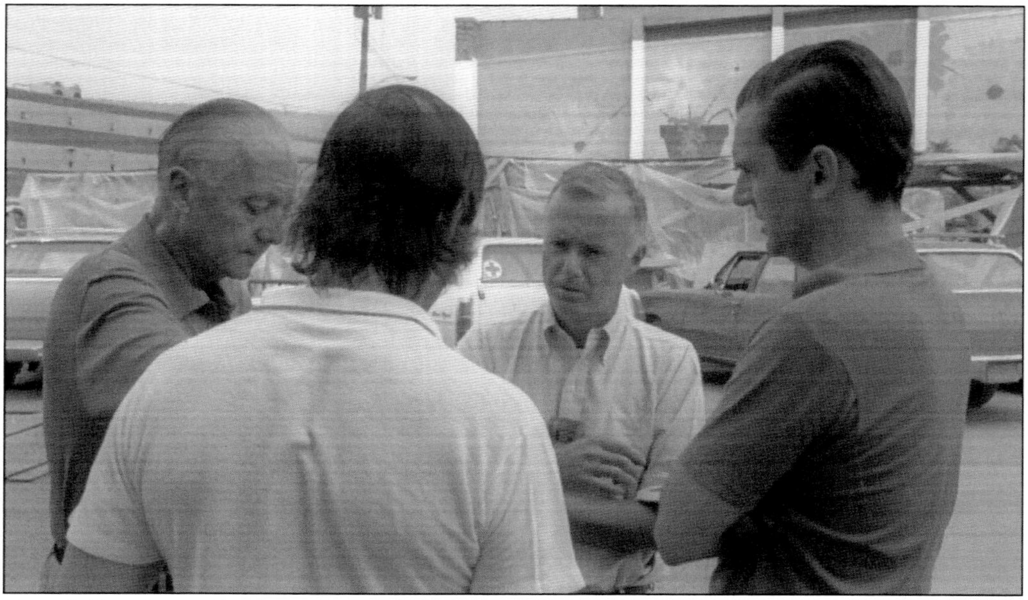

"Amo" Houghton (facing camera), his brother James Houghton (right), and their father the Honorable Amory Houghton Sr. (left) confer in the midst of the crisis. The eldest man was a former Glass Works chairman and a former US ambassador to France. Amo would later serve, as his grandfather had, in Congress. "Jamie" would later be chairman and chief executive officer of Corning Incorporated, as the company was renamed in 1989. The Republican family used its political connections to make sure the region's post-flood needs were remembered in Washington. (CI.)

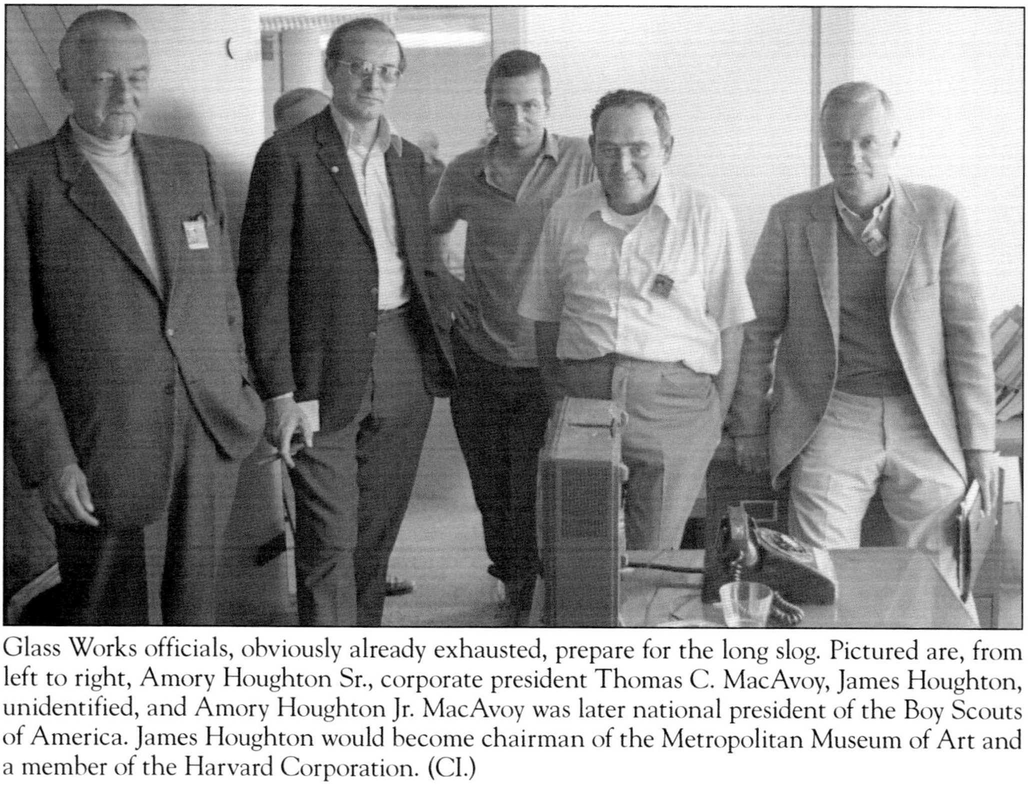

Glass Works officials, obviously already exhausted, prepare for the long slog. Pictured are, from left to right, Amory Houghton Sr., corporate president Thomas C. MacAvoy, James Houghton, unidentified, and Amory Houghton Jr. MacAvoy was later national president of the Boy Scouts of America. James Houghton would become chairman of the Metropolitan Museum of Art and a member of the Harvard Corporation. (CI.)

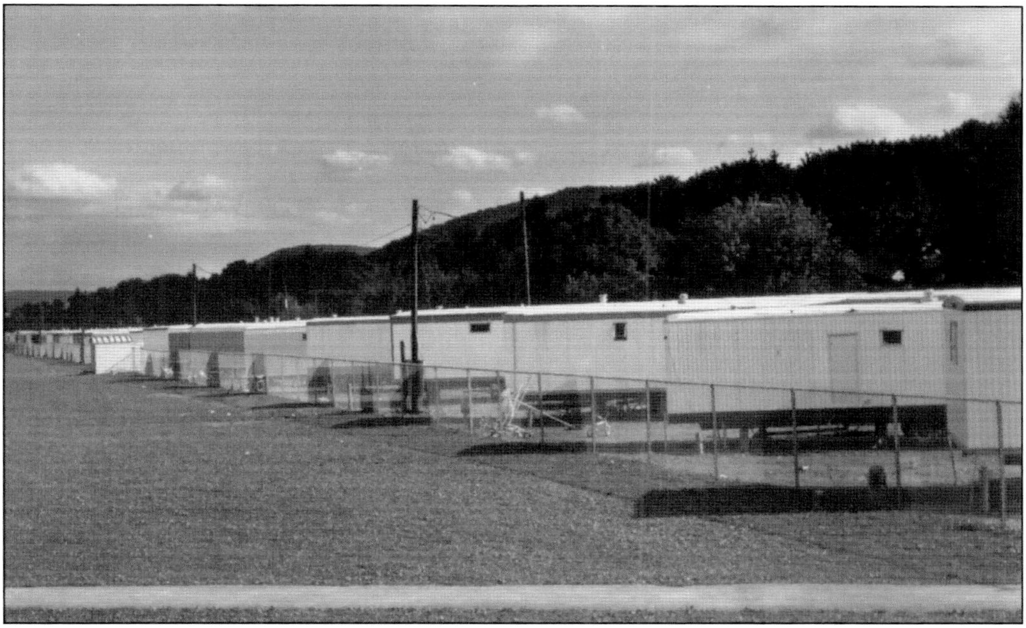

Craig Park, located on Victory Highway in Painted Post, became a temporary home to trailers from the federal Department of Housing and Urban Development (HUD). HUD brought in almost 2,000 of these mobile homes. (CPP.)

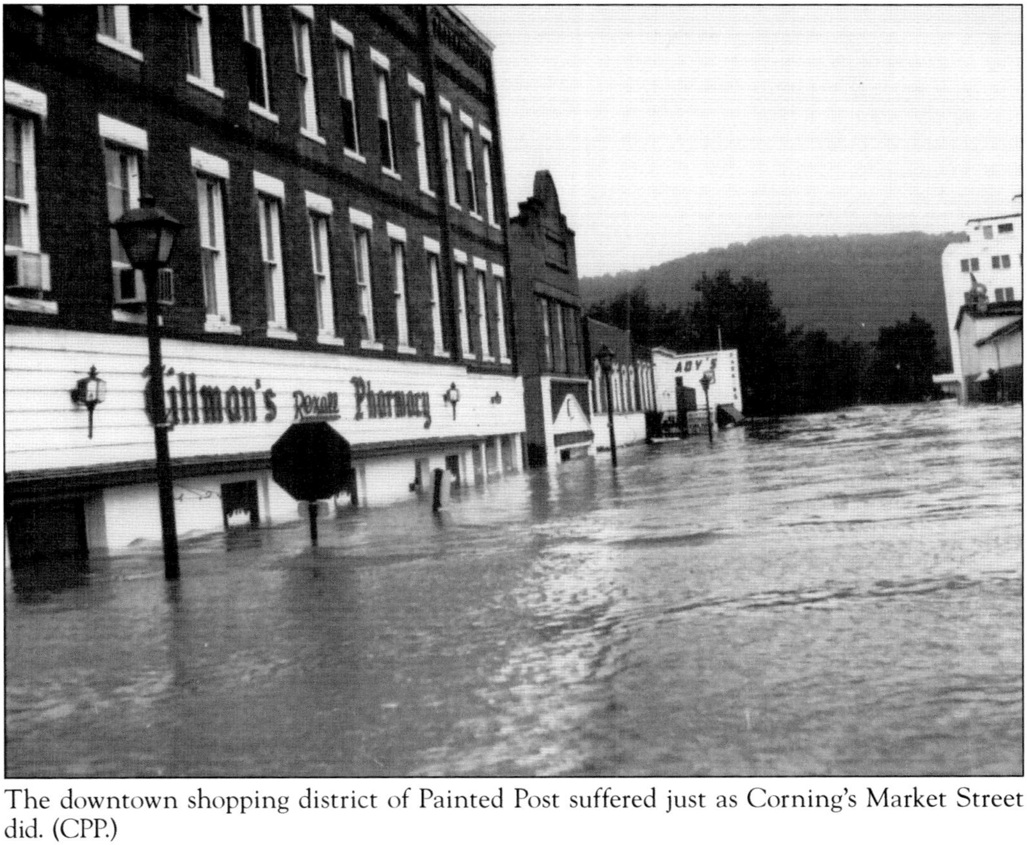

The downtown shopping district of Painted Post suffered just as Corning's Market Street did. (CPP.)

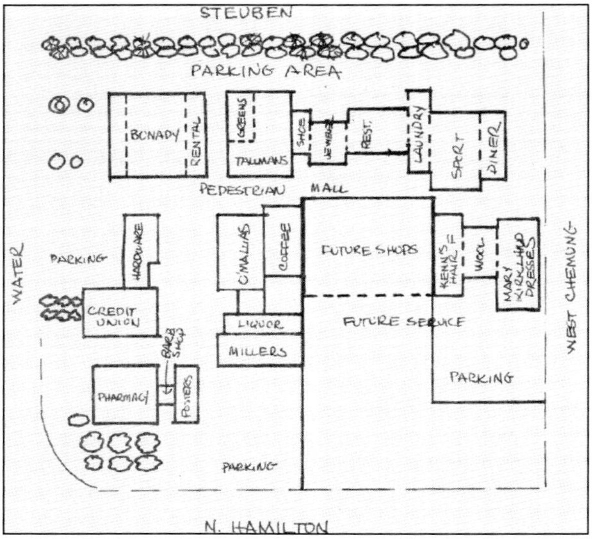

Urban Renewal planned a new $6.4 million shopping center for Painted Post. Village Square, including Tallman's, is still busy today. (CPP.)

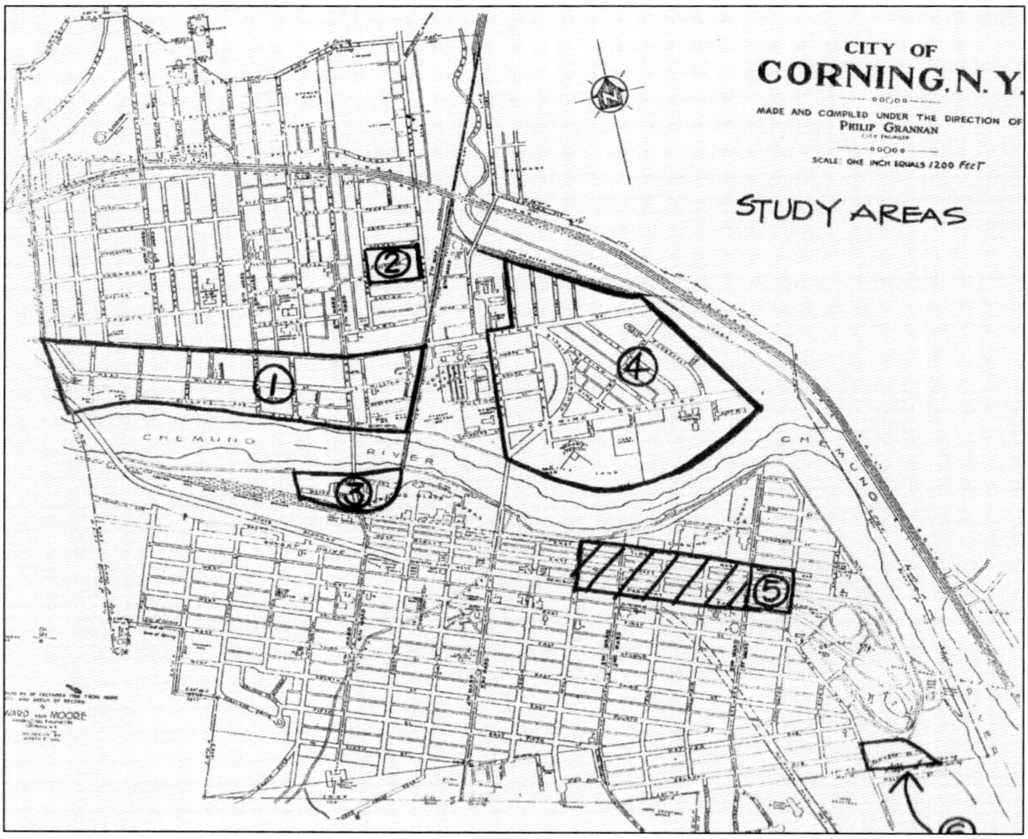

All the marked areas of Corning city needed extensive architectural reviews following the flood. The Tioga and Conhocton Rivers come together to form the Chemung River just west of this map, with the Tioga having just received the Canisteo River. Post Creek can be seen coming down from the north. Houghton Plat is roughly the area bounded by Post Creek, the Chemung River, and Centerway. Glass Works production facilities were on the riverbank near sections No. 5 and 3. Headquarters and the glass center were between sections No. 1 and 4. (SCHS.)

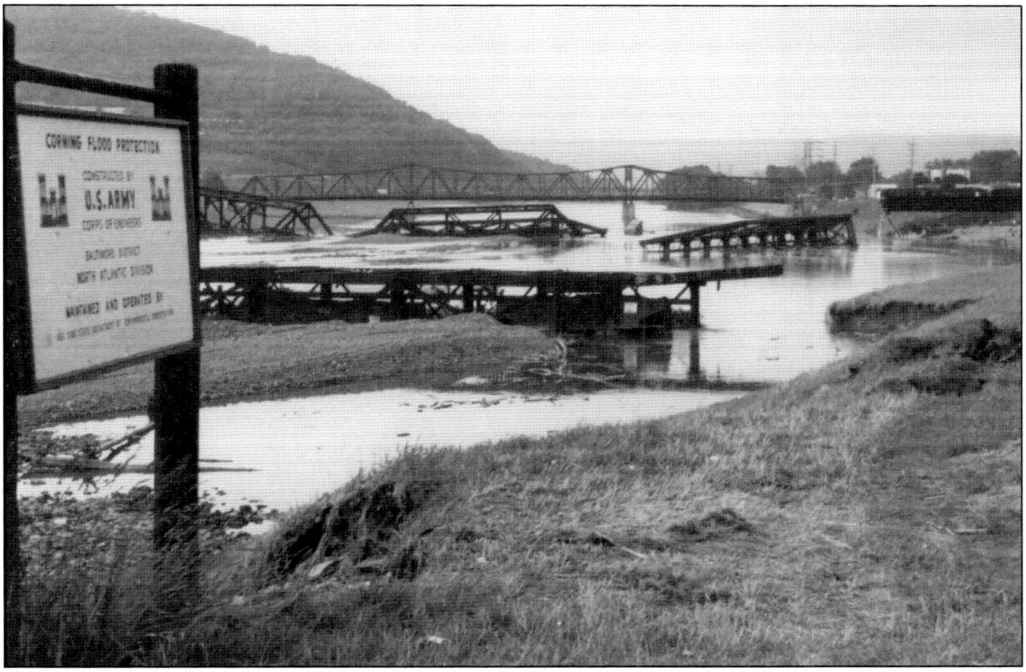

A long history of flooding had inspired 20th-century alterations designed to protect the Chemung and Canisteo Valleys. Hurricane Agnes was beyond what anyone had planned or prepared for, so the US Army Corps of Engineers was back on the job. (CPP.)

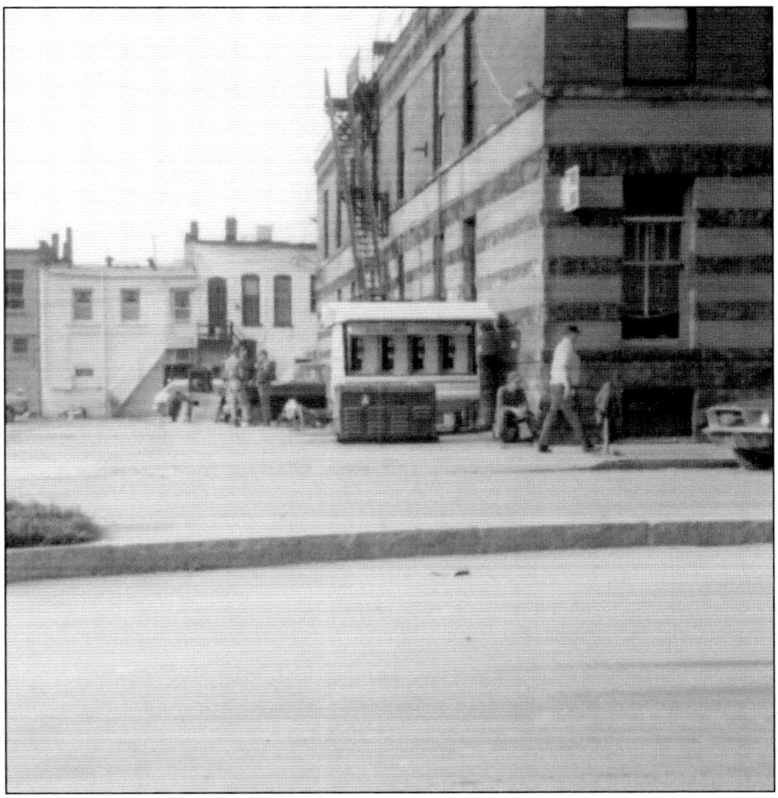

The small trailer is an emergency telephone station outside the police station in Corning's city hall (now the Rockwell Museum of Western Art). (AB.)

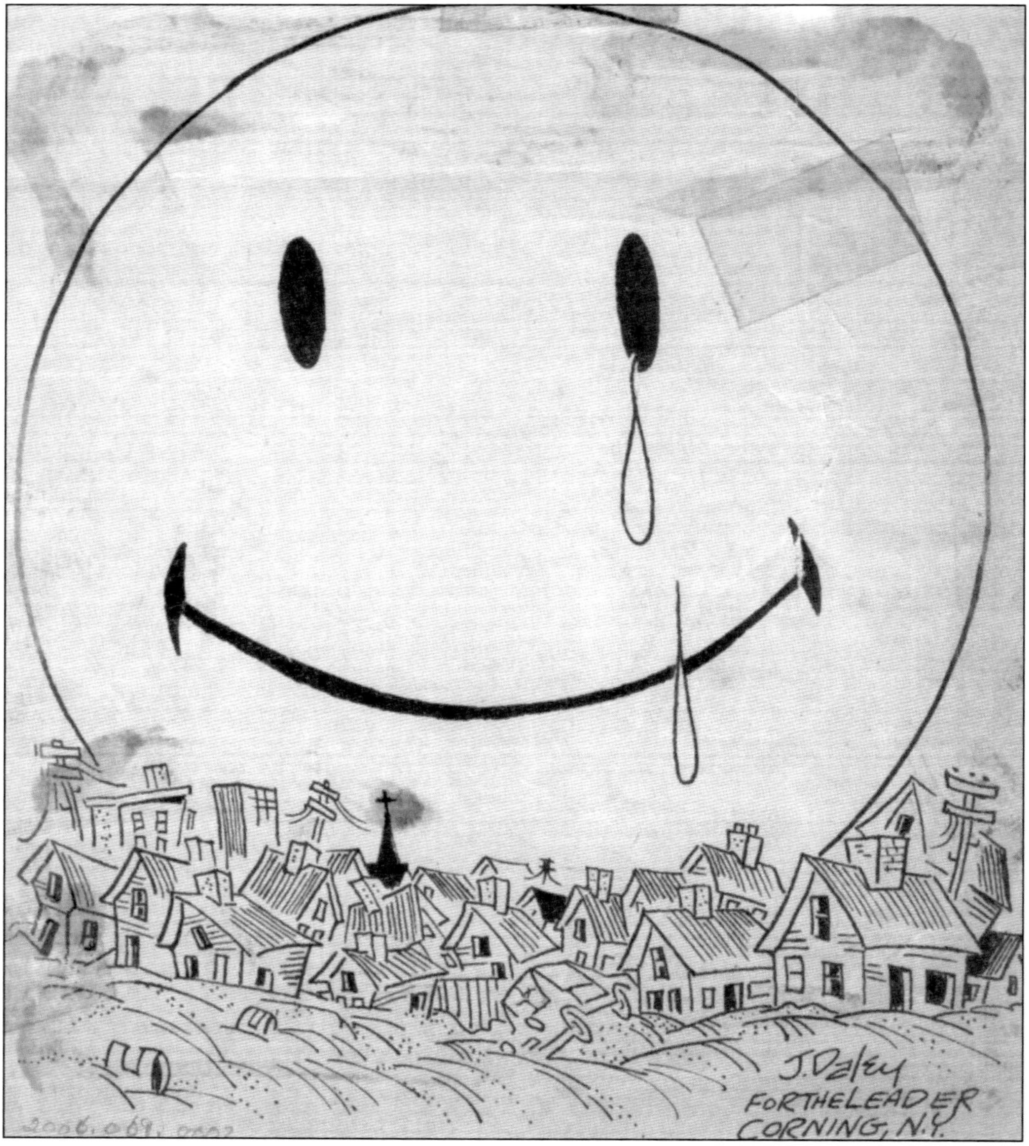

Like Snoopy, the smiley face was an unavoidable 1970s icon. This *Leader* cartoon captured the sorrow and the hope both at once. (CPP.)

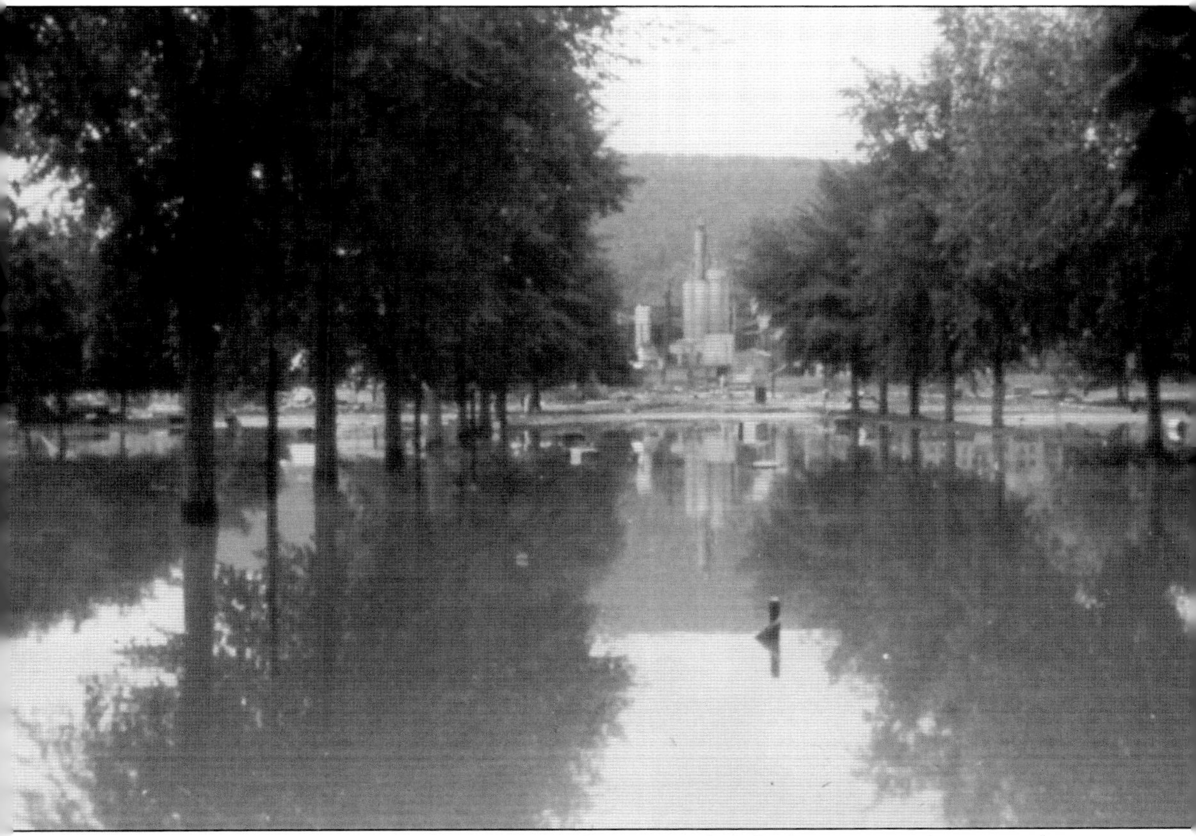

A sharp eye and an open imagination could do the same. While looking upon a disaster with an industrial background, a photographer has captured a reflection pool and monumental architecture worthy of a world capital. (RET.)

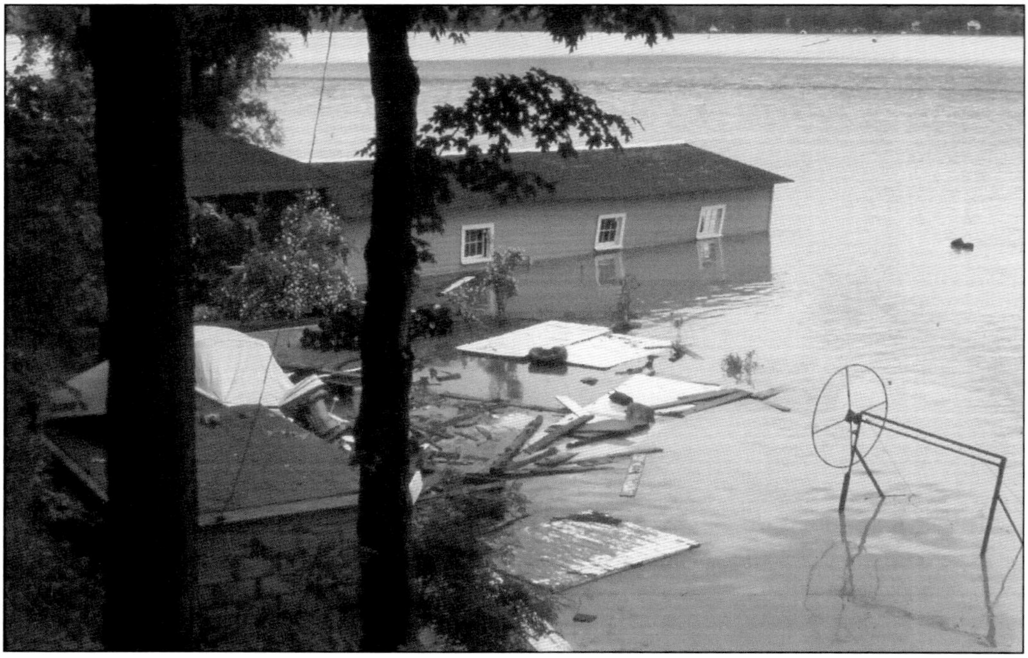

Elsewhere in Steuben County, the storms also took their toll. Keuka Lake rose three feet in two days, an event requiring apocalyptic rainfall. It flooded this boathouse and its surroundings at Corning Landing on the east side. (RET.)

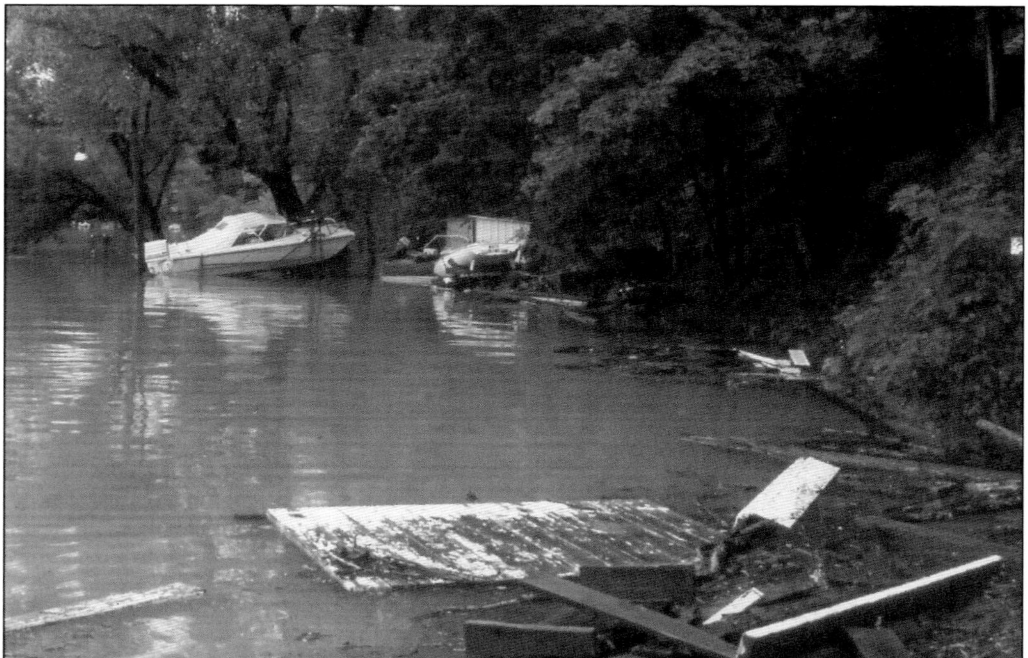

Bob and Liz Turissini spent much of the night of the flood corralling drifting boats and securing them to whatever was handy. (RET.)

Flabbergasting though it may have seemed locally, life went on outside. This carton appeared in the Corning *Leader*. (CPP.)

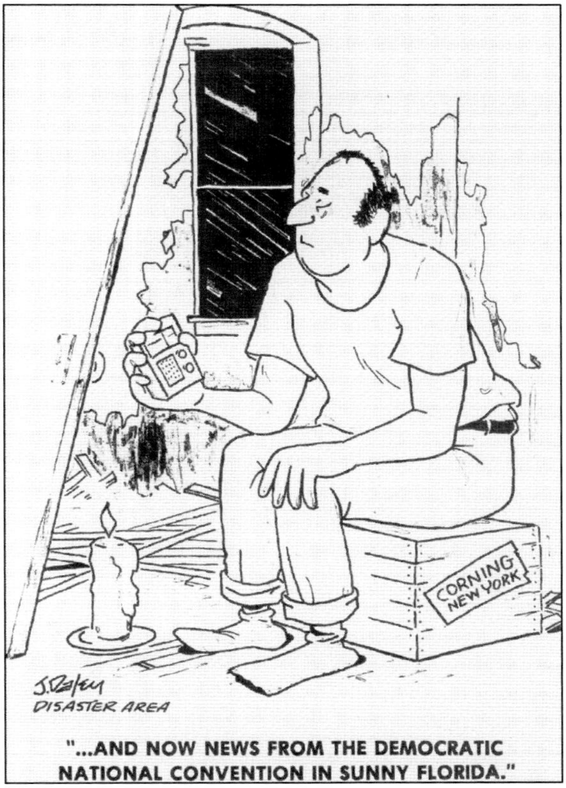

The Glass Works recruited hundreds of teenagers and put them to work on paid community cleanup. Besides military and government responders, groups such as the American Red Cross, Salvation Army, and Mennonite Disaster Service hurried to the region. Some stayed on the job for years. (CPP.)

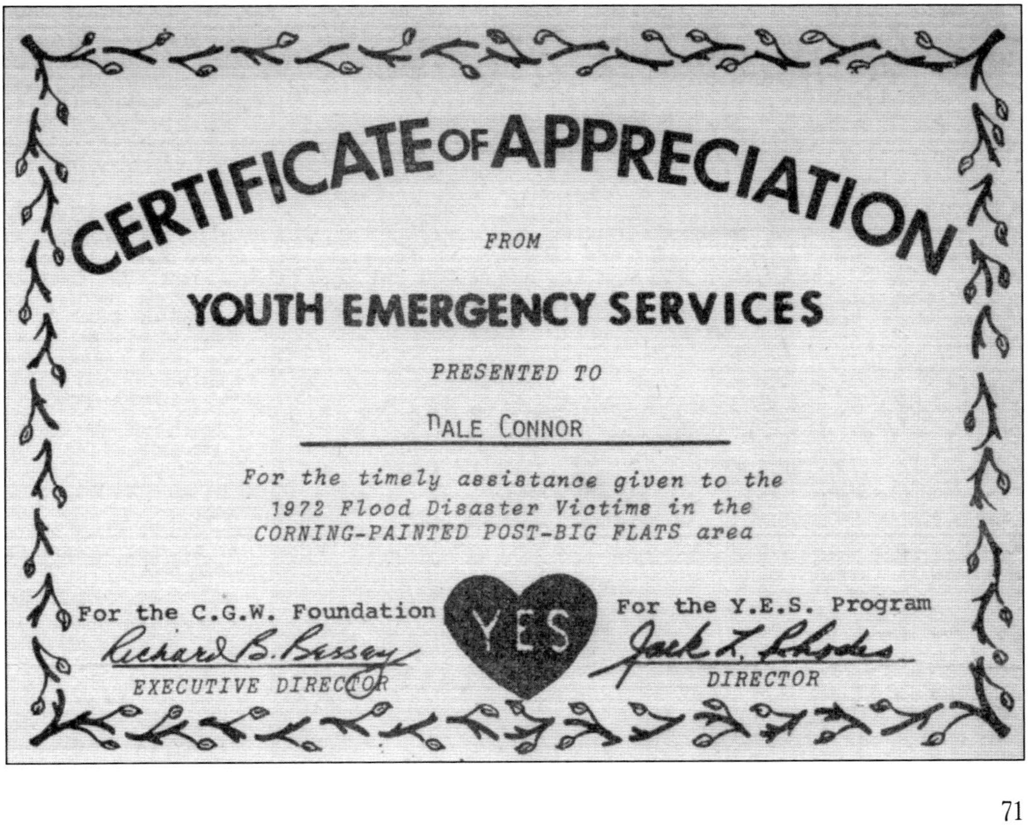
CERTIFICATE OF APPRECIATION

FROM

YOUTH EMERGENCY SERVICES

PRESENTED TO

DALE CONNOR

For the timely assistance given to the 1972 Flood Disaster Victims in the CORNING-PAINTED POST-BIG FLATS area

For the C.G.W. Foundation
Richard B. Bessey
EXECUTIVE DIRECTOR

YES

For the Y.E.S. Program
Jack L. Rhodes
DIRECTOR

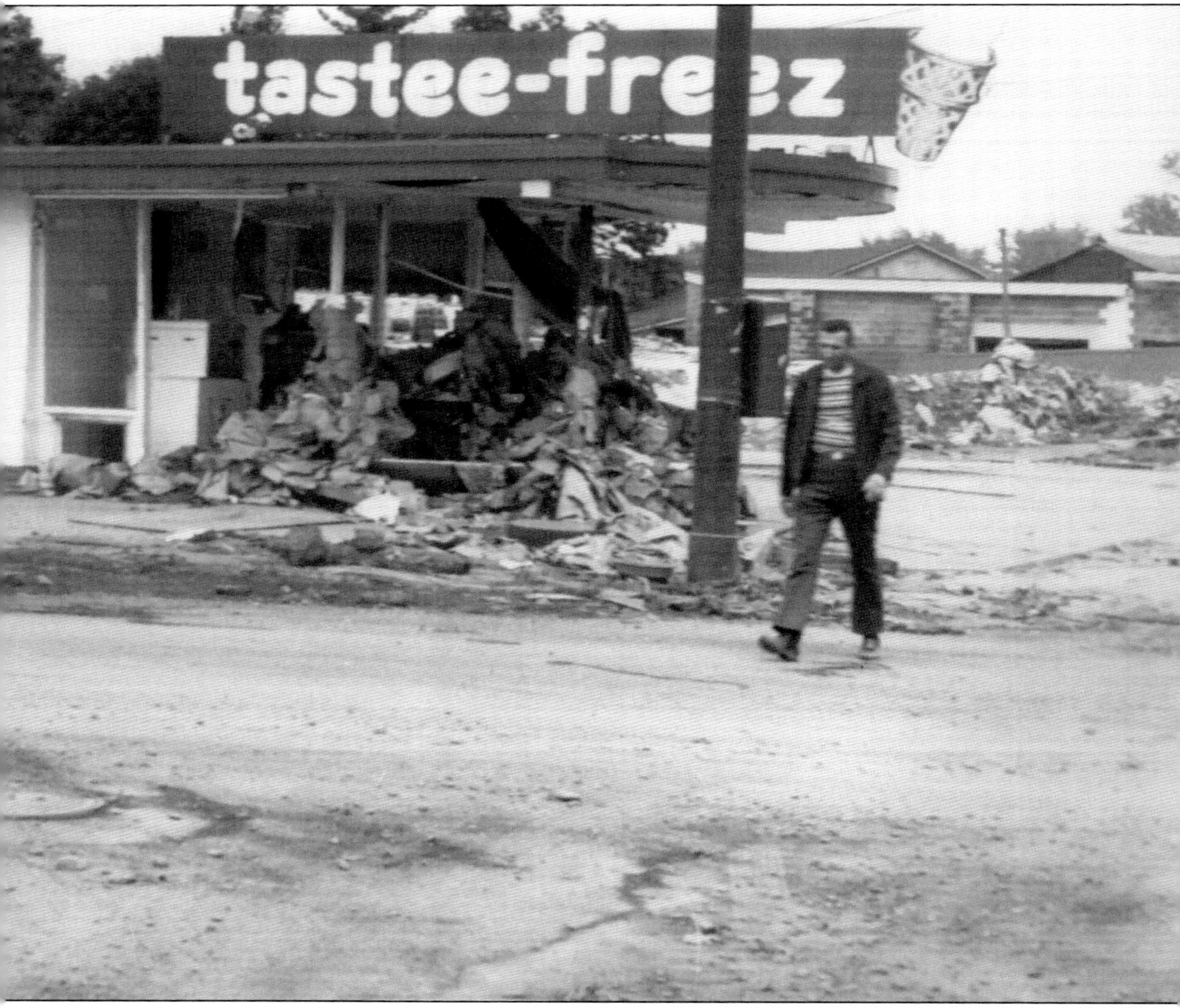

The city may lie in ruins, the clothes may be borrowed, and the drinking water may come by truck. But it is time to rebuild. (CPP.)

Two

The Corning Museum of Glass

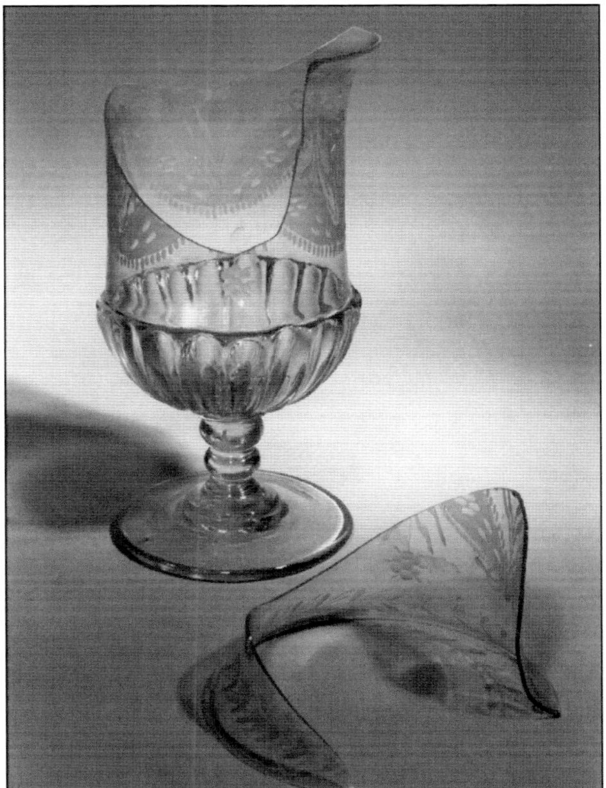

The flood also devastated a world-level cultural resource; the Corning Museum of Glass was the first major American museum to suffer such an inundation. CMOG benefited from the support of a major corporation but also from expertise the art world had wrung from the previous decade's flooding of the Arno River in Florence. (CMOG.)

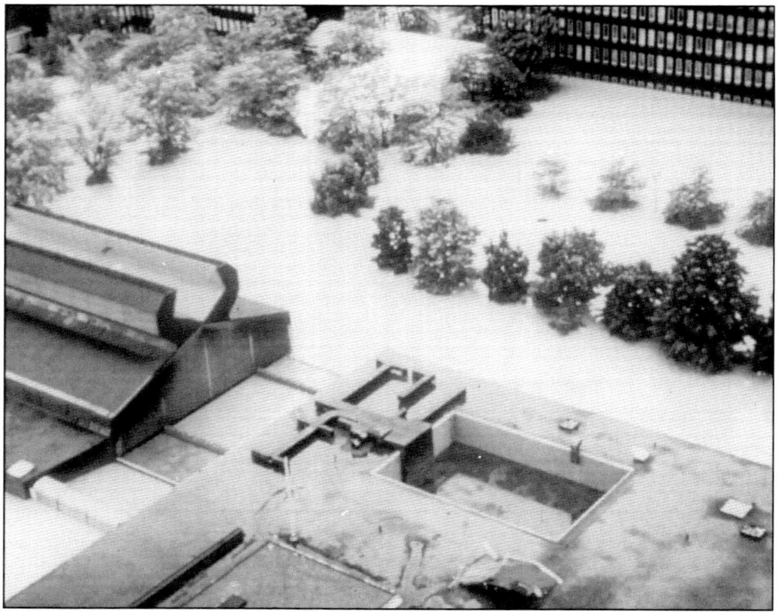

In 1972, the Corning Glass Center housed the museum, a hall of science and industry, an auditorium, and the Steuben Glass factory, which produced art glass. When the waters rose, the Corning Glass Center and surrounding Glass Works headquarters facilities were among the first casualties. (CMOG, copyright by Tom Gill.)

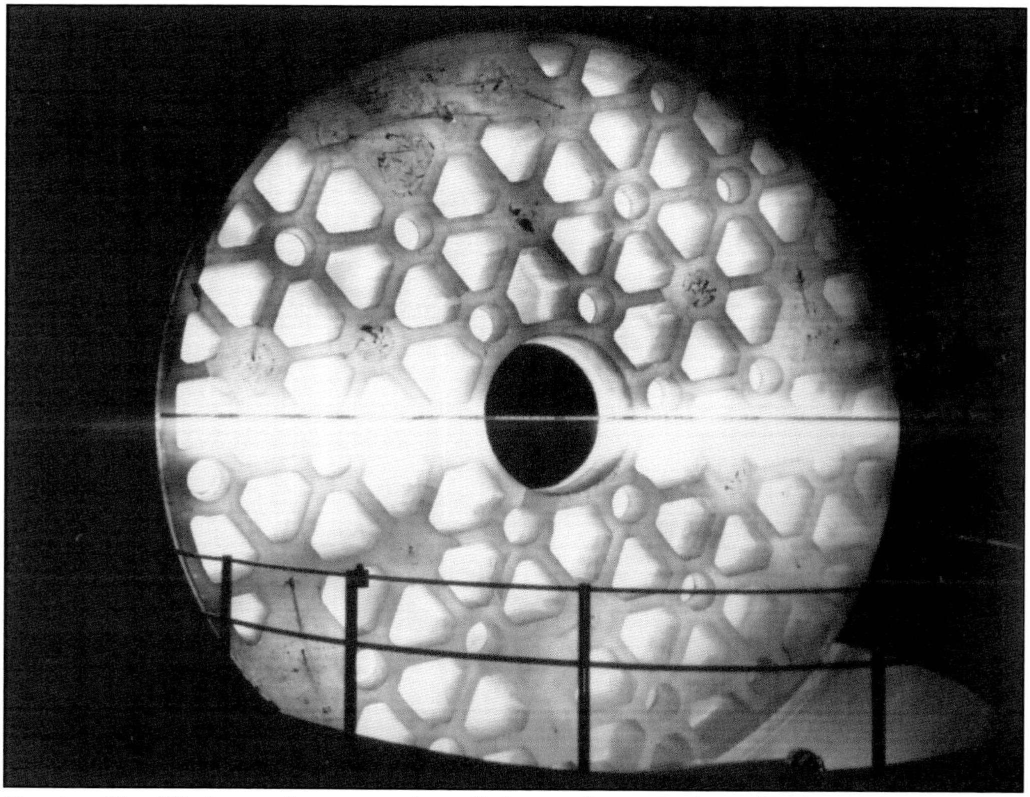

Corning Glass Works cast the unprecedentedly huge reflector for the Hale Observatory on Mount Palomar, California, in the 1930s. The first attempt failed, and the second, though successful, was threatened by the 1935 flood. The flawed 200-inch original, which became a tourist attraction, was flooded in 1935 and again in 1972, by which time it had become an anchor exhibit at the Museum of Glass. That ribbon across its diameter represents the 1972 high-water mark. (CPP.)

That high-water mark is also visible on these exhibition cases. (CMOG.)

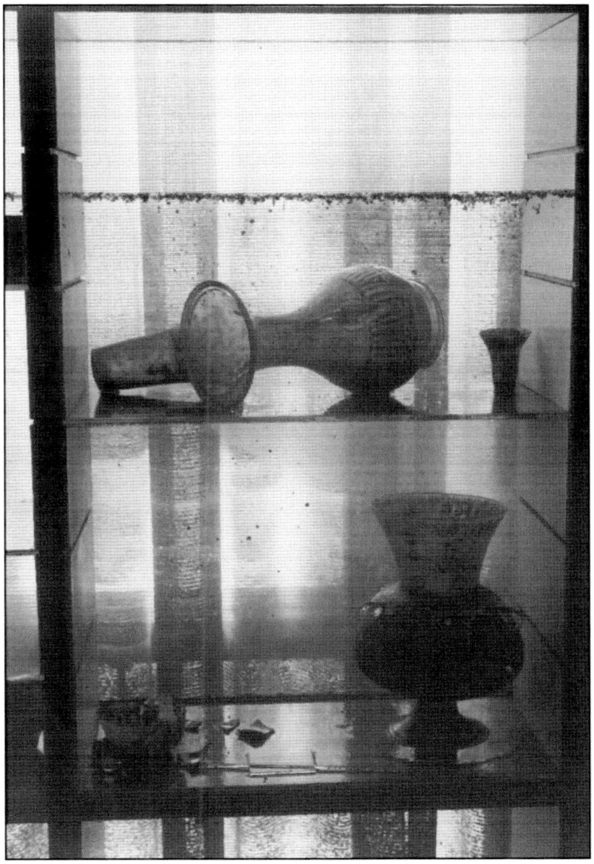

Notice the broken artifacts within. Some treasures were irretrievable. But, many others would be rescued and restored through long, hard, costly work. (CMOG.)

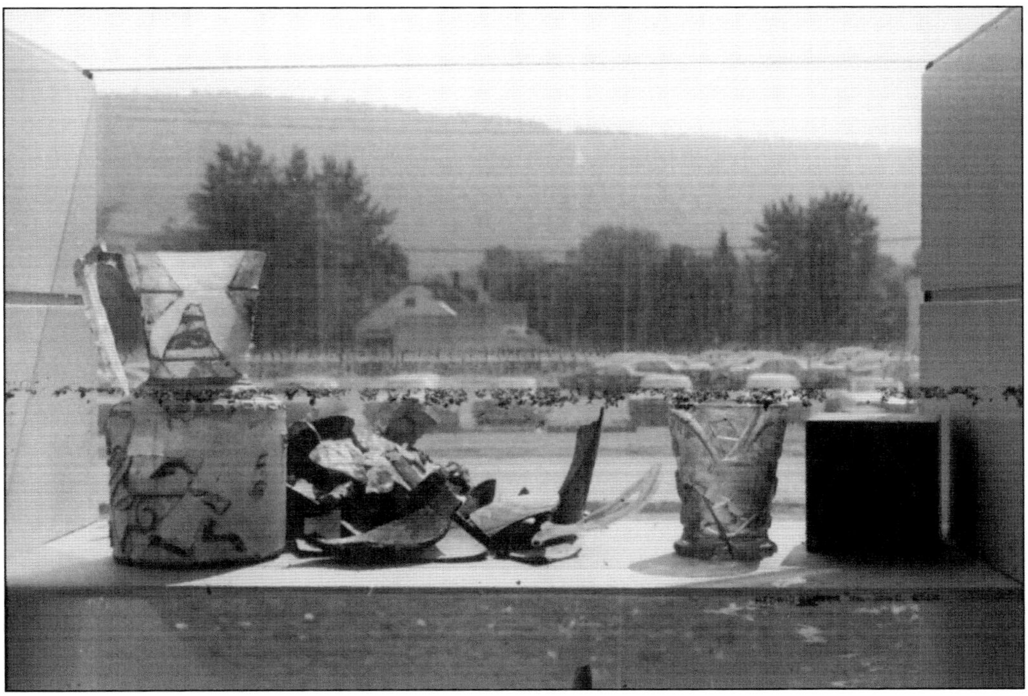

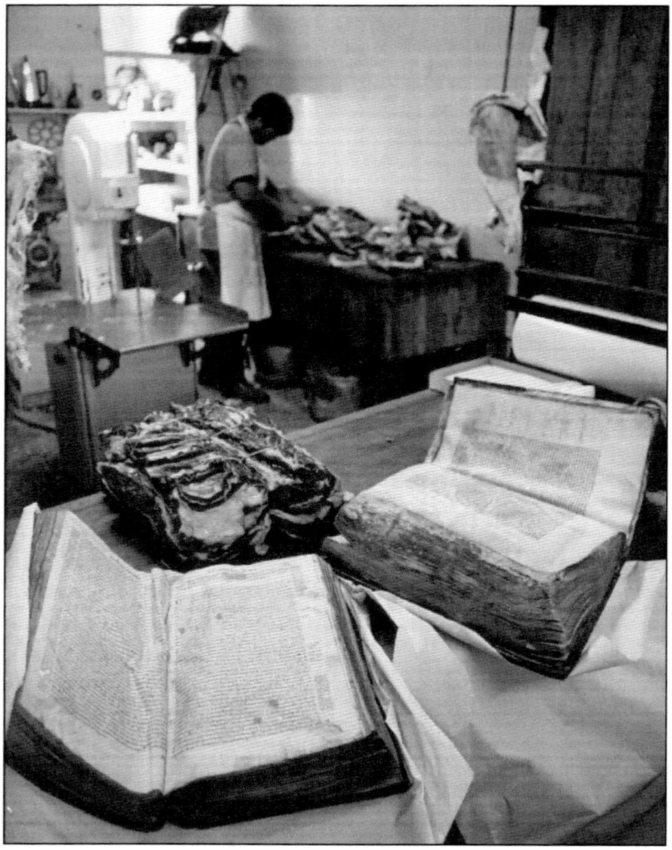

In many ways, the museum's Rakow Library fared worse than the main artifact collection. Where not actually broken, many of the glass treasures were cleaned rather simply, which was not the case with books. These volumes were taken to a butcher shop for freezing to arrest deterioration until they were attended to. (CMOG.)

The destruction stretched far and wide. Offices, in this case Bob Brill's, were ruined. (CMOG.)

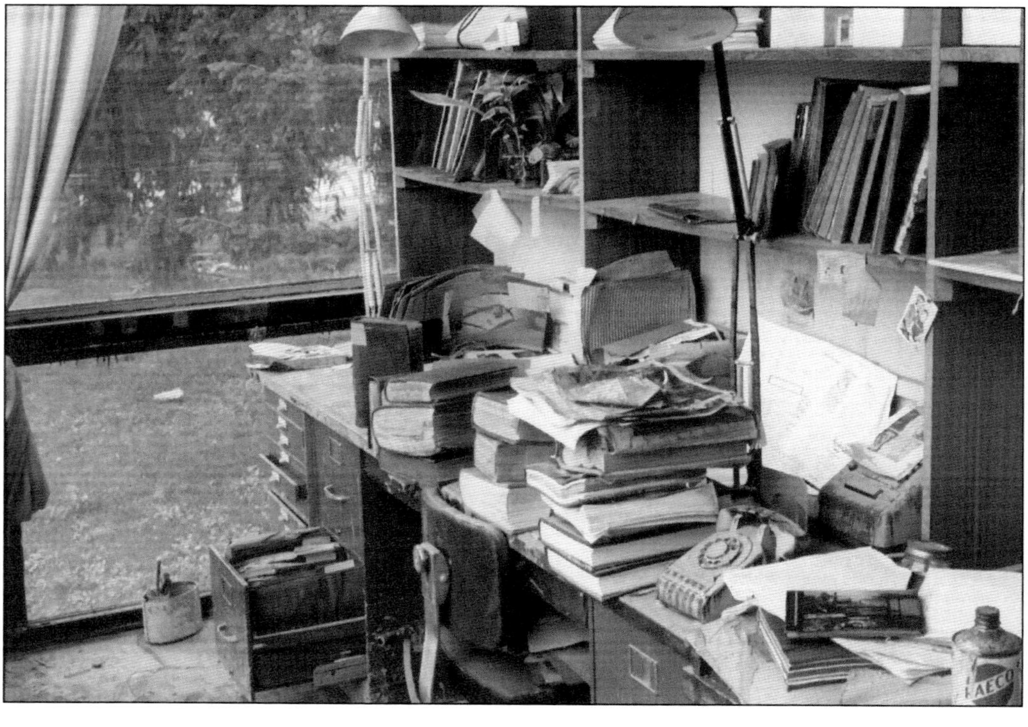

Once important furnishings and supplies were now junk. (CMOG.)

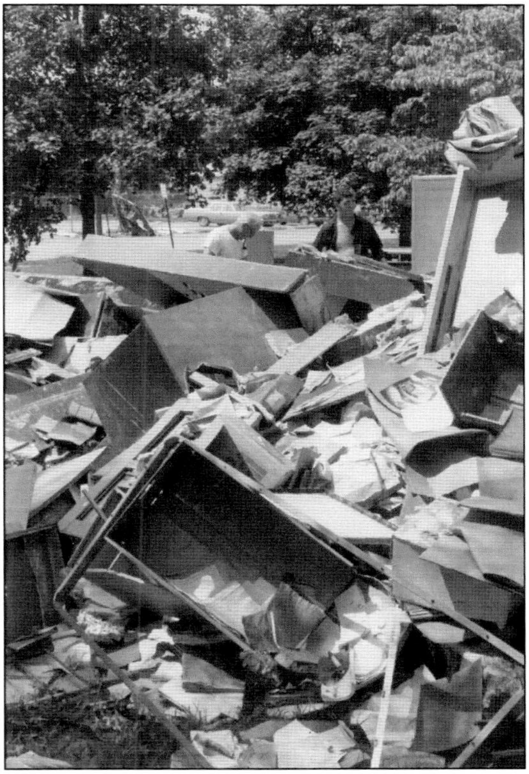

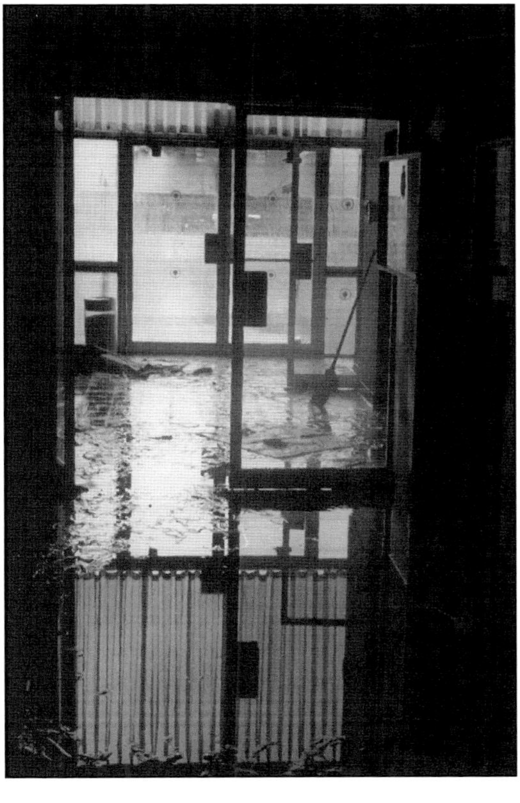

The facility's structural integrity had to be evaluated after the flood. (CMOG.)

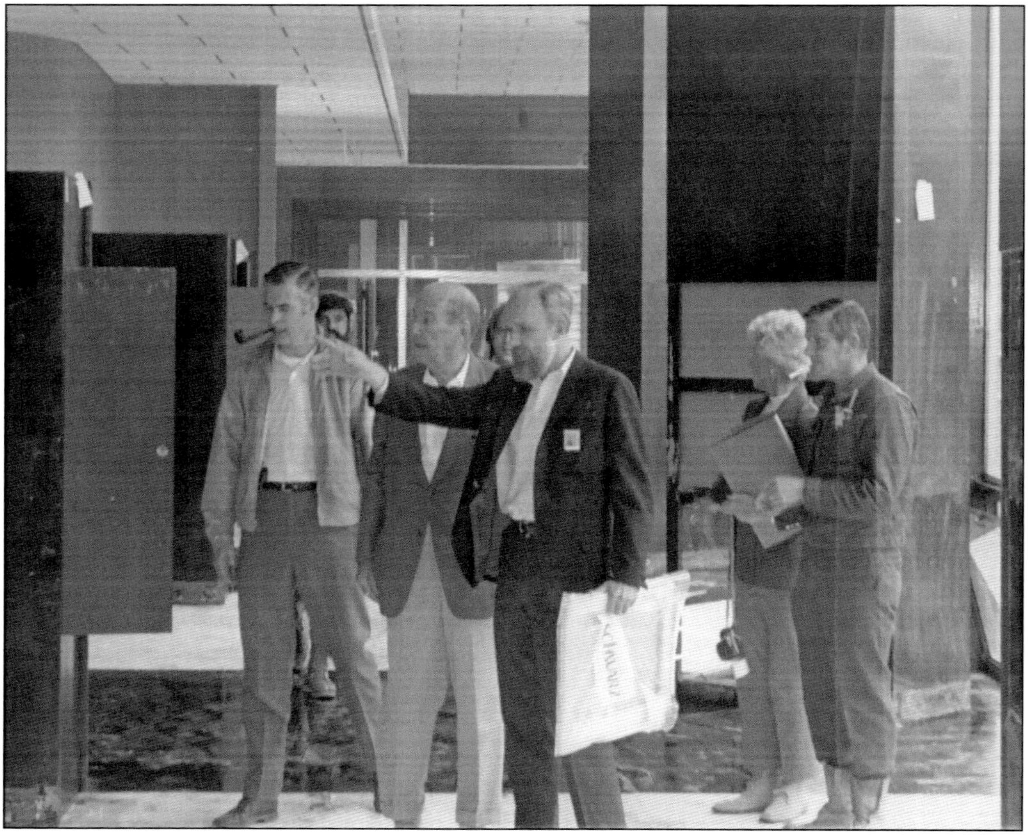

Museum president Thomas Buechner (third from left), along with his staff and supporters, had to cleanse and rebuild a major cultural resource. With Buechner are Amory Houghton Sr. (second from left), a former ambassador and former chairman of the board for the Corning Glass Works, and other Houghton family members. (CMOG.)

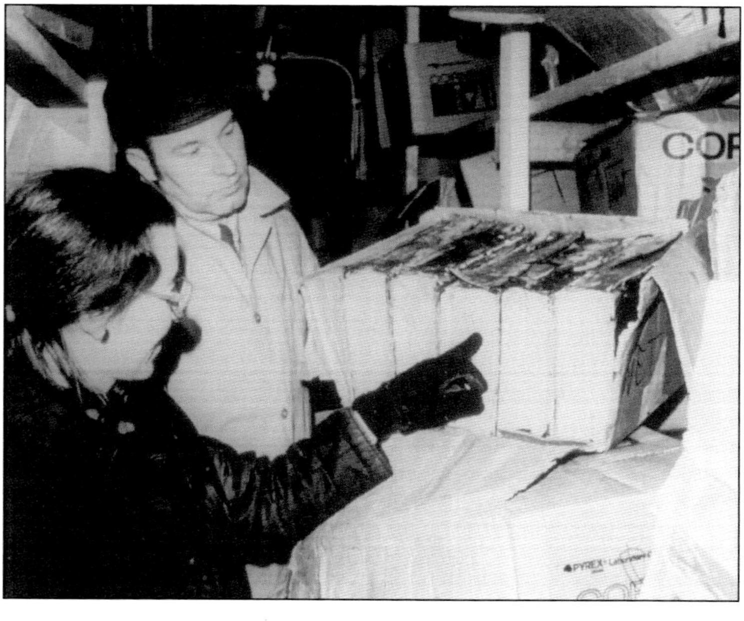

With the museum's huge collection in dire need of immediate attention, it would be impossible to address all the needs at once. These items were placed in a freezer truck for preservation until their turn arrived, perhaps years in the future. Assistant librarian Virginia Wright and physical scientist Dave Frazier are examining the freeze-dried items for mold. (CMOG.)

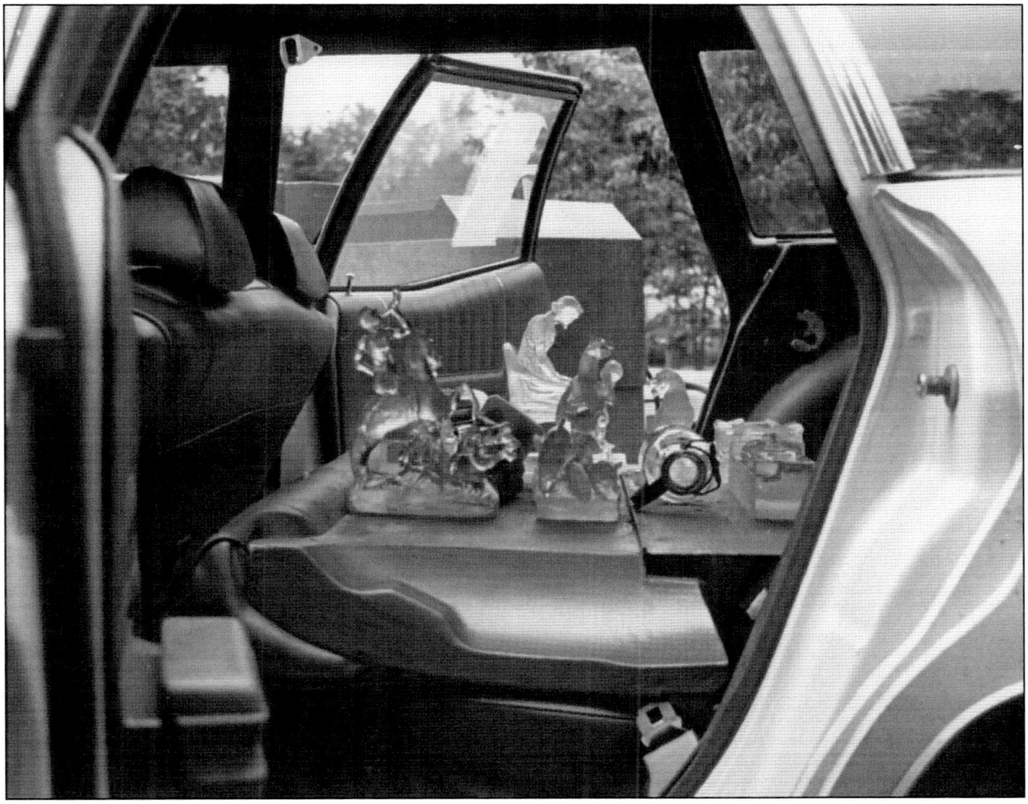

The Frederick Carder Collection was transferred to the Acme Supermarket, dried out, sorted, and evaluated. Carder was the creator of the art glass Steubenware and founder of the company that made it. By 1972, it was a division of the Glass Works. Carder had served for many years on a rural school board. In 1957, one of the consolidated district's modern new elementary schools was named for him. Corning Incorporated announced the end of Steuben production in 2011. (CMOG.)

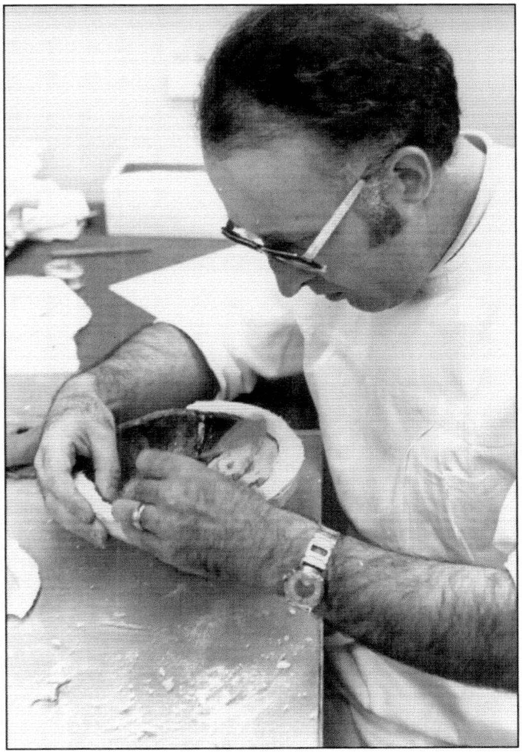

Experts from around the globe flocked to meet the Glass Museum's needs. Rolf Wihr came from Germany. (CMOG.)

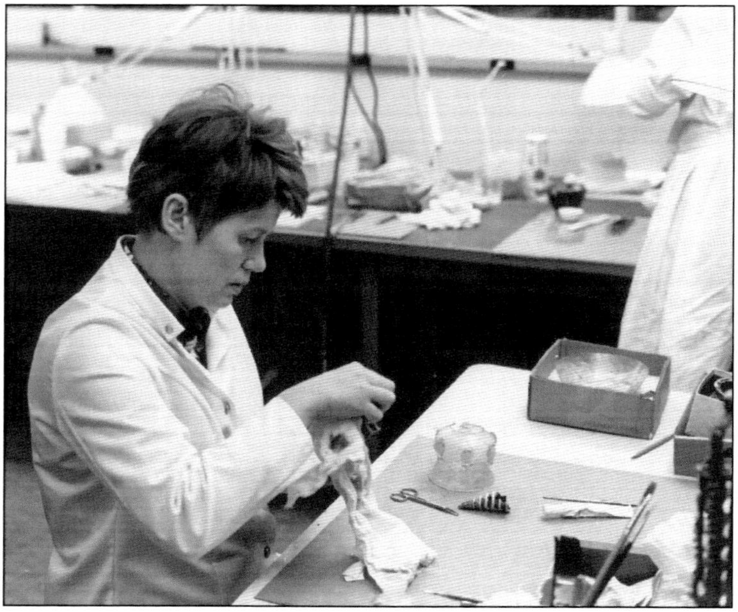

The work was painstaking and meticulous. Here, Dorothea Wihr assists with glass conservation. (CMOG.)

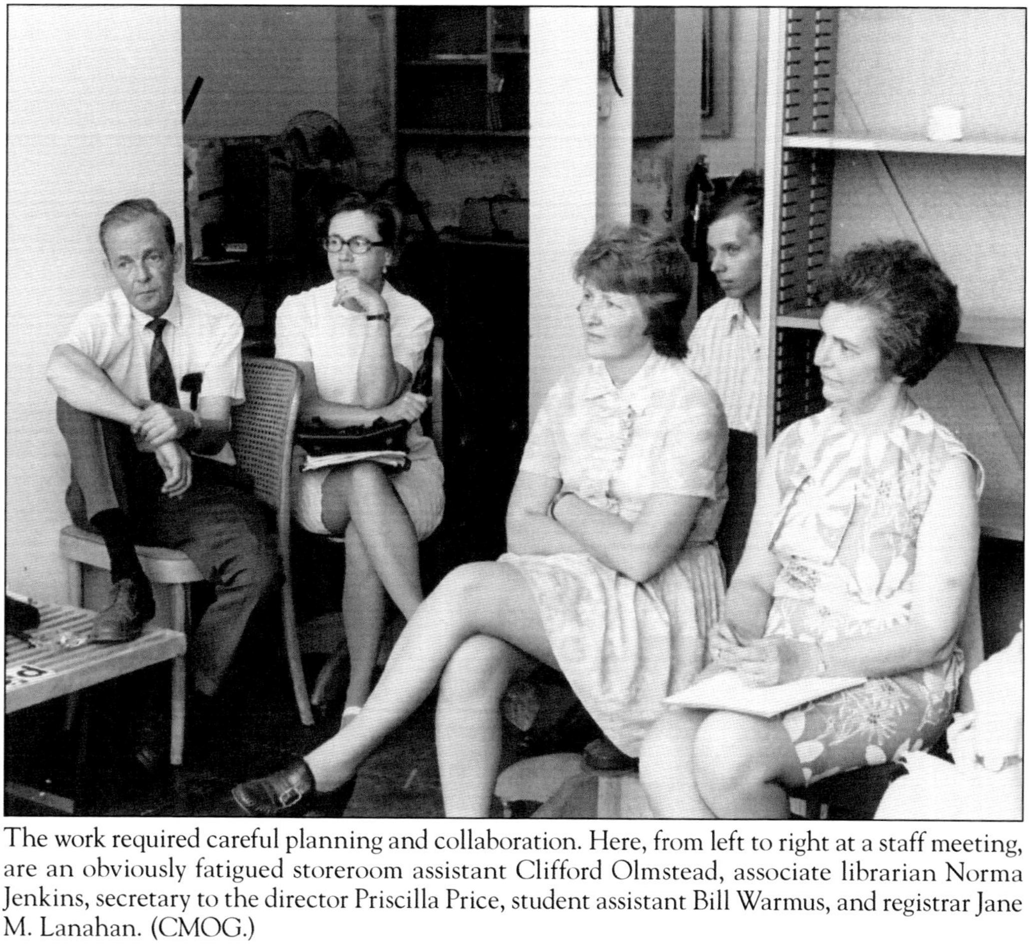

The work required careful planning and collaboration. Here, from left to right at a staff meeting, are an obviously fatigued storeroom assistant Clifford Olmstead, associate librarian Norma Jenkins, secretary to the director Priscilla Price, student assistant Bill Warmus, and registrar Jane M. Lanahan. (CMOG.)

Restoring the museum was also exhausting. Assistant librarian Virginia Wright (left), paper conservator Carolyn Horton, and director Paul Perrot plan the restoration of rare books. (CMOG.)

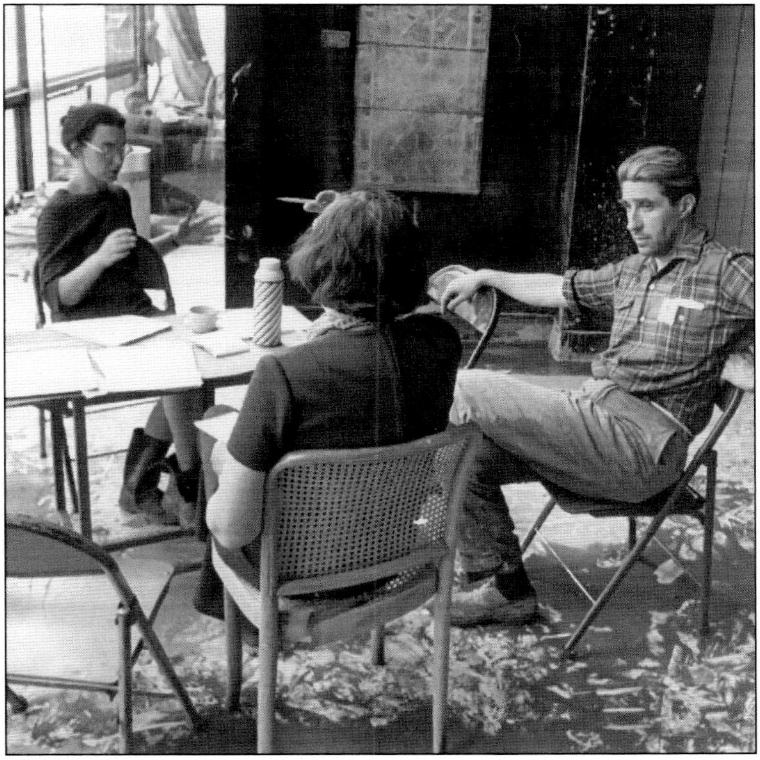

It was filthy work, as this unidentified student worker and his surroundings show. (CMOG.)

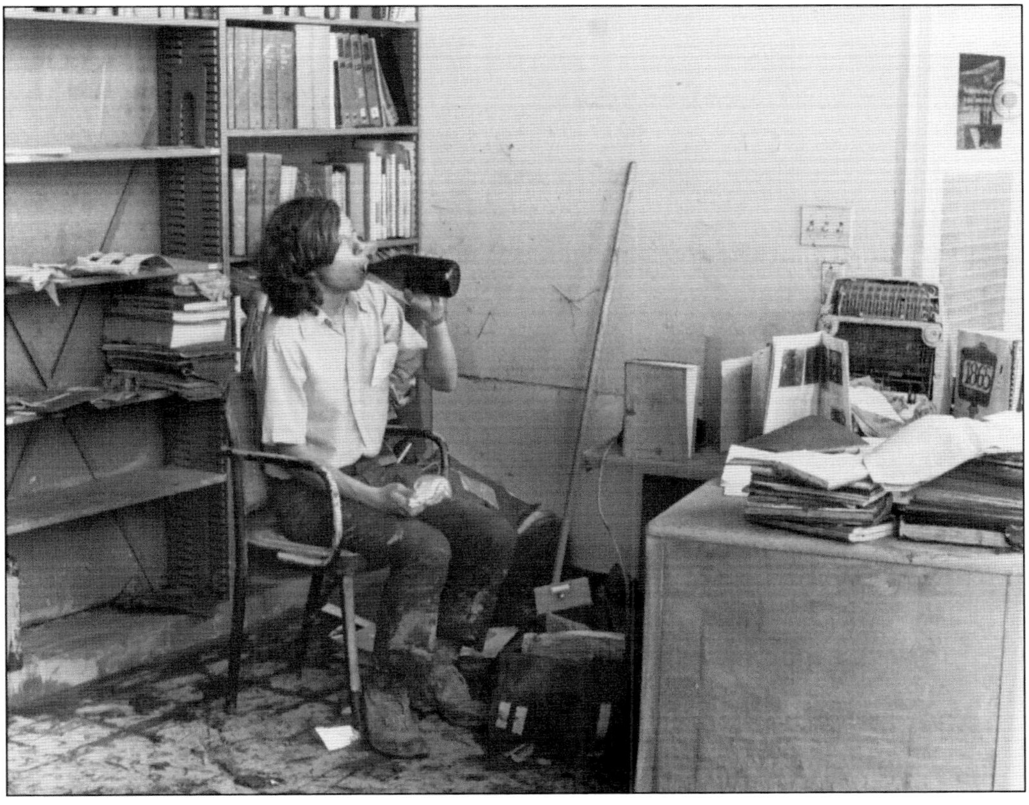

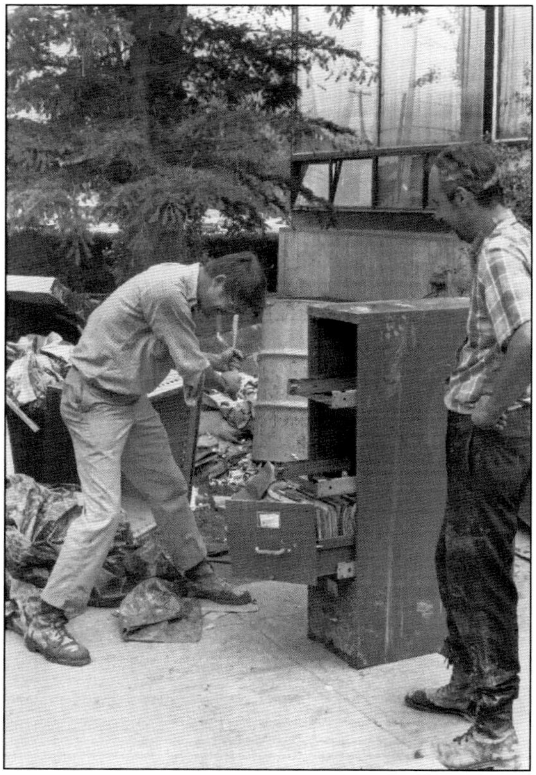

Eventually, as these workers show, people started to laugh again. (CMOG.)

The museum was closed, but as the sign indicates, it was only temporary. Years of recovery work lay ahead, but the doors reopened within two months. The Corning Museum of Glass is still a major attraction (300,000 visitors a year) in Western New York and still a major American museum, preserving its collection of 40,000 objects. (CMOG.)

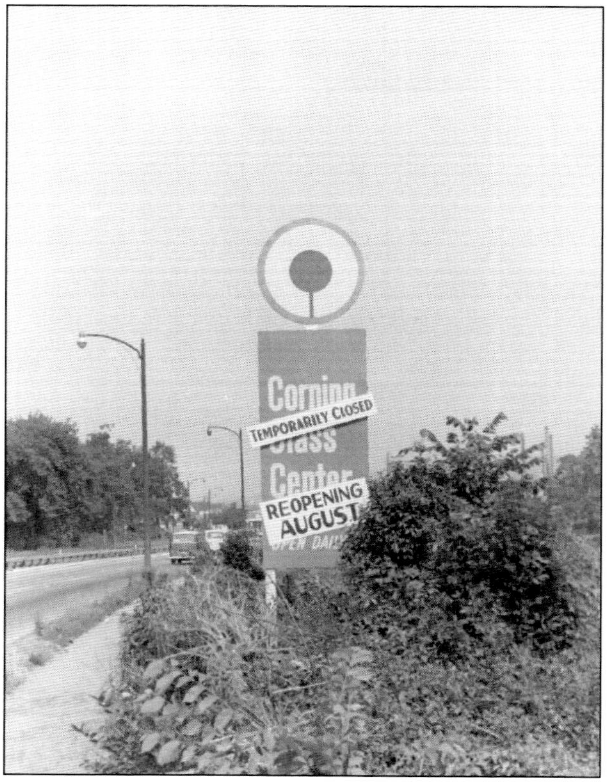

Three

Chemung County

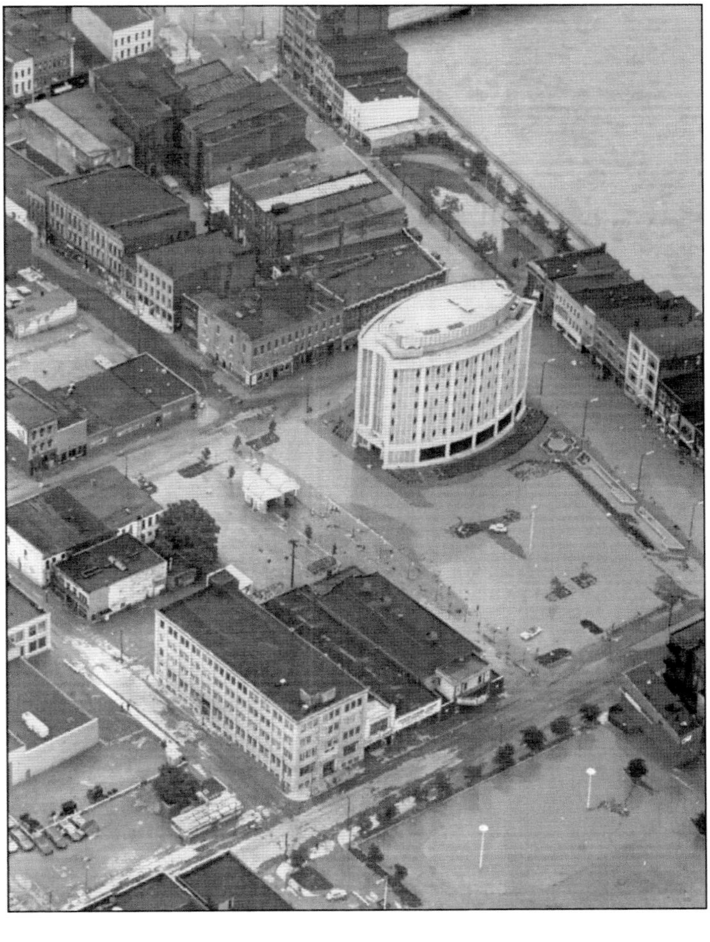

A few miles below Corning, the Chemung River's flood roared across the line into its namesake Chemung County. Riverside communities such as Big Flats suffered, and so did towns along smaller streams. But, just as the Chemung River flows right through Corning, it also bisects the much larger city of Elmira (pictured). The flood would tear a gash through Elmira, then roll on through rural Chemung County and finally cross the state line into Pennsylvania. (CC.)

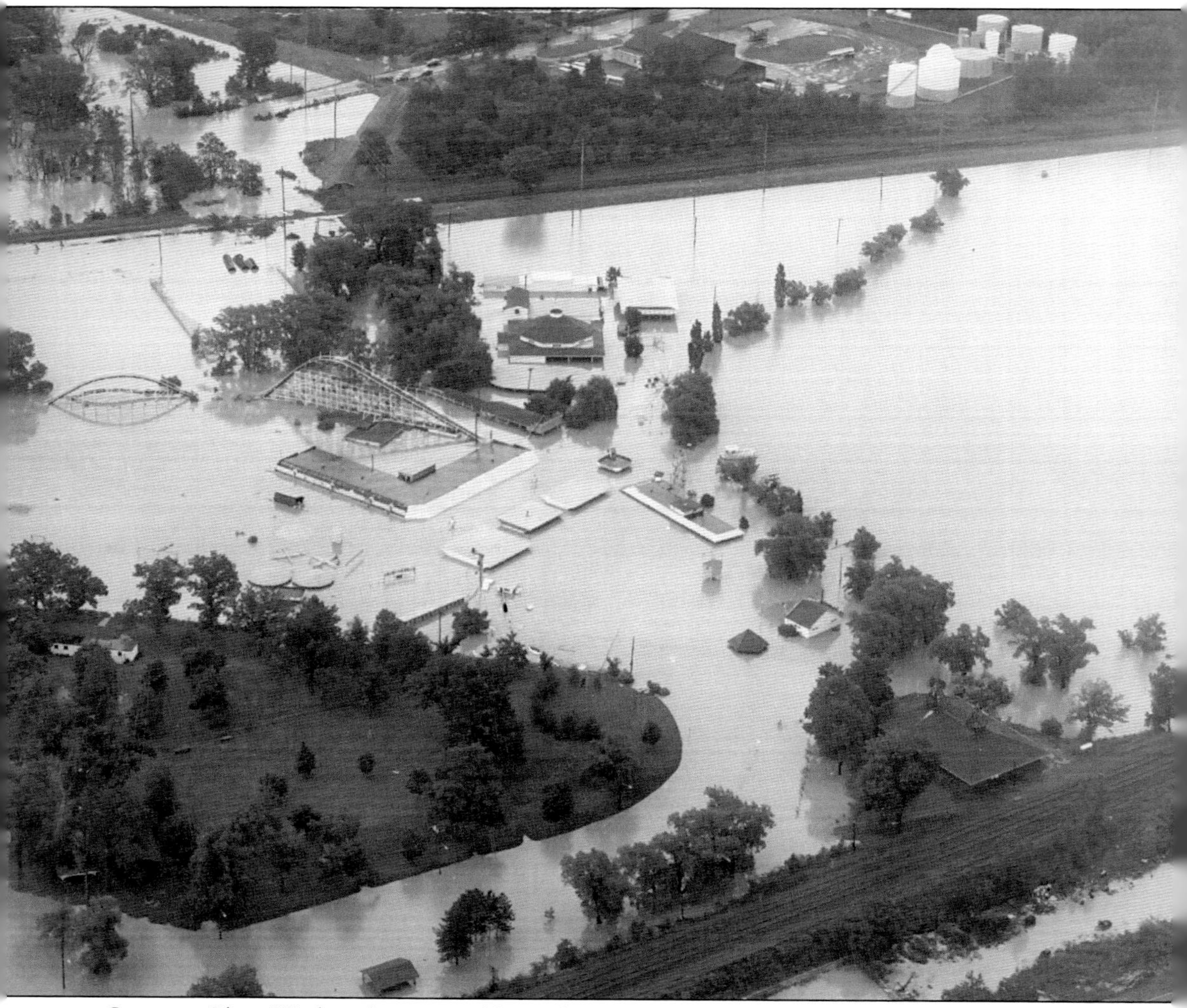

Corning Glass Works pilot Lee Robbins photographed damage from the air. Eldridge Lake in Elmira has taken over Eldridge Park. After being closed for almost 20 years, the park has been experiencing a revival since reopening in 2006. The historic 1890s Loof carousel (the octagonal building near center of photograph), with its 56 animals, has been restored and was reopened at the same time. (CC.)

At this time, the river has receded behind and below the retaining wall, but look at the damage left behind. The rear of these buildings along Elmira's Water Street caught the brunt of the flood, and many of them would not survive. (CC.)

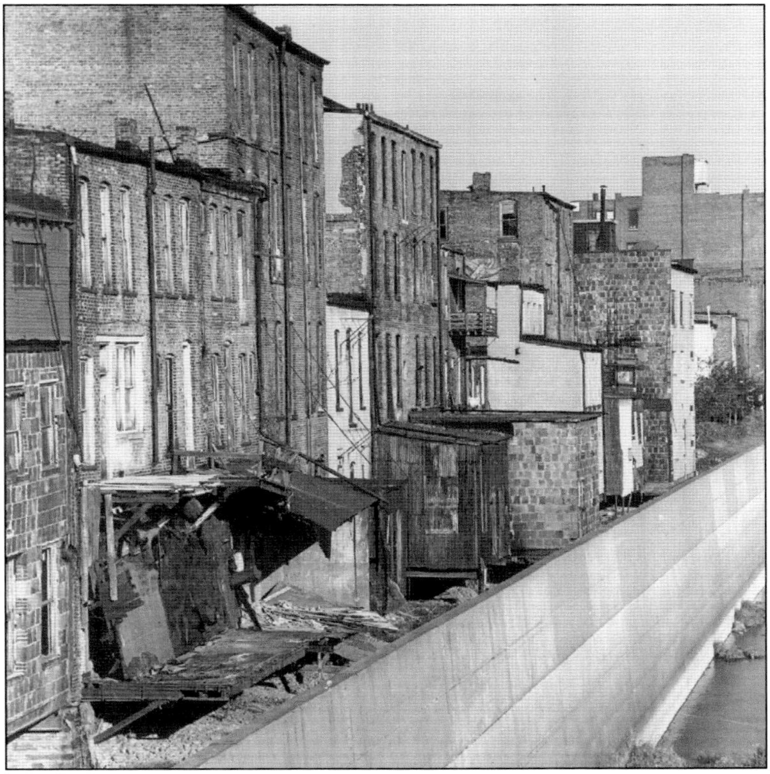

Coping with the flood was a daunting task. Everybody had to pitch in. (CC.)

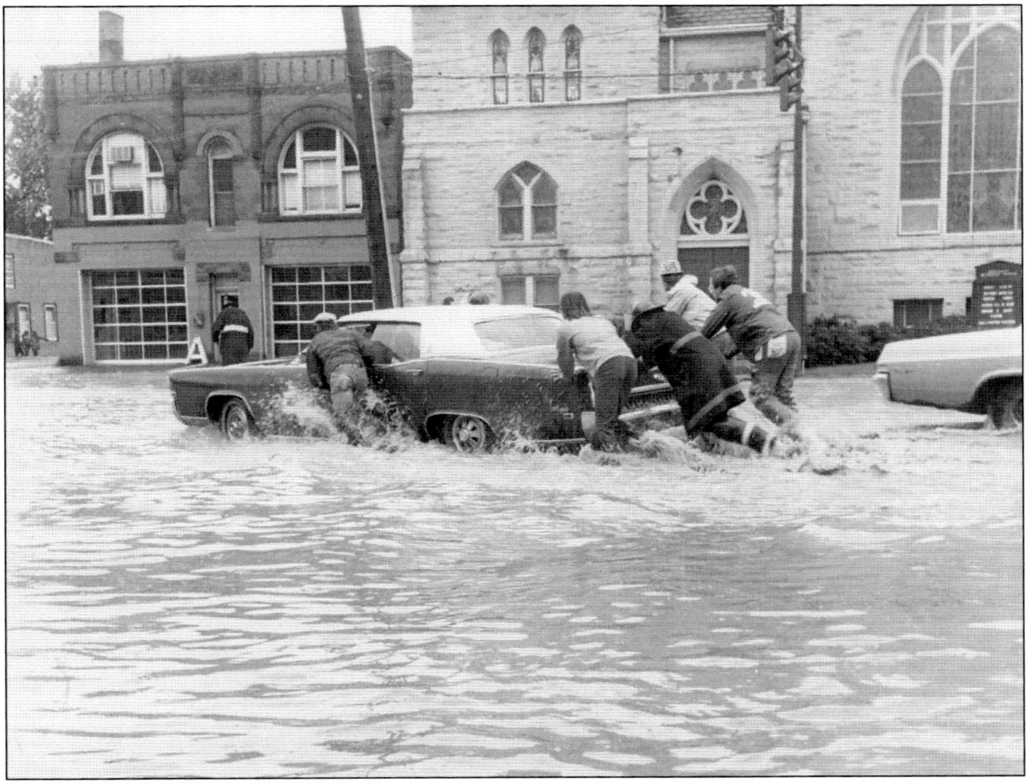

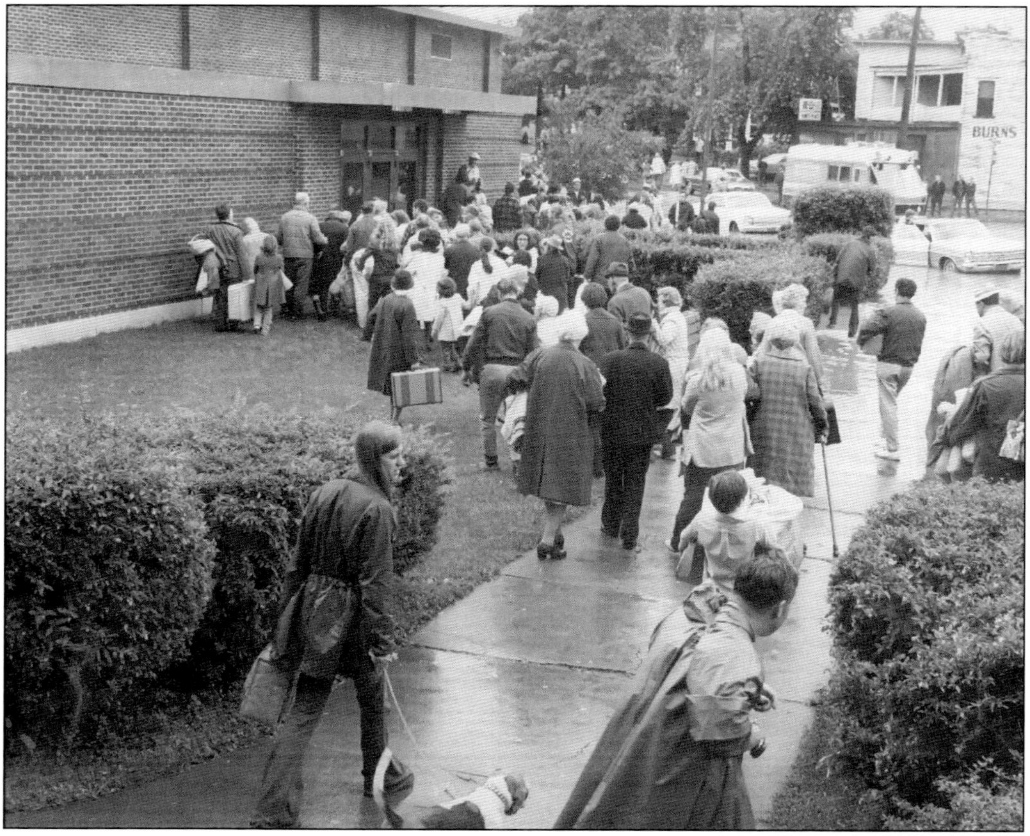

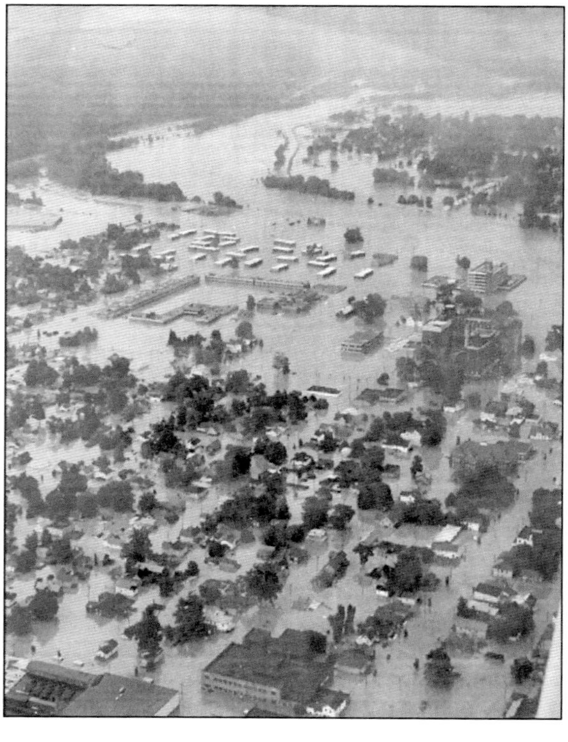

Victims were evacuated first to Southside High (seen here) and later to Broadway. Notice that the car at right is up to its axles in water. Out of 40,000 city residents, half were suddenly homeless. These folks have managed to get away with suitcases, bedding, and pets. An emergency vehicle is parked across the street next to King's Place and Burns Grocery. (CC.)

At this point, the waters have flowed so wide that there is really no longer any distinction between the city and the river. (CC.)

Miller's Pond, pictured in the foreground, has taken over its neighborhood, as seen in this photograph by Lee Robbins. (CC.)

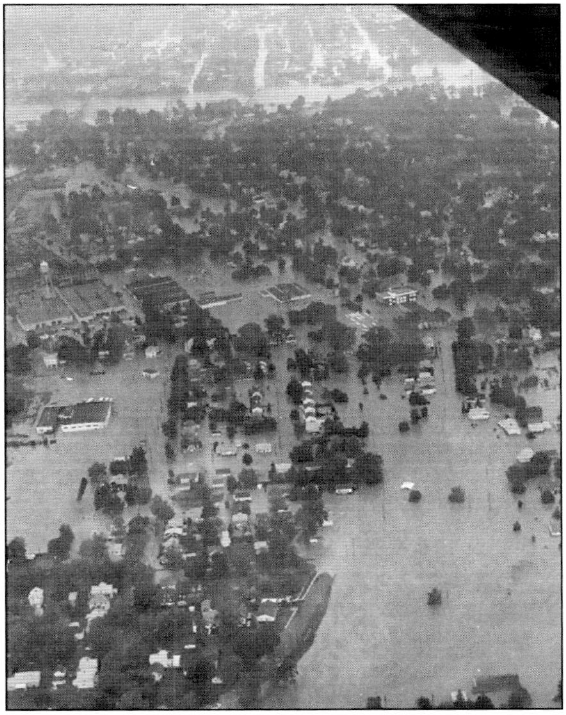

The flood engulfed St. Joseph's Hospital, along with the next-door church and all the homes in the neighborhood. A helicopter is just visible on the white pad at center. (CC.)

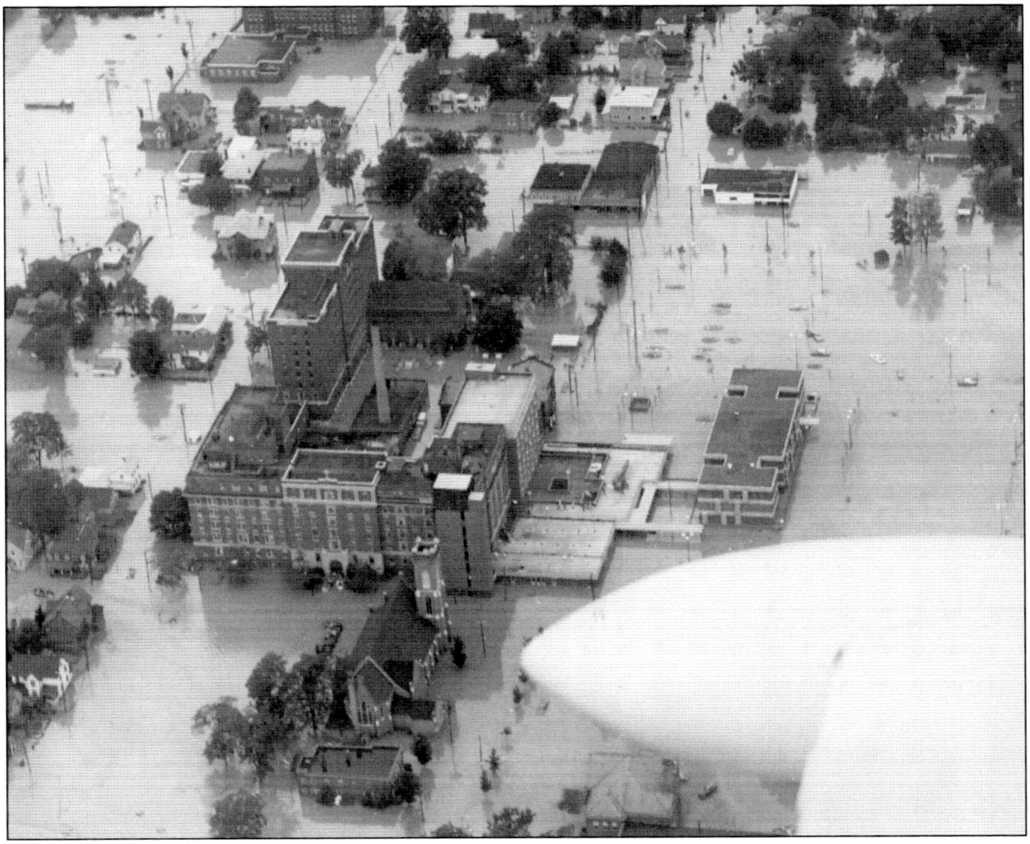

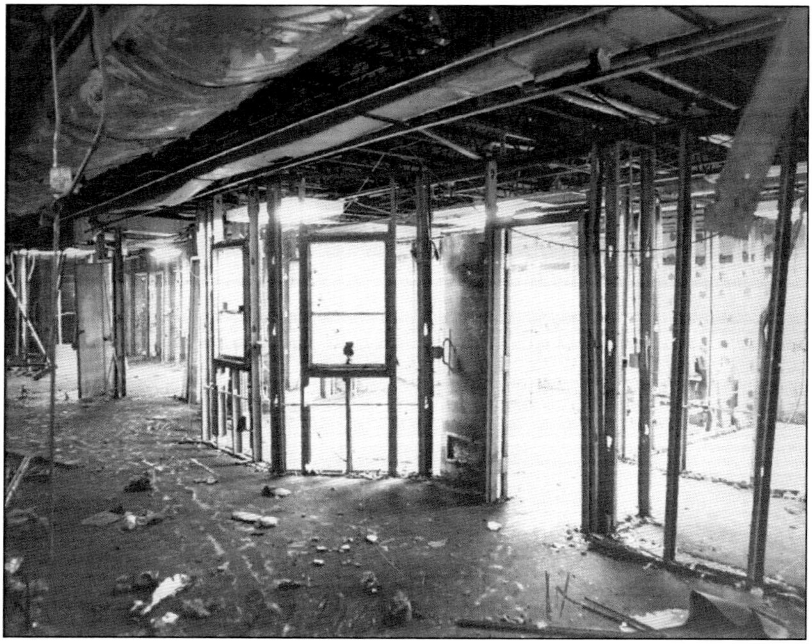

The destruction at St. Joseph's Hospital was extensive. (CC.)

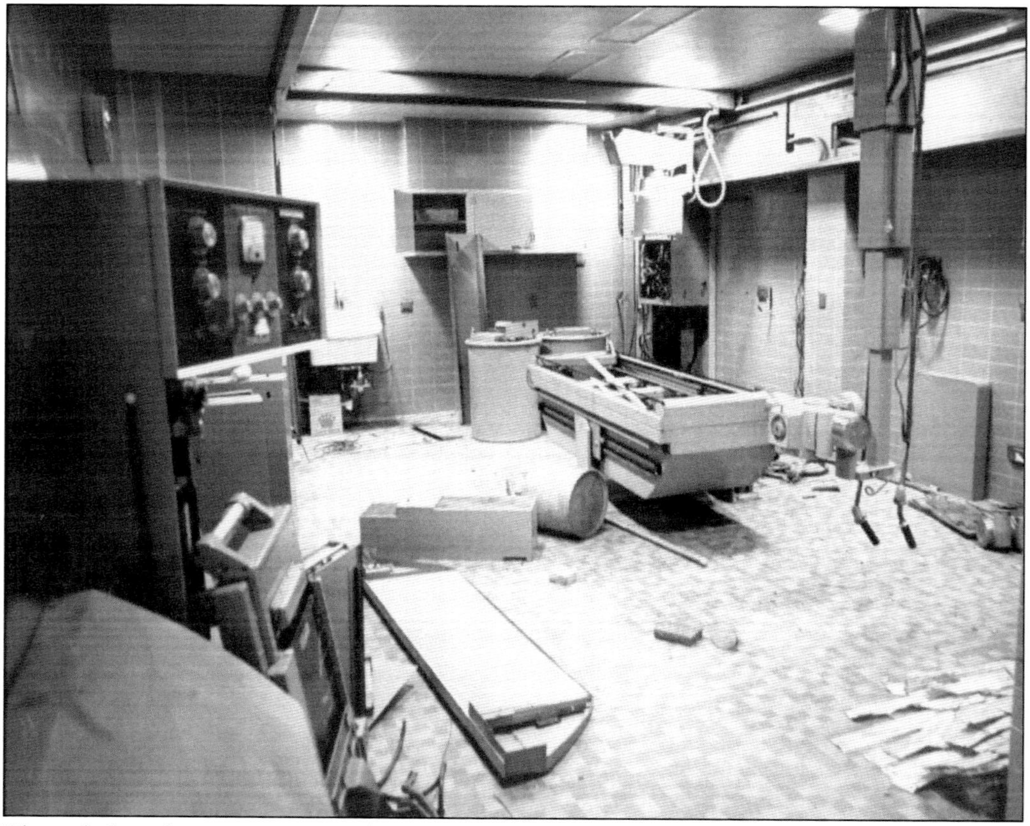

The radiology department was only one of those essentially destroyed. (CC.)

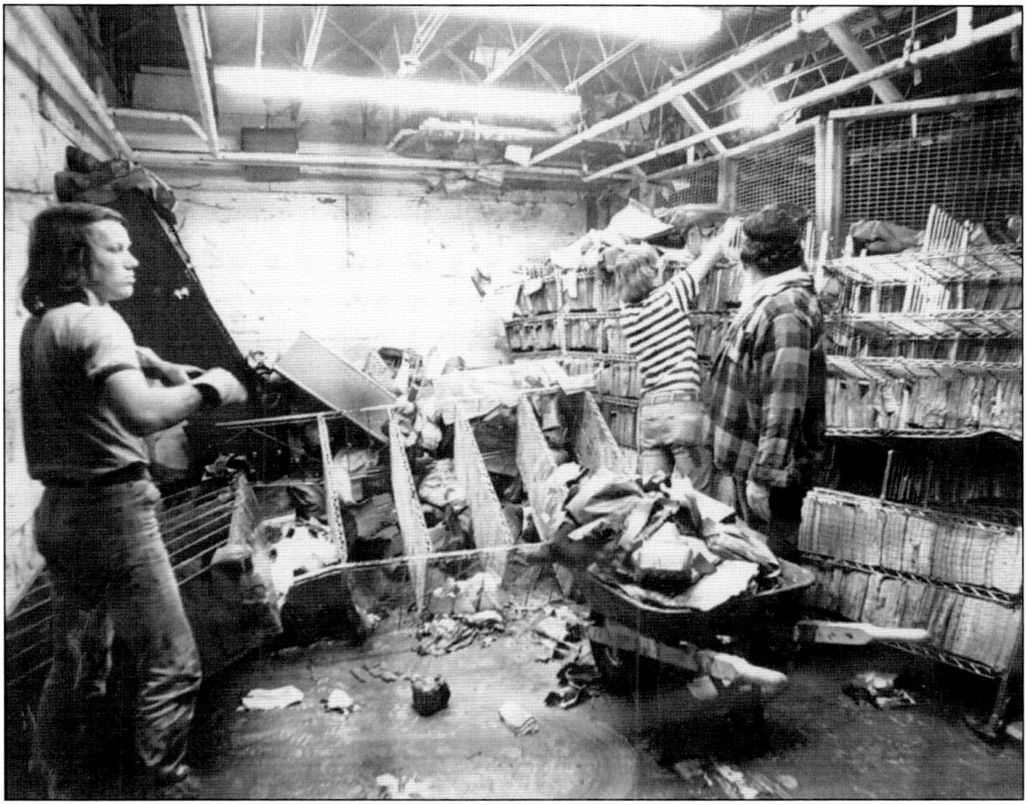

Medical records would be lost, or at least long inaccessible, as well. The depth of such disasters is always more than meets the eye. These tired, unidentified workers are taking ruined records out in a wheelbarrow. (CC.)

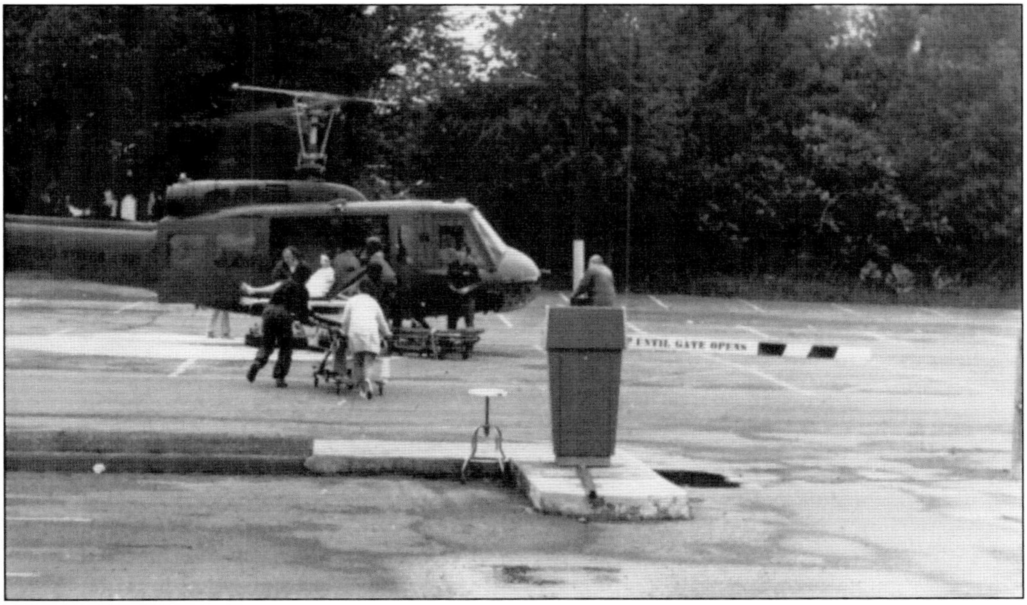

Unlike Corning, Elmira had a second hospital, outside the flood zone. Helicopters (this one from the US Army) and other vehicles ferried patients to nearby Arnot-Ogden Medical Center. (CC.)

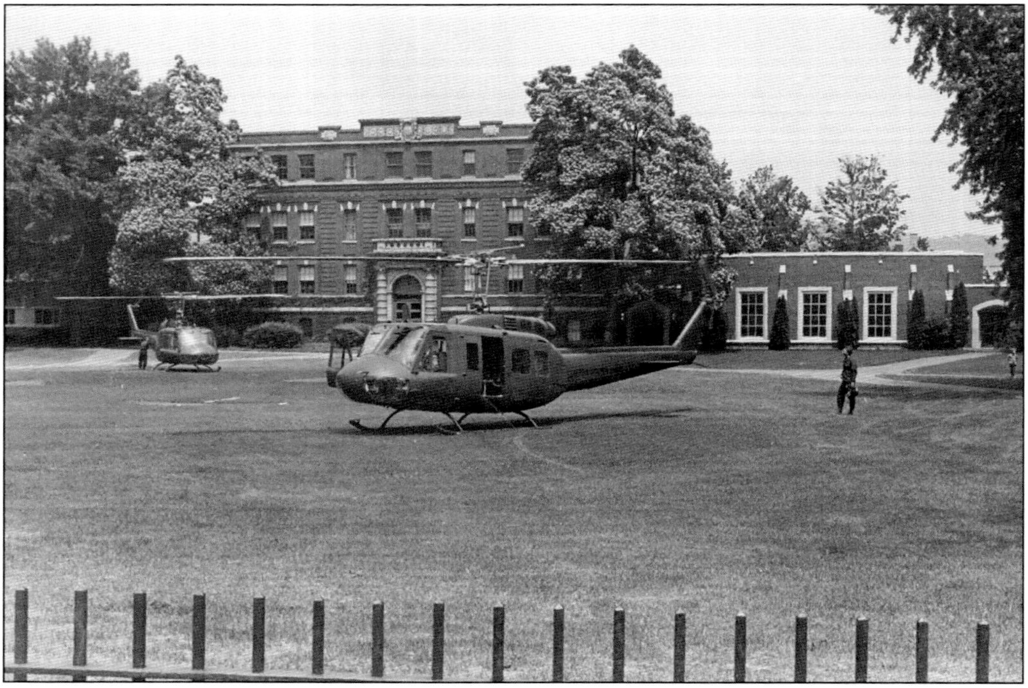

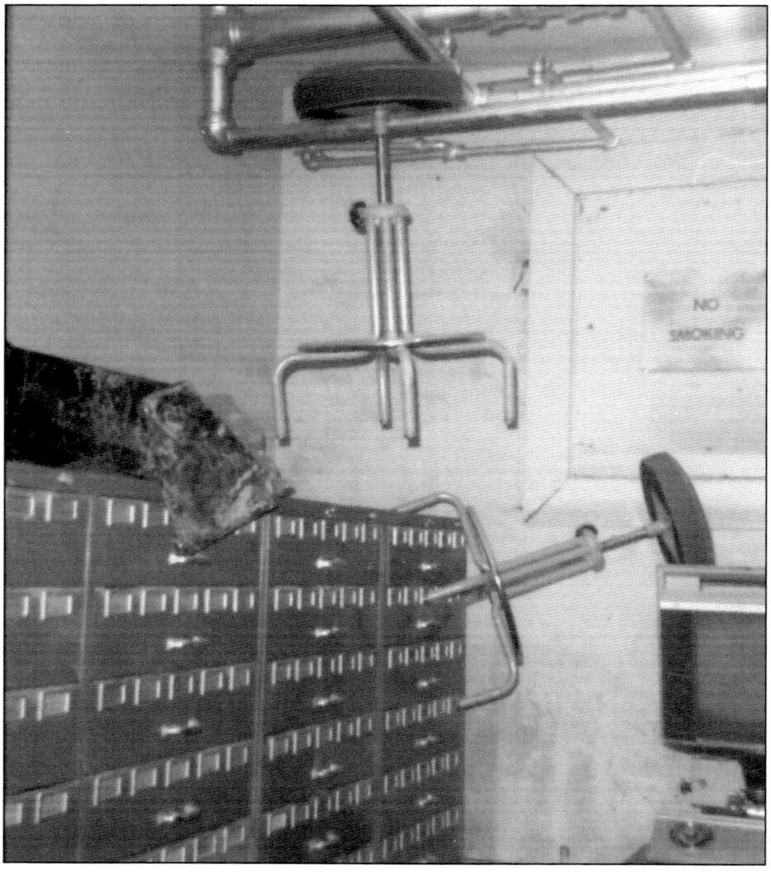

Green space at center-city Elmira College made a convenient multi-aircraft helipad. Founded in 1852, Elmira was the first college in the United States to grant full baccalaureate degrees to women. (CC.)

Steele Memorial Library, the largest library in a six-county region, was scoured by the waters. Notice how a stool floated to the ceiling in the census and microfilm room. (AB.)

Steele Library was then at its old location on Church and Lake Streets. The magazine level was wiped out. (AB.)

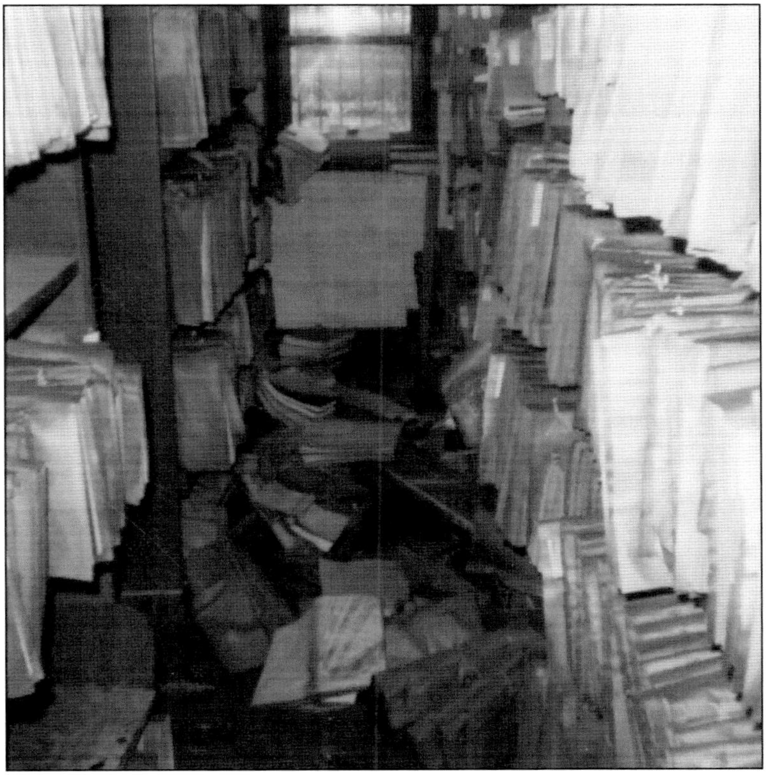

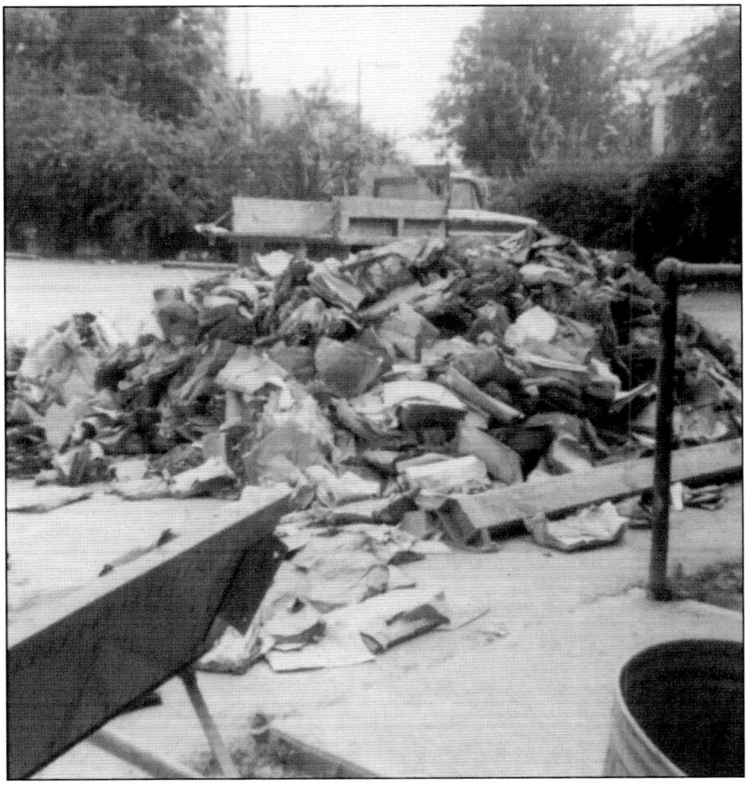

This photograph captures what was left of the magazines. (AB.)

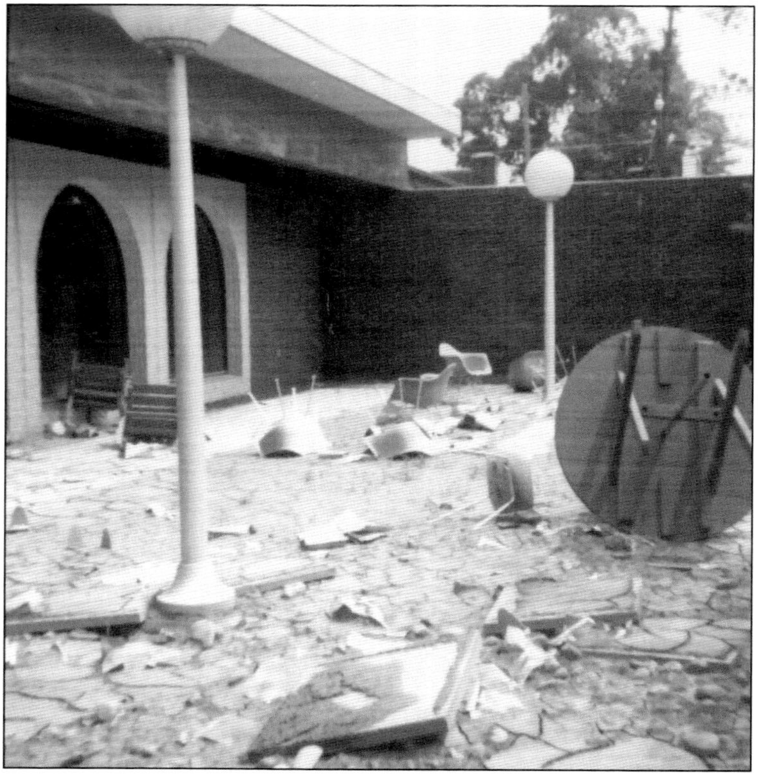

At Steele Memorial Library's Southside Branch, which is no longer in operation, the reading patio was still untouched three weeks later. Too many needs were far more pressing. (AB.)

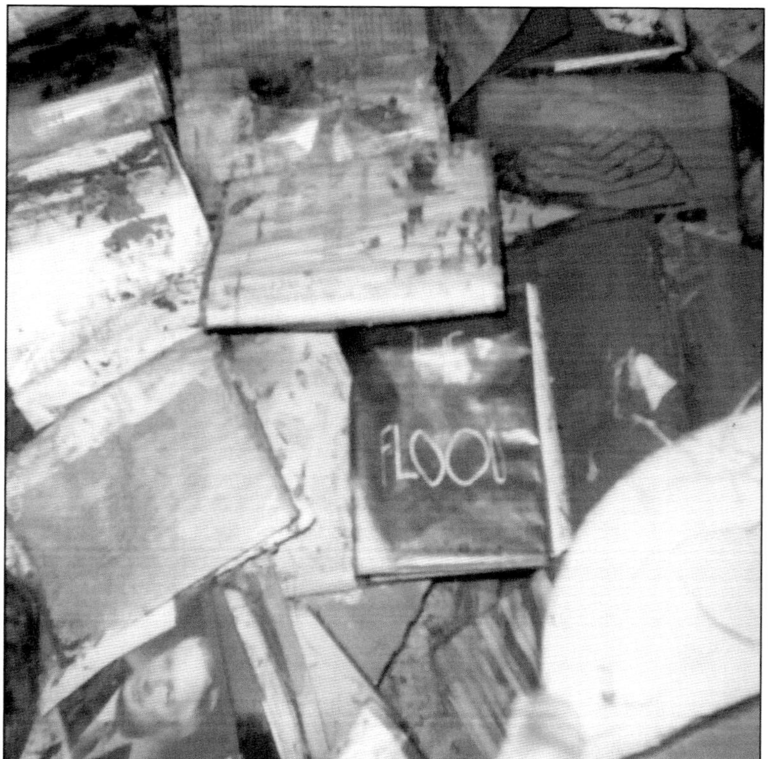

A pile of destroyed or damaged books is enough to break the heart of any librarian. But Ann Brouse still found a little amusement in the title on the top of this pile. (AB.)

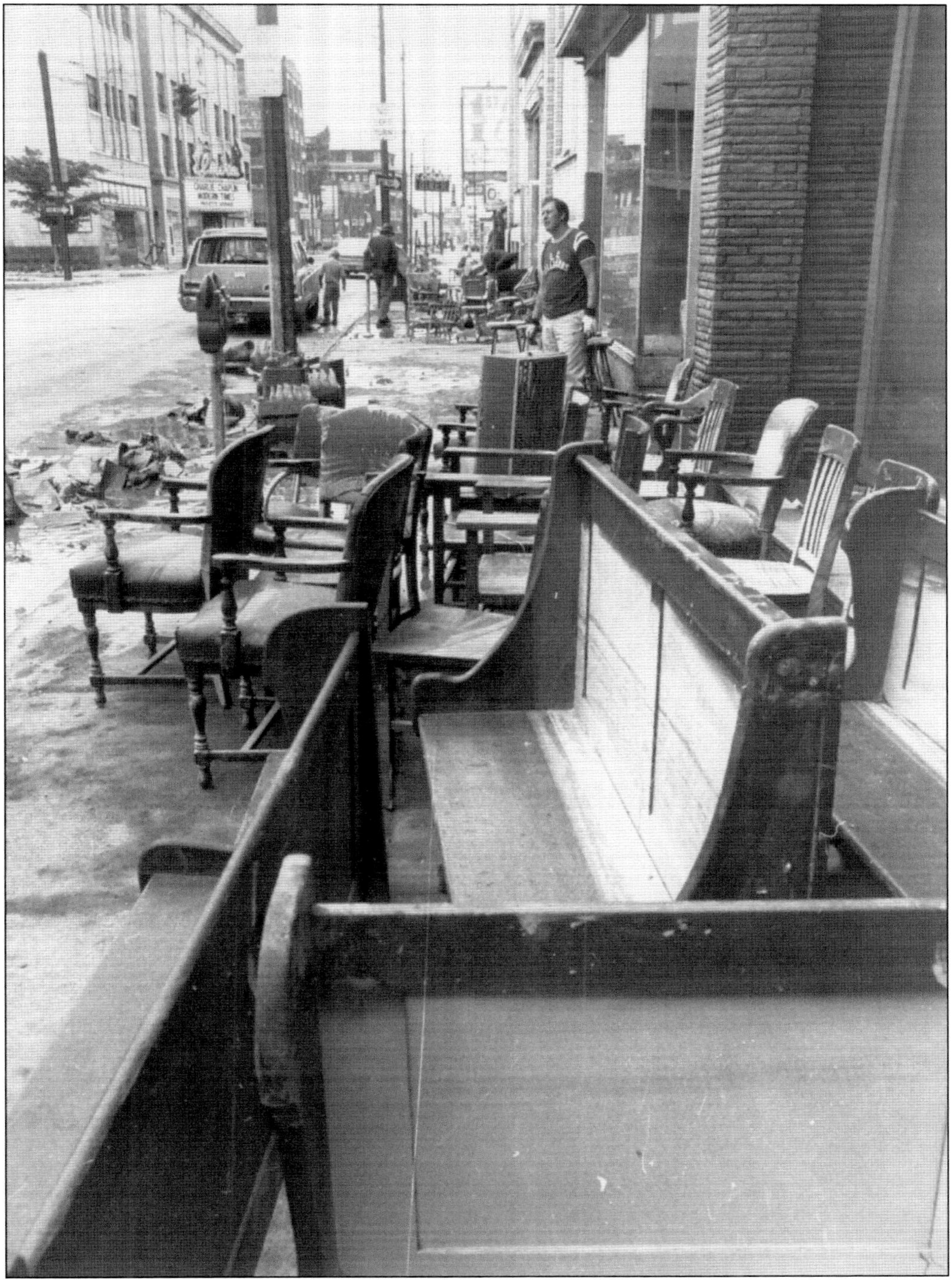

Millions of dollars in property was lost. The Elmira Theater, seen in the left background, had been showing a rerelease of Charlie Chaplin's *Modern Times*. Signs farther back advertise Arco gasoline and a diner. The fellow wearing work gloves at the right has a shirt that reads, "C.C. Billiards." (CC.)

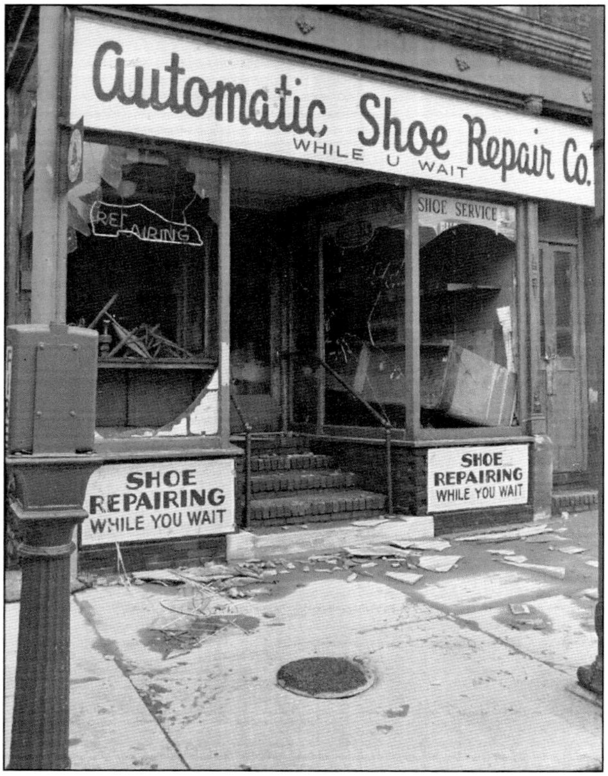

"Repairing while you wait" is just what this downtown business needs. Notice how the display case has gone adrift in the right-hand window, besides the fact that the plate glass itself is all gone. The flood wrecked 40 percent of Elmira's commercial space. (CC.)

Business, residential, and church properties all suffered, as this image shows. The fellow with the backhoe now had considerable job security. (CC.)

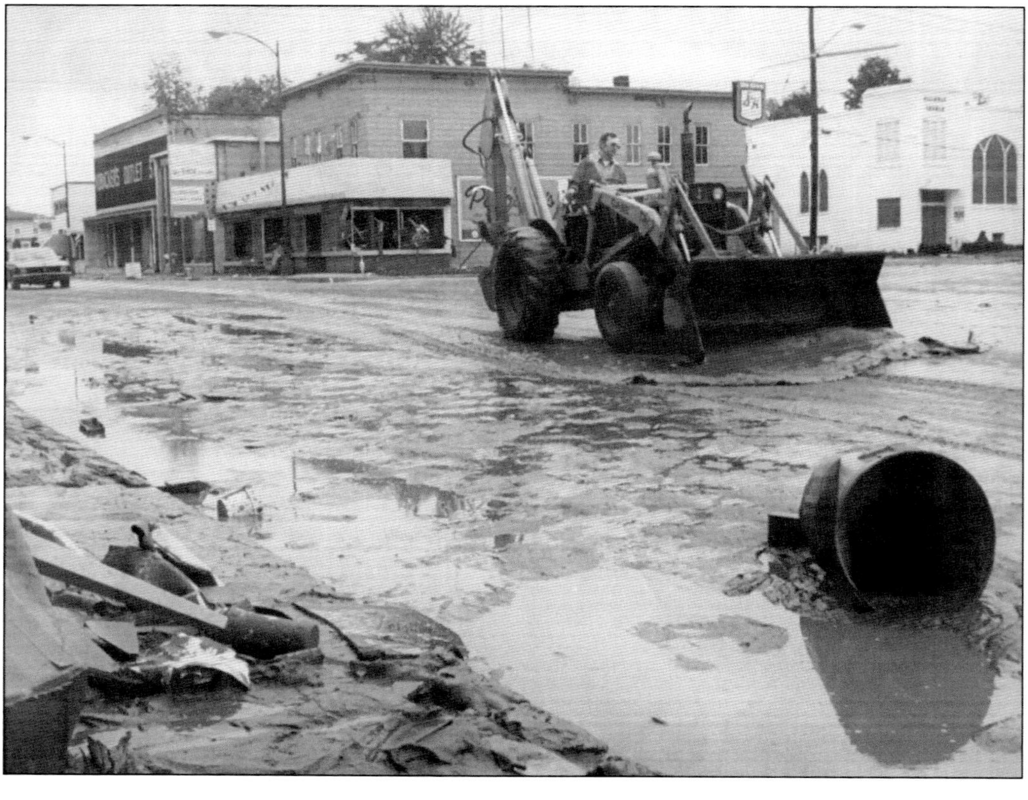

The newspaper business has a long-standing tradition of always hitting the streets no matter what the challenges. The *Corning Leader* and *Elmira Star-Gazette* joined forces to bring out a three-page joint edition datelined noon the next day—by hand-cranked mimeograph. (CPP.)

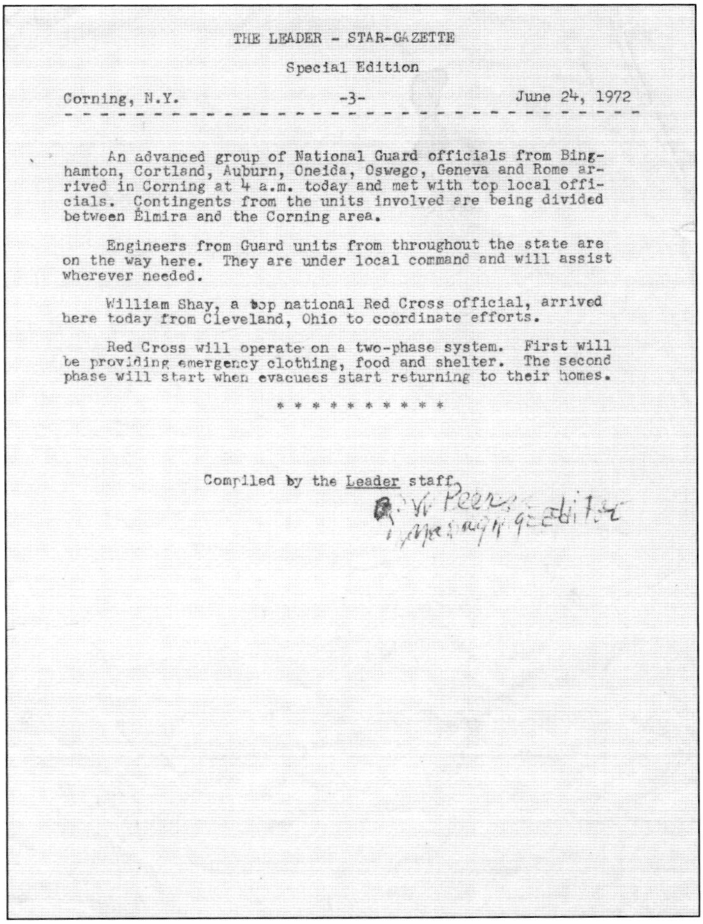

THE LEADER - STAR-GAZETTE

Special Edition

Corning, N.Y. -3- June 24, 1972

An advanced group of National Guard officials from Binghamton, Cortland, Auburn, Oneida, Oswego, Geneva and Rome arrived in Corning at 4 a.m. today and met with top local officials. Contingents from the units involved are being divided between Elmira and the Corning area.

Engineers from Guard units from throughout the state are on the way here. They are under local command and will assist wherever needed.

William Shay, a top national Red Cross official, arrived here today from Cleveland, Ohio to coordinate efforts.

Red Cross will operate on a two-phase system. First will be providing emergency clothing, food and shelter. The second phase will start when evacuees start returning to their homes.

* * * * * * * * * *

Compiled by the Leader staff.

National Guardsmen salute in the background as Vice Pres. Spiro Agnew (just right of center, carrying a rolled-up paper) visits the Southern Tier, saying, "Conditions are worse than anything I have seen anywhere." Pres. Richard Nixon toured Pittsburgh, greeting thousands of suddenly homeless families with a tone-deaf announcement that the important thing was to get the steel mills open again. (CC.)

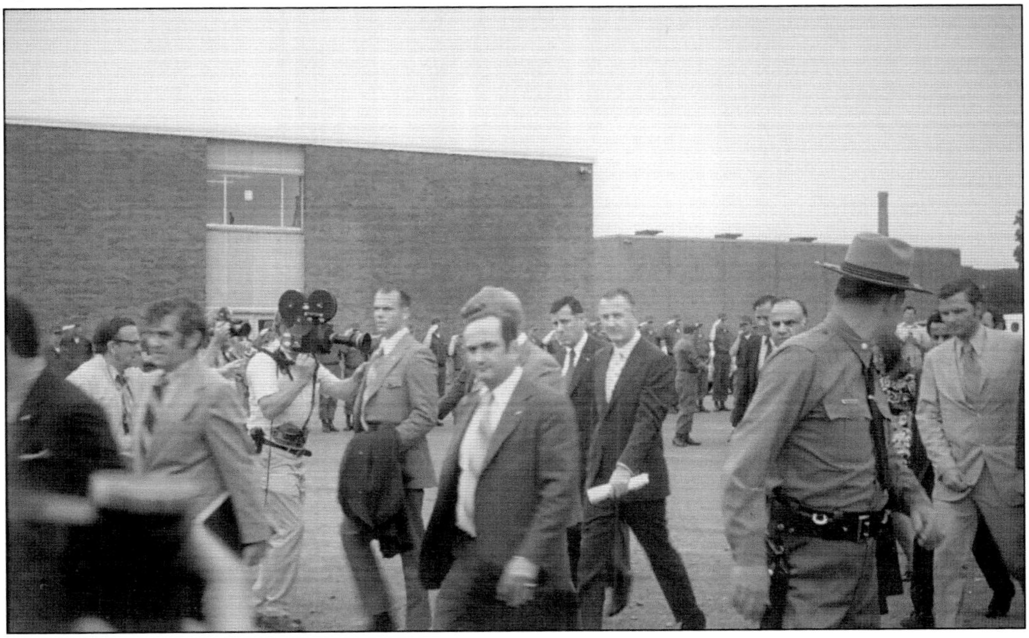

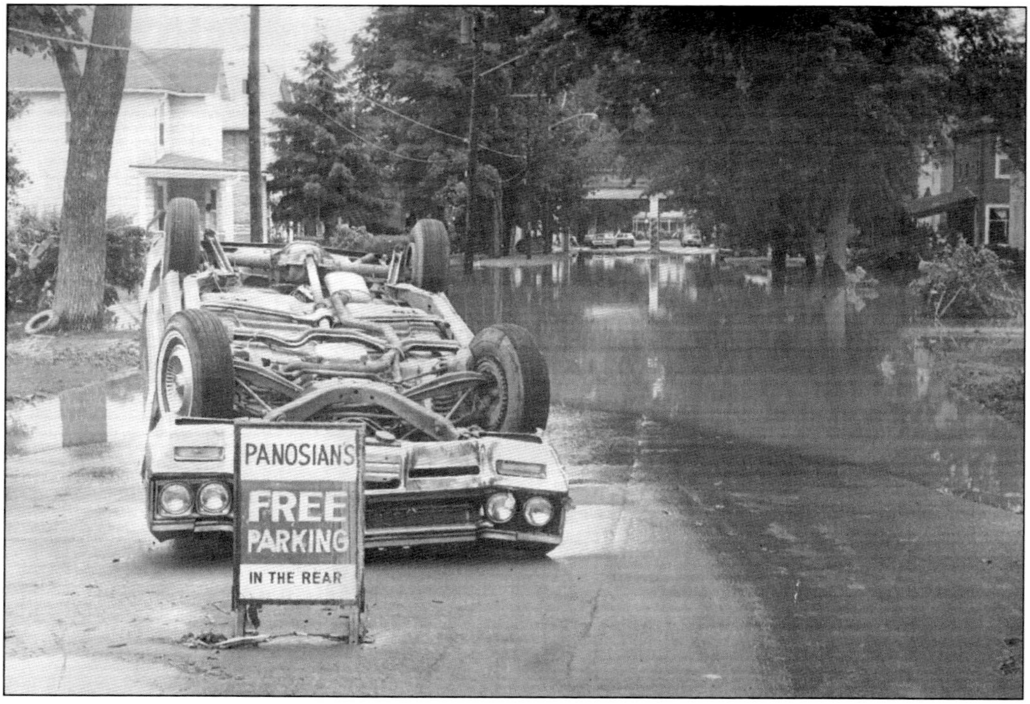

Traffic patterns (both road and rail) were snarled throughout New York, New Jersey, Maryland, and Pennsylvania. In September 2011, the one-two punch from remnants of Hurricane Irene and Tropical Storm Lee would again make much of the region impassable for days, especially in the Broome County–Binghamton area. (CC.)

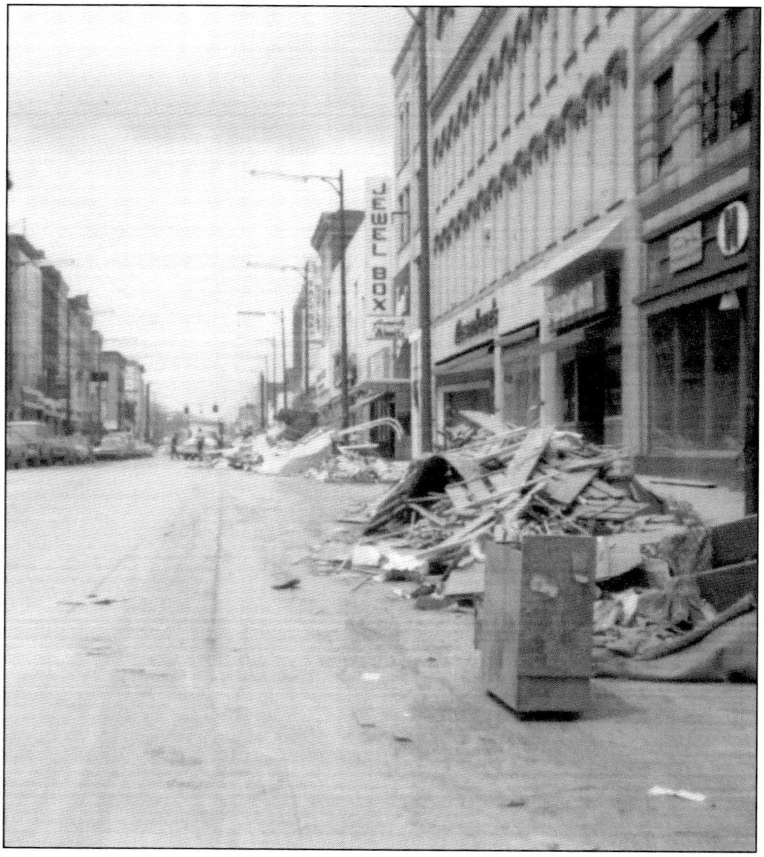

On July 10, three weeks after the disaster, Water Street in Elmira was clear for passage. But weeks or months of cleanup remained for these businesses. (AB.)

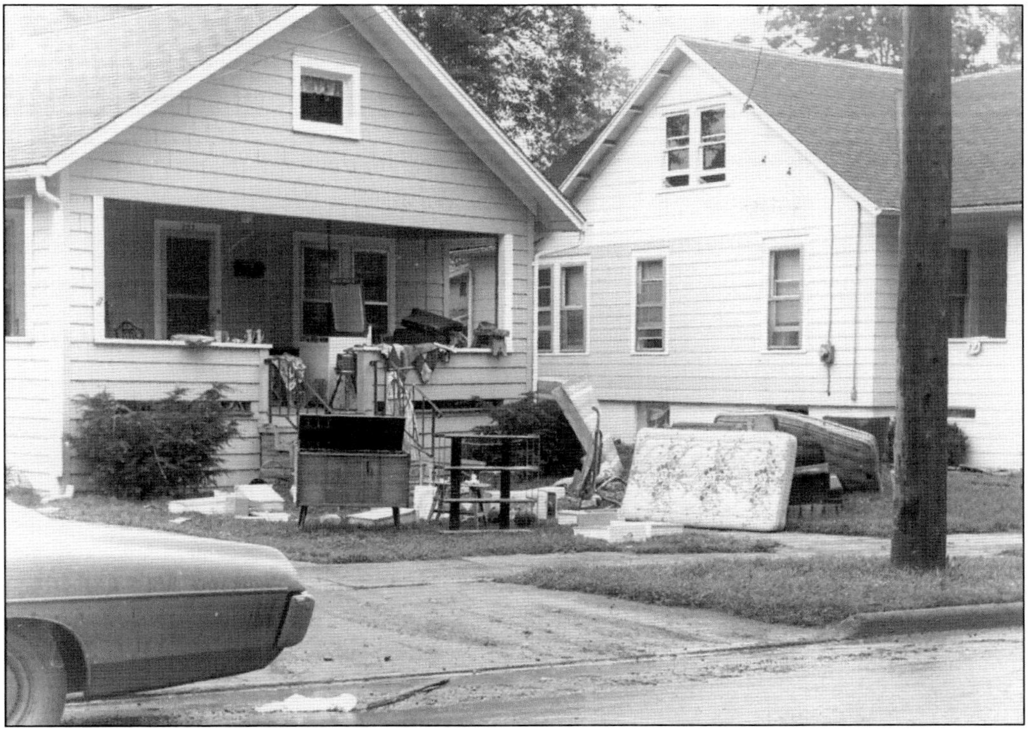

Homes and residential areas lost their contents just as the shops and business districts did. (CC.)

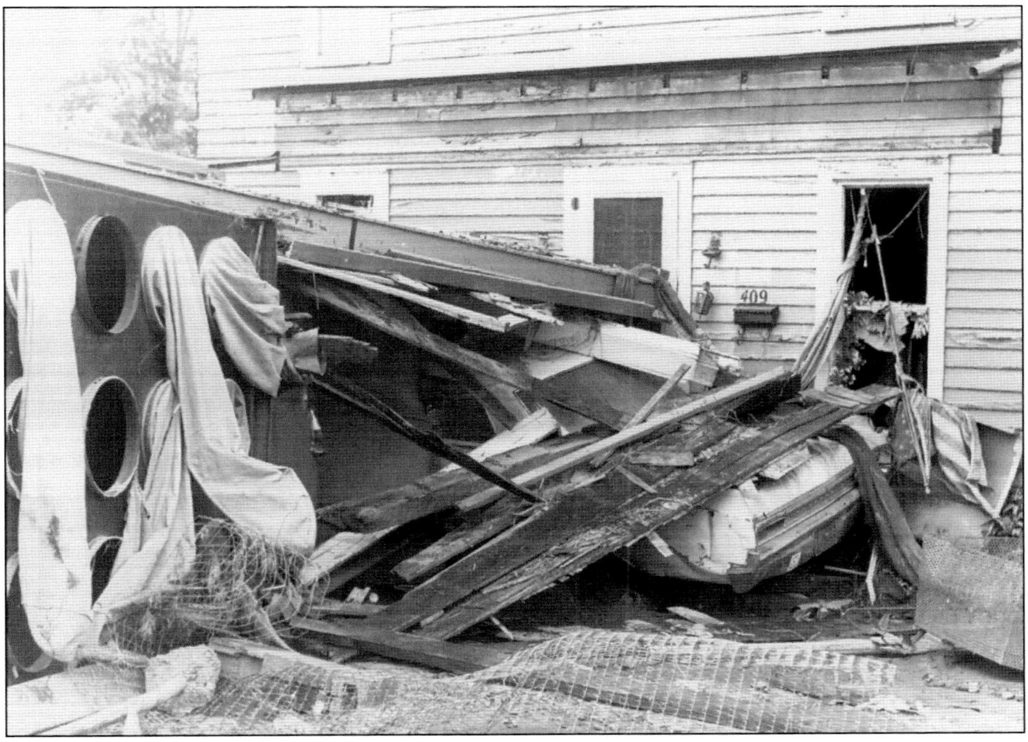

Neither car nor garage survived in this case, and the house does not look good either. (CC.)

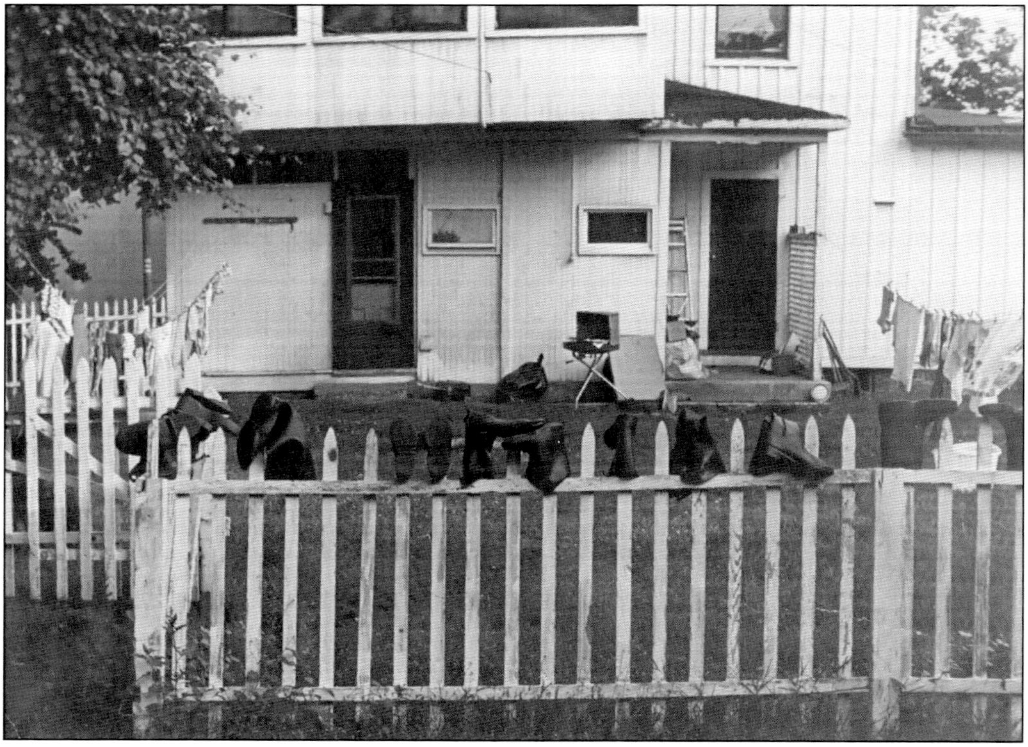

There was still a lot of drying-out to do, and the residents needed outdoor grills to get any cooking done. Here, boots on the fence form a sort of statement about the struggle and also mark a commitment to persevere. (CC.)

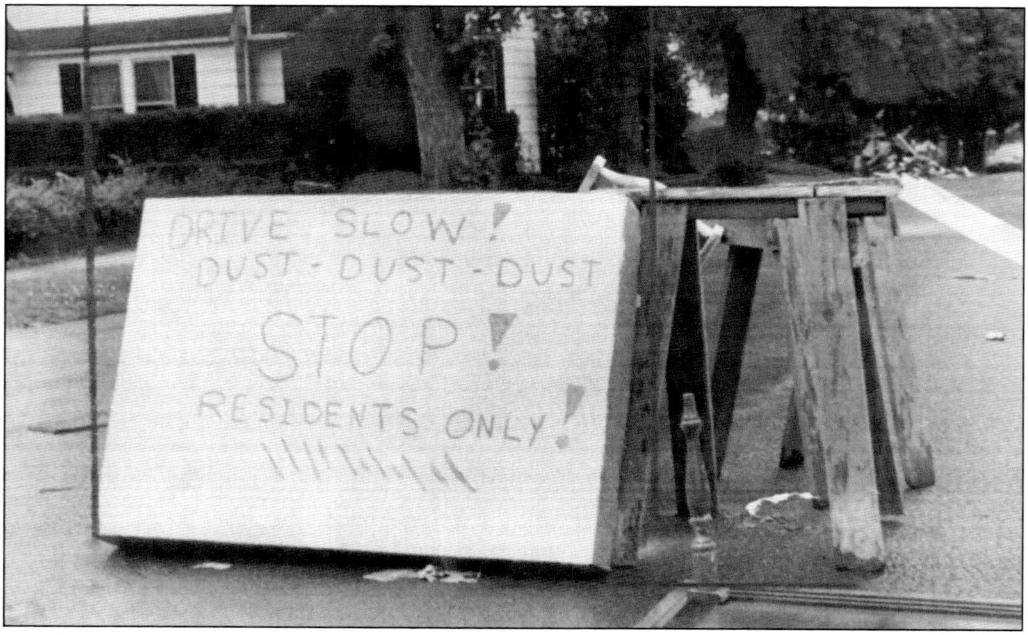

Speaking of statements, aside from worrying about looters and predators, area residents were also understandably annoyed by the gawkers and rubberneckers who unaccountably swarm to other peoples' tragedies. (CC.)

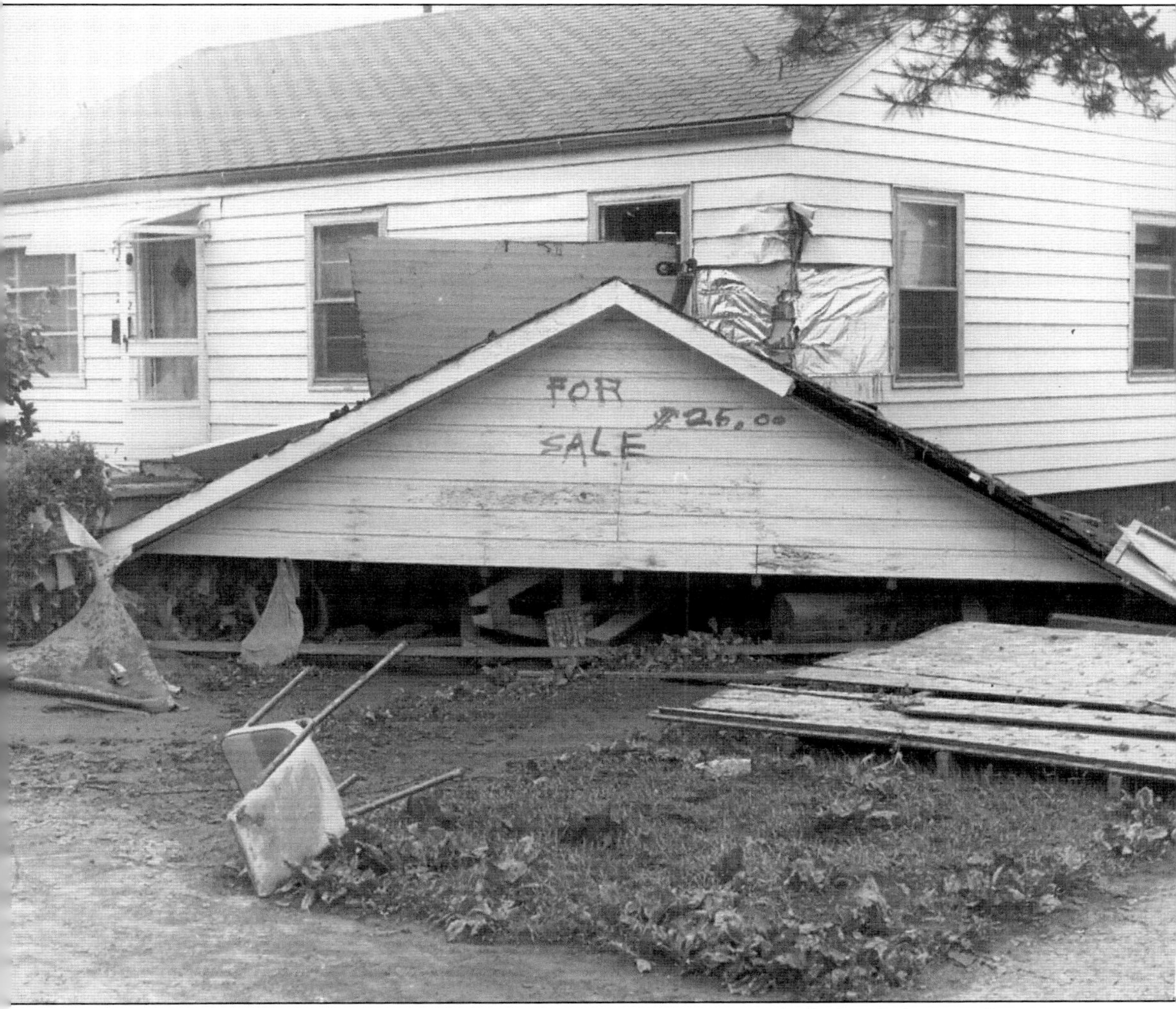

This frustrated owner is making his own sardonic statement: "For sale $25.00." A water heater is under the wreckage, insulation is exposed, a dinette chair is cast aside in the foreground, and a perfectly sized piece of sheeting has gone through the window. (CC.)

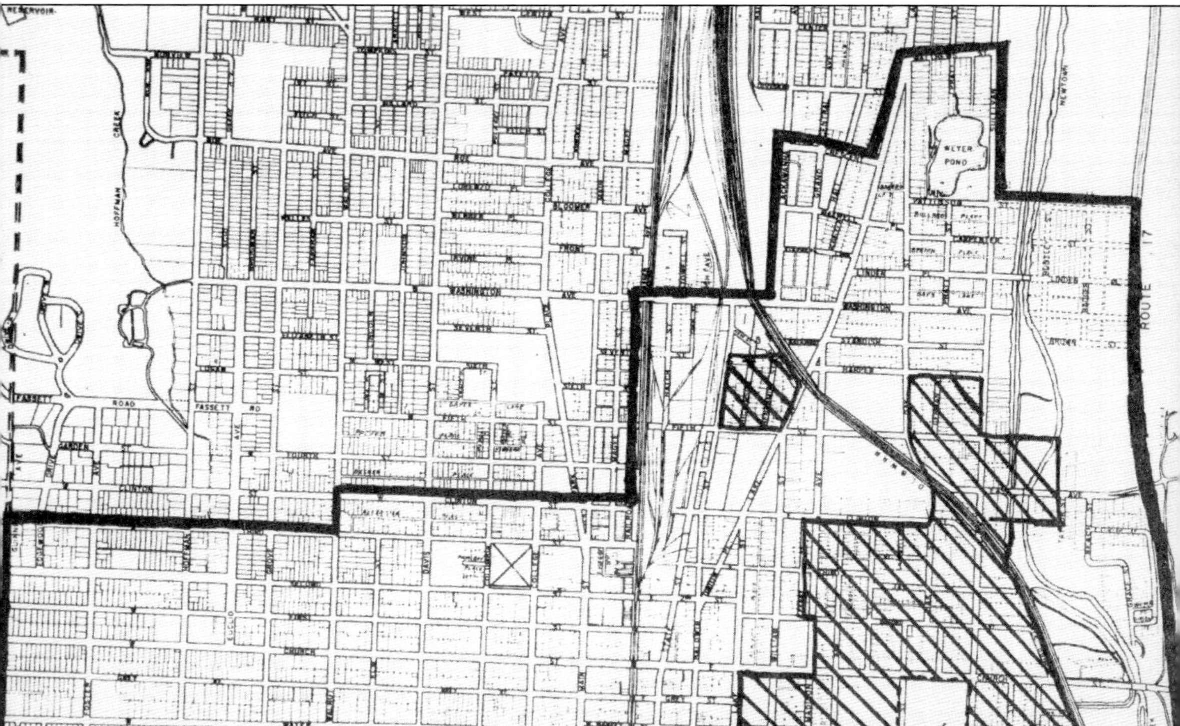

All the outlined area of Elmira's Northside was scheduled for review and urban renewal after the flood, with the crosshatched sections getting priority. Notice the Newtown Creek (which also flooded, of course) coming south from the top of the map, just inside Route 17. Notice also the extensive rail lines. (SCHS.)

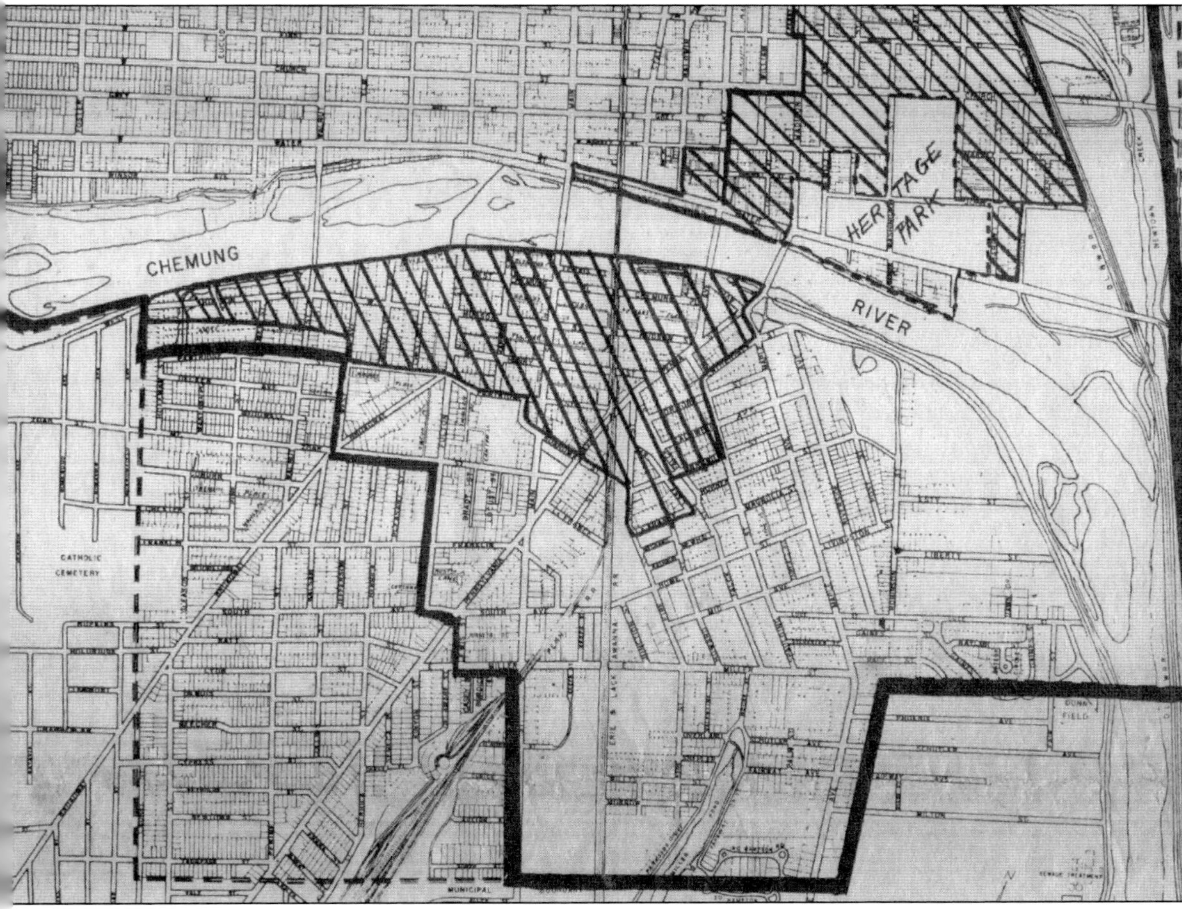

The Southside got similar attention, as this overlapping map shows. (SCHS.)

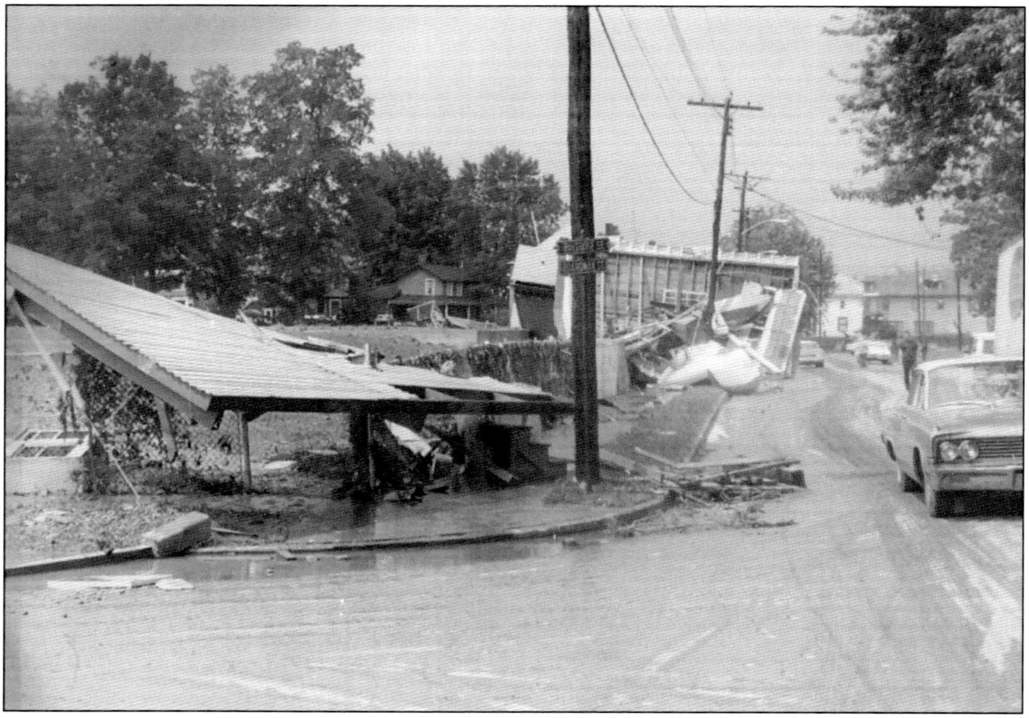

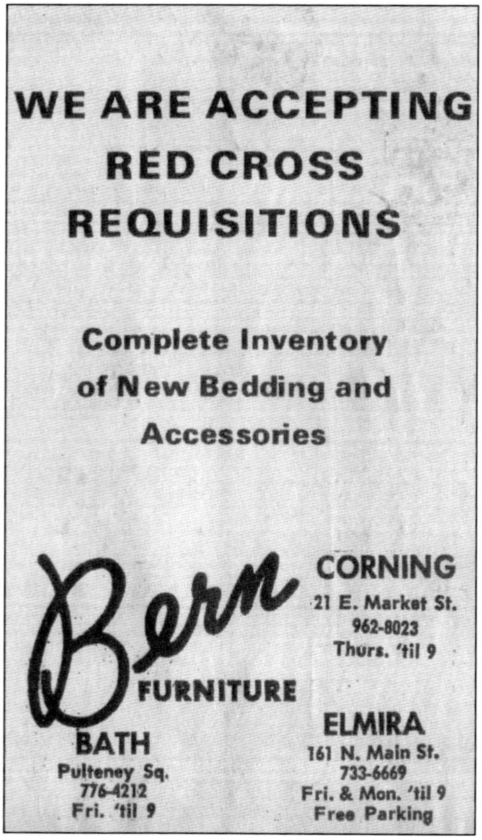

Things are still a mess at Partridge and Boardman Streets on the Southside, but at least the traffic is starting to move again. (CC.)

Post-flood realities included accepting help from the Red Cross and other agencies, such as religious, civic, and governmental groups. The Small Business Administration processed well over 10,000 loan applications for the area. (SCHS.)

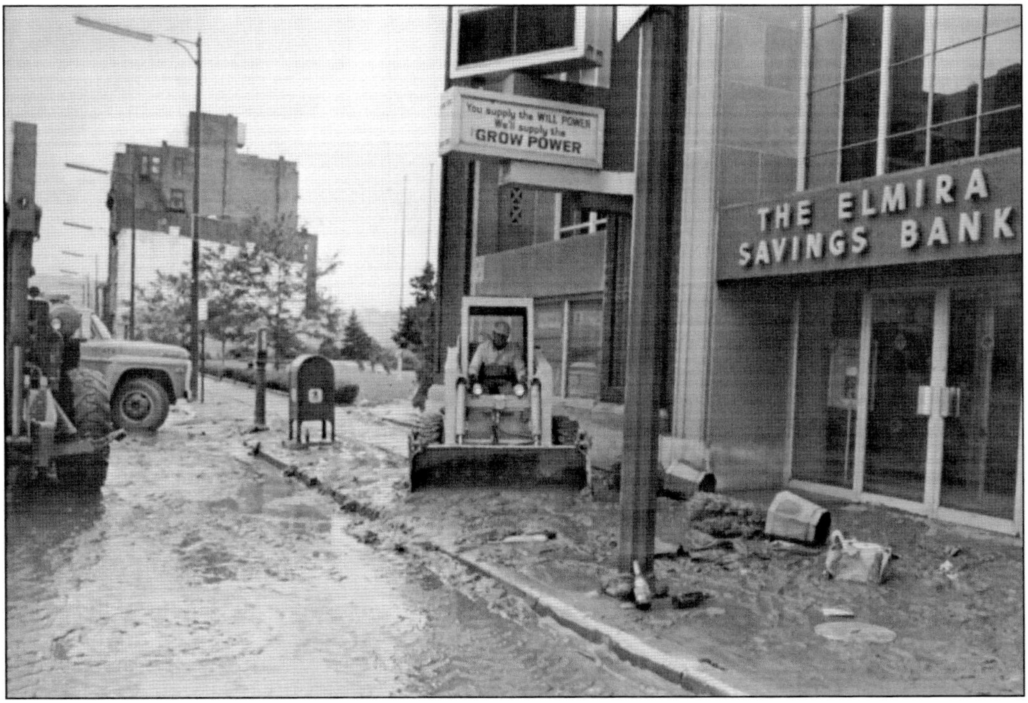

"Grow power" was now a vital need for the community. The mailbox is a reminder that the postal service was snarled. (CC.)

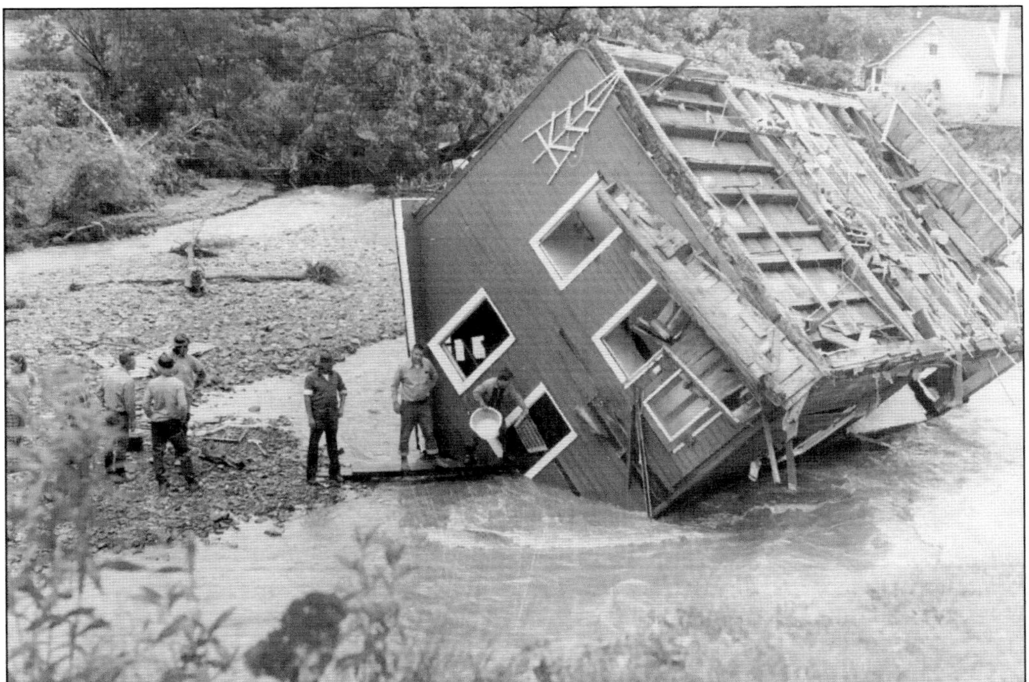

On Bird Hill Road near Millport in the northern end of the county, the northward-flowing Catharine Creek (which feeds Seneca Lake) took this house away nearly intact, including the trellis but not the roses. (CC.)

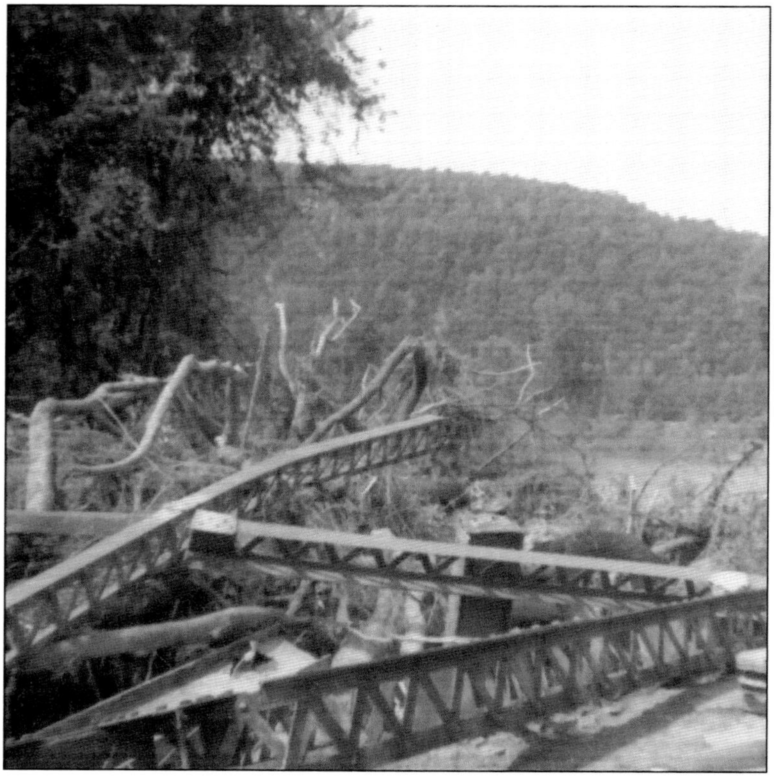

Fitch's Bridge in Big Flats is a wreck. Notice the trees that have crashed into the bridge. (AB.)

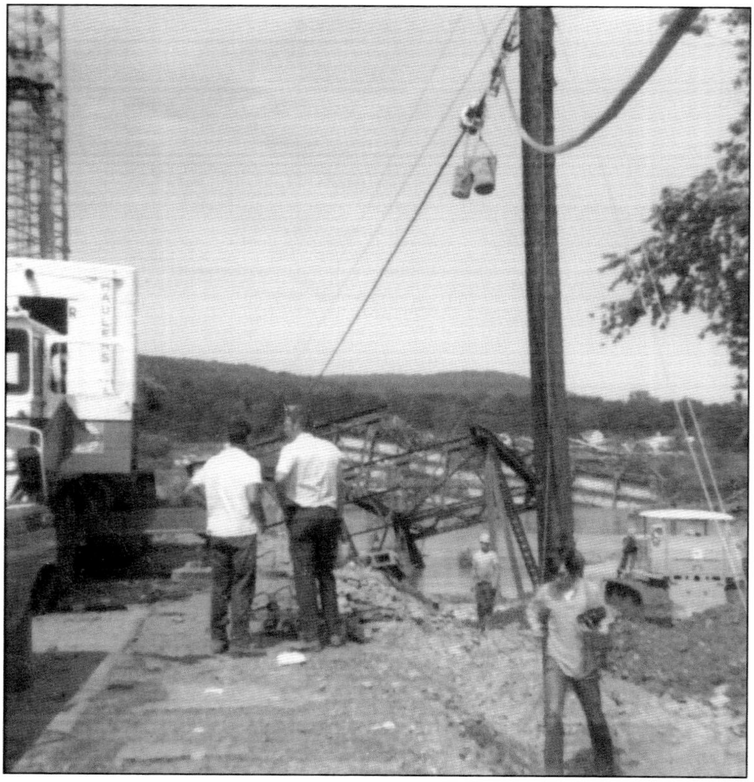

Repairs would take copious amounts of money, equipment labor, and time, even for just this one bridge. (AB.)

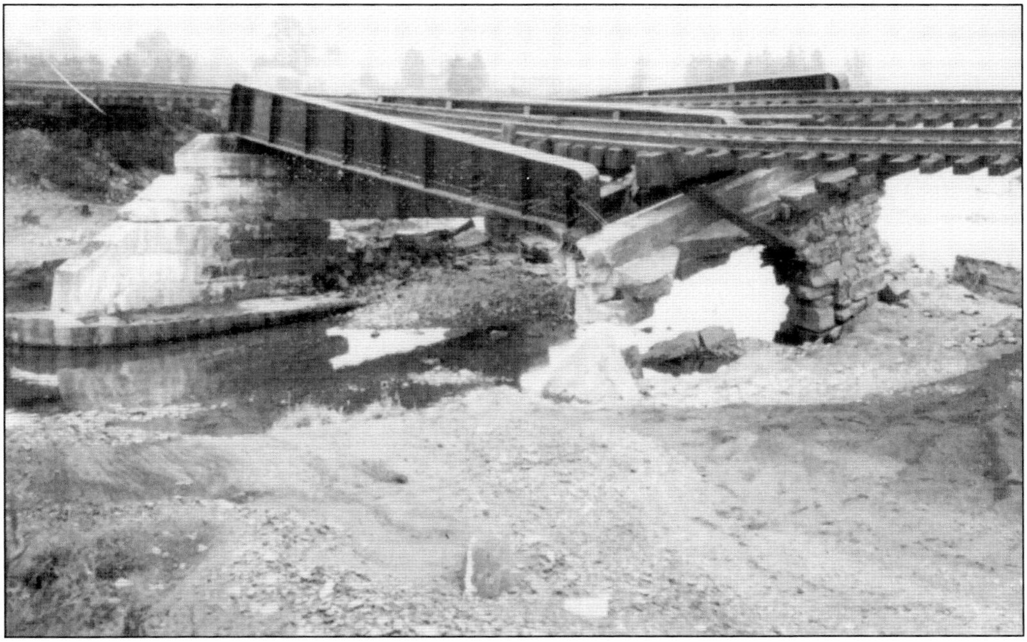
Also in Big Flats, these Erie Lackawanna tracks were left suspended in space. (EL.)

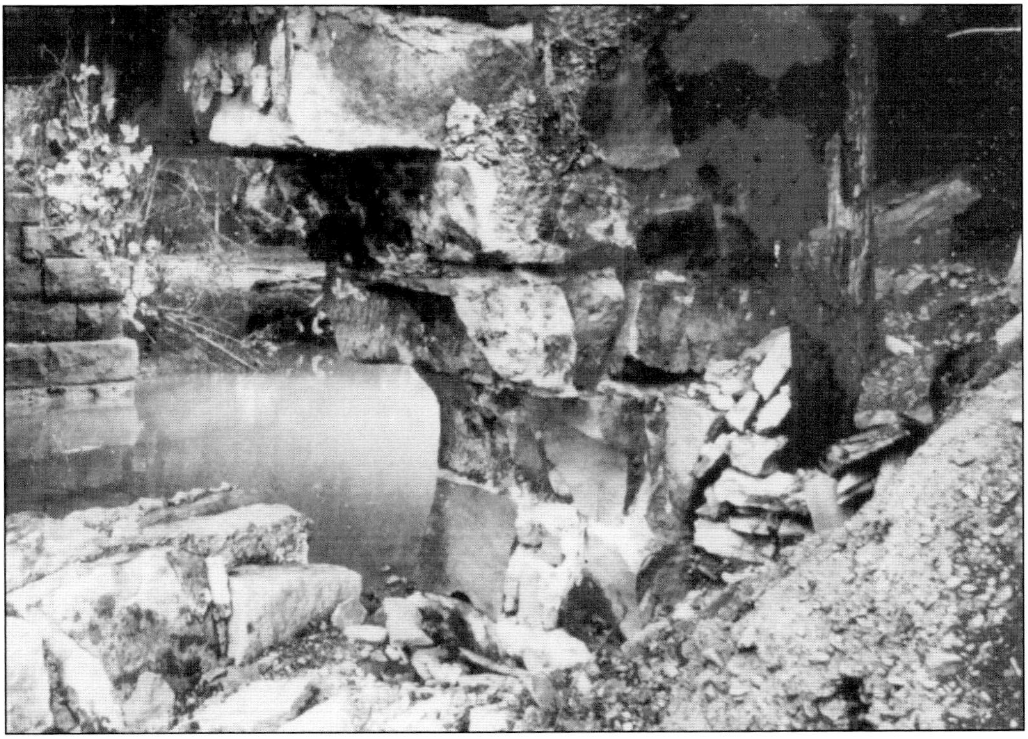
At Canal Street in Big Flats, the flood gouged out the stone railroad abutments. (EL.)

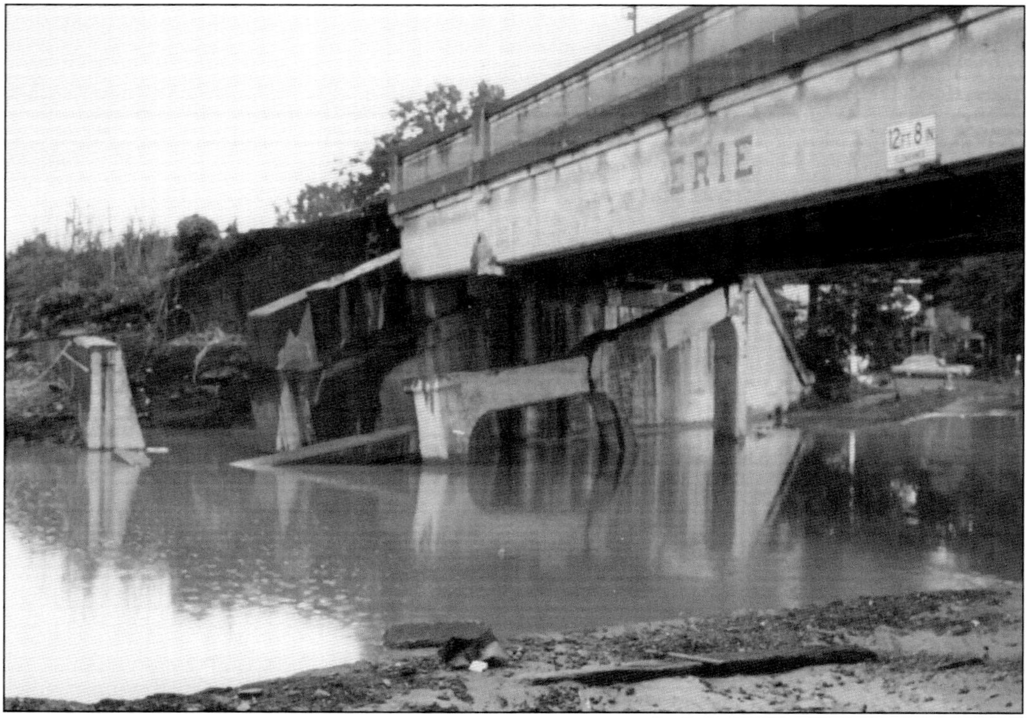

The flood has ripped the underpinnings from this railroad bridge at Pennsylvania Avenue in Elmira. (EL.)

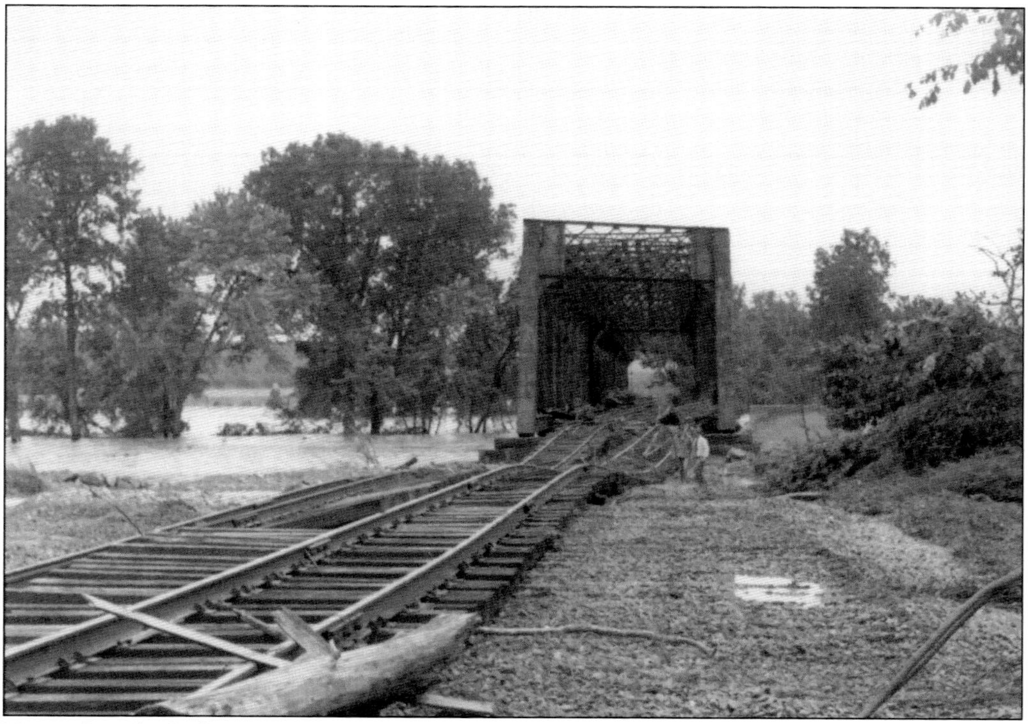

Notice how high the river still is under this Erie Lackawanna Bridge in the town of Chemung. The tracks themselves look as though they are floating on water. (EL.)

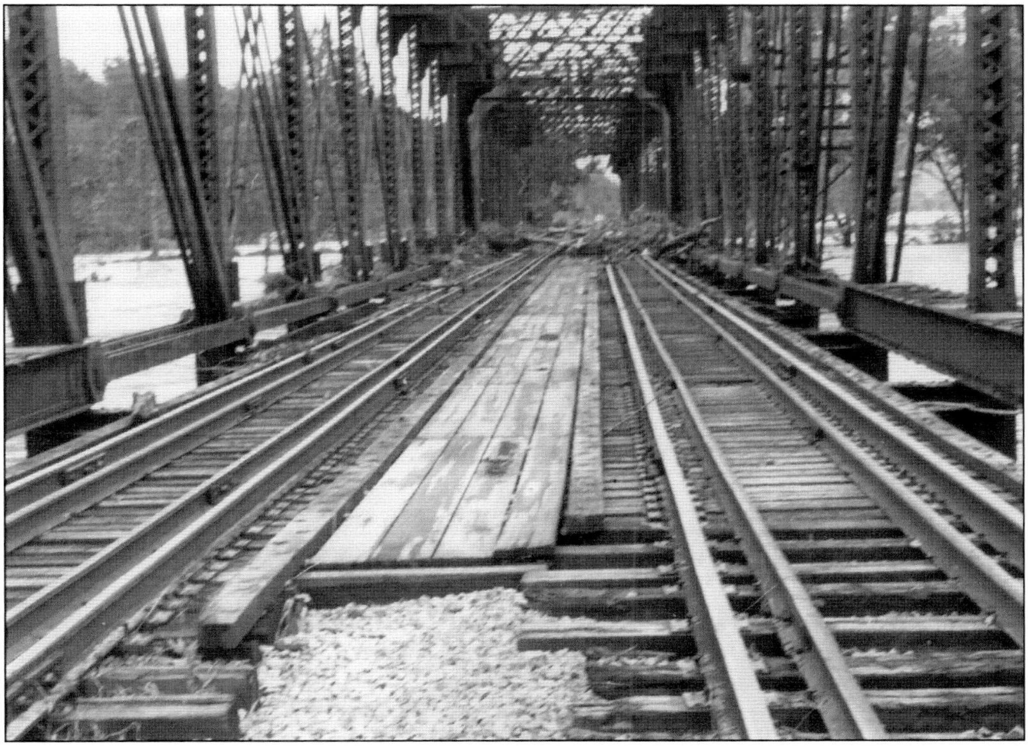

Waterborne debris piled up in the bridge itself. (EL.)

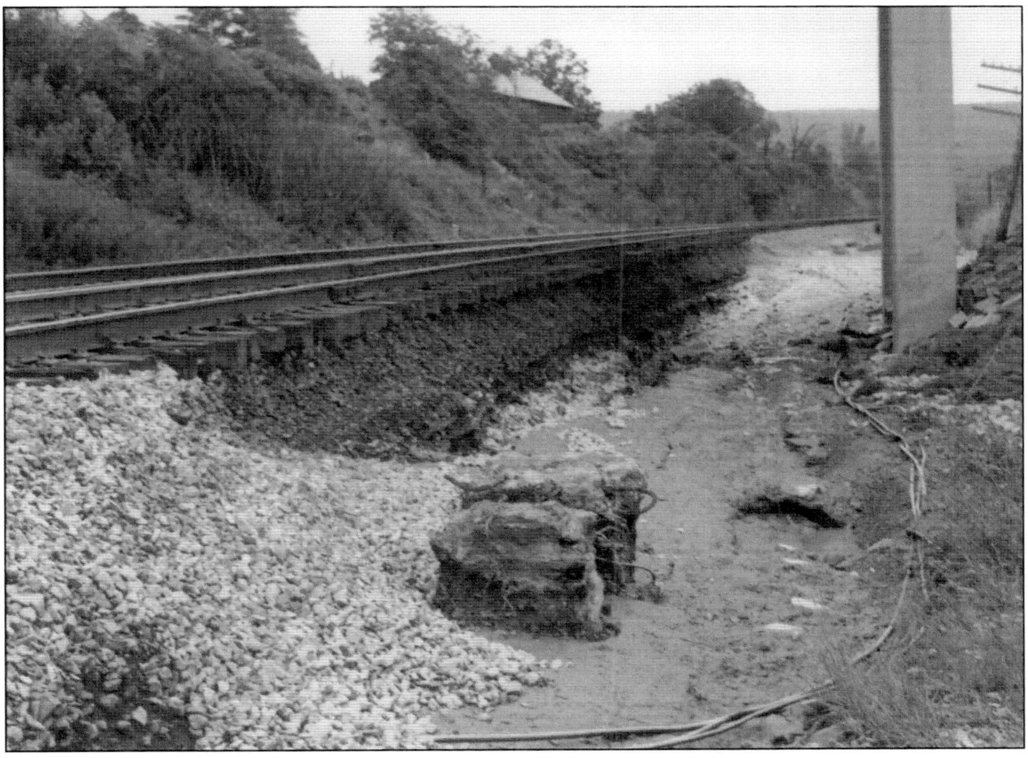

Not far from the bridge, the embankment has been carried away. (EL.)

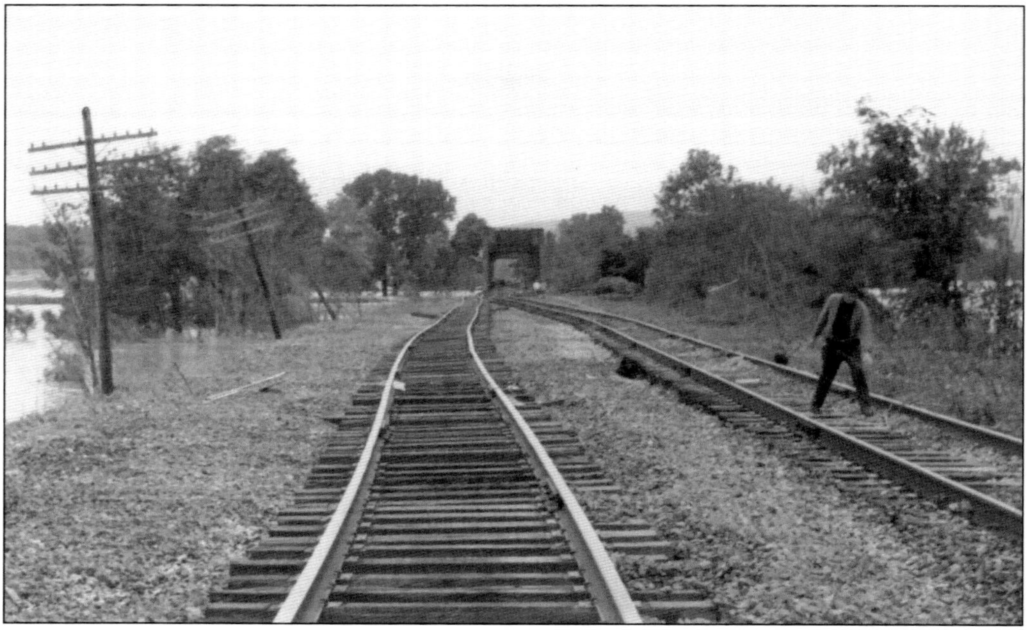

Tracks and utility poles alike are swaying, and the river has widened across the countryside. (EL.)

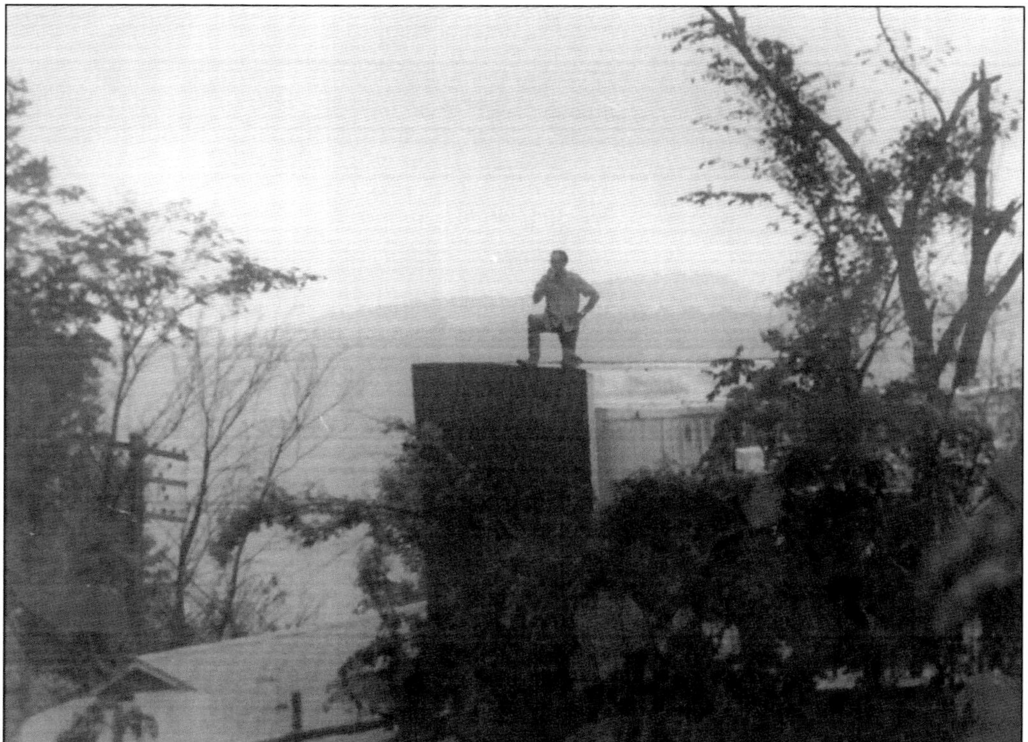

In the town of Chemung, the Chemung River finally slides out of New York and into Pennsylvania to add its waters to the Susquehanna River. This unidentified resident has plenty to contemplate about the river's passing. (CC.)

Once the waters receded, a long haul still lay ahead. Those most closely affected needed help and care, while the whole region would need to repair and recover. Inmates at Elmira's state prison baked 3,000 loaves of bread for the homeless. Remington Rand (shown here) became a staging area for donated clothes, of which Montgomery Ward sent a large load. (CC.)

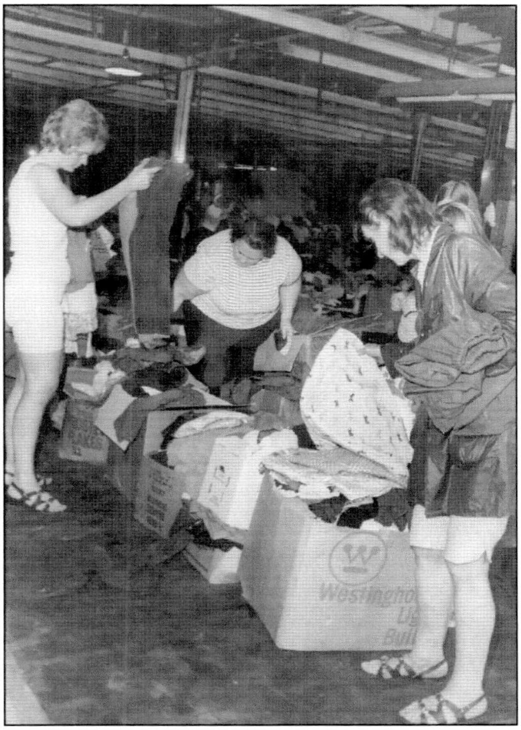

Trailers from the federal Department of Housing and Urban Development proved a godsend for hundreds of families. Despite the work of numerous agencies and individuals on the local, state, and federal levels, the flood's destructiveness only contributed to a trend being experienced across the Northeast. Elmira's population, around 40,000 in 1972, was 31,000 at the census 38 years later. (CC.)

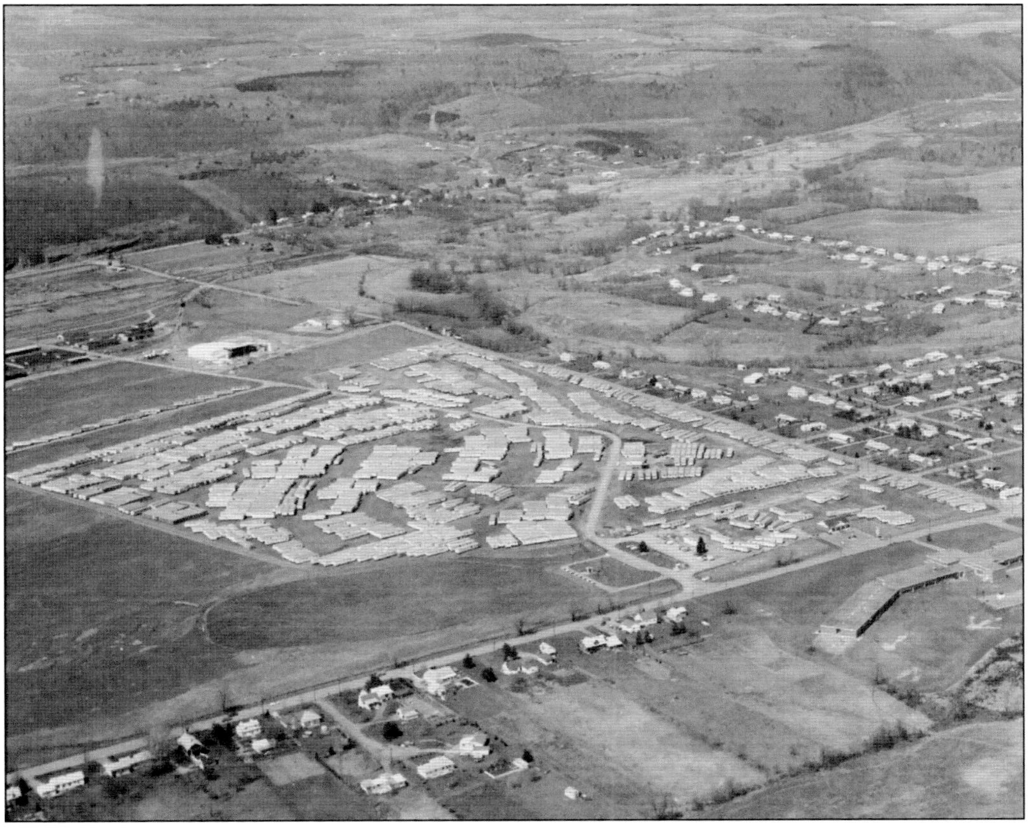

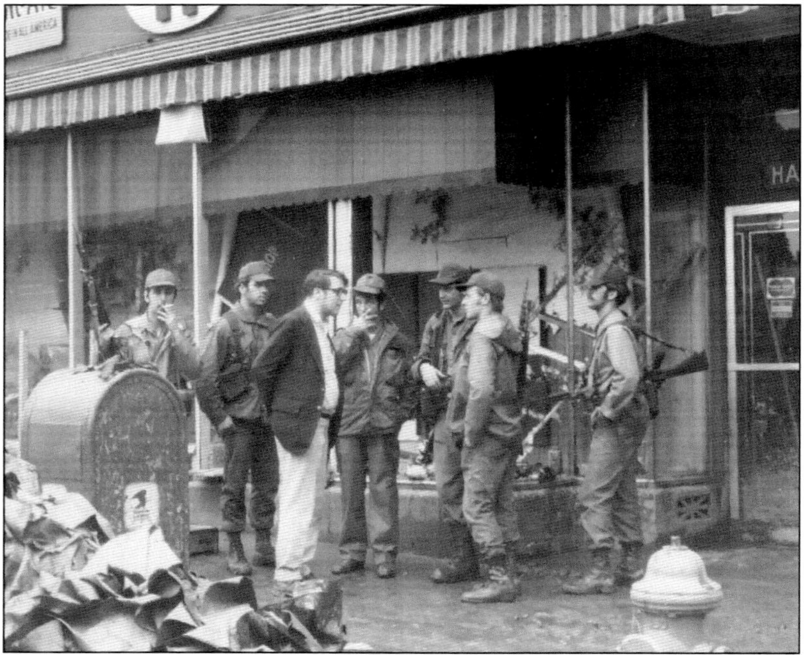

The National Guard was on the job throughout the Southern Tier, helping with evacuations and police functions. (CC.)

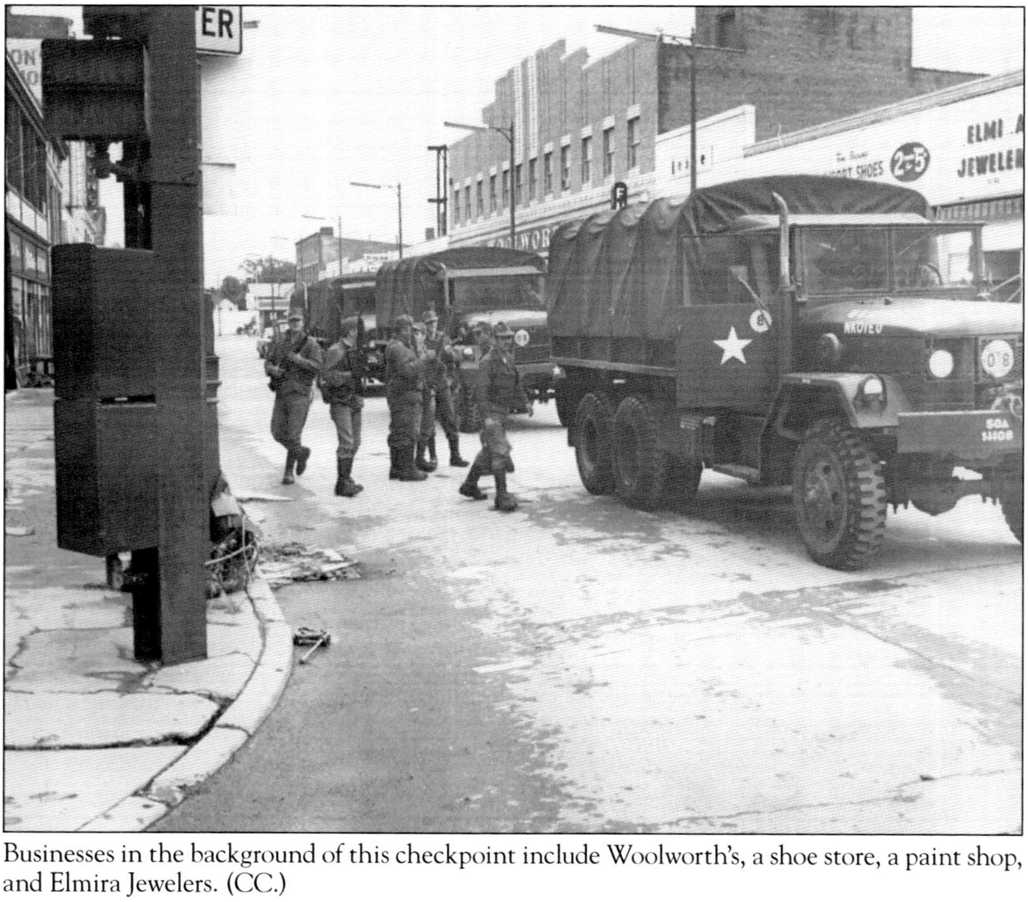

Businesses in the background of this checkpoint include Woolworth's, a shoe store, a paint shop, and Elmira Jewelers. (CC.)

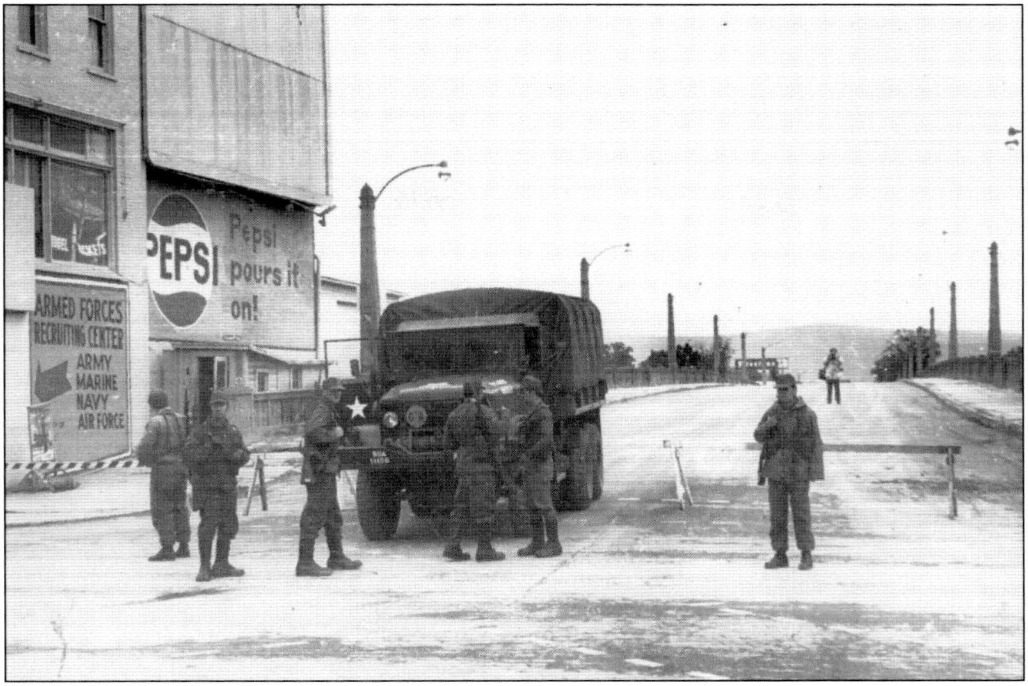

The bridges across the Chemung River in Elmira all had to be reevaluated for safety. The second-floor business above the recruiting billboard sells model rockets. The photographer has immortalized a colleague or competitor on the bridge snapping the same shot from the reverse angle. (CC.)

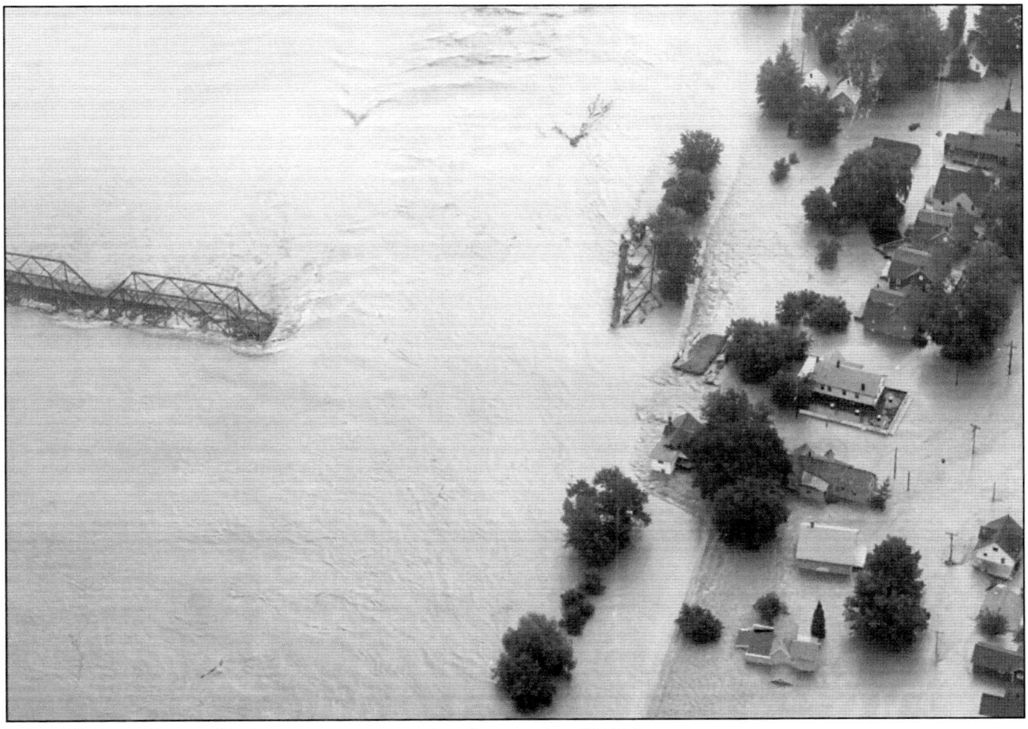
The Walnut Street Bridge gave way under the strain. (CC.)

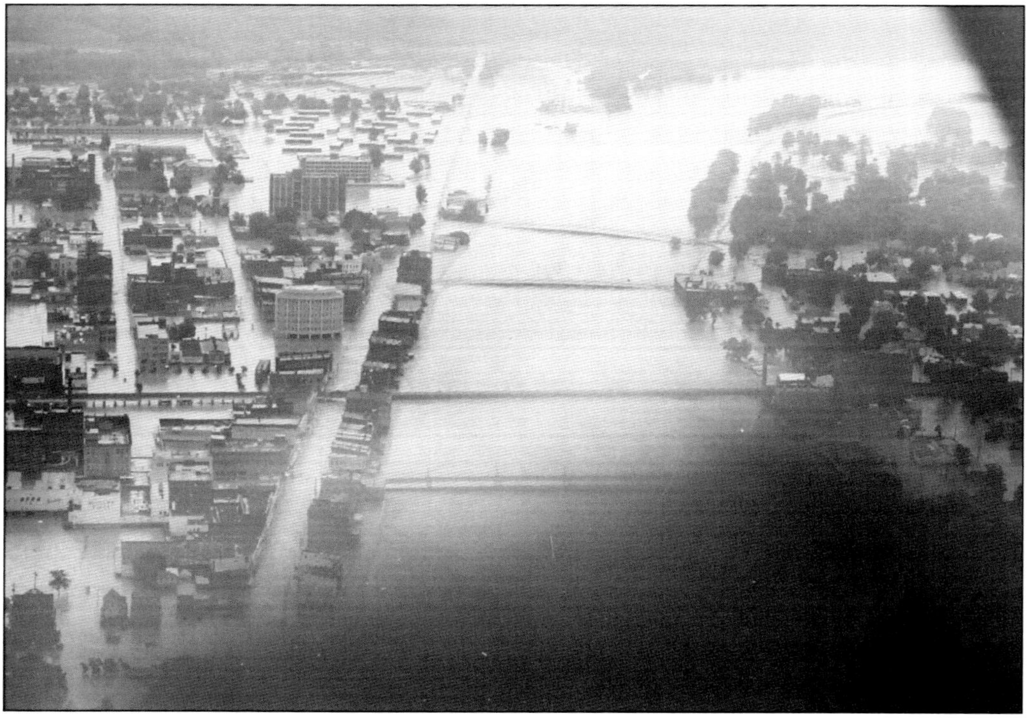

The Chemung River flows from bottom to top in this photograph, with Elmira's Southside on the right, and the overflowing Newtown Creek just discernible running horizontally beyond the city. The foremost bridge is for Walnut Street, while the next carries the Erie Lackawanna Railroad. Notice the overhead viaduct running off to the left. Just beyond the railroad is the oval Chemung Canal Trust Building. A long row of structures is islanded between Water Street and the river; only a few, if any, exist today. (CC.)

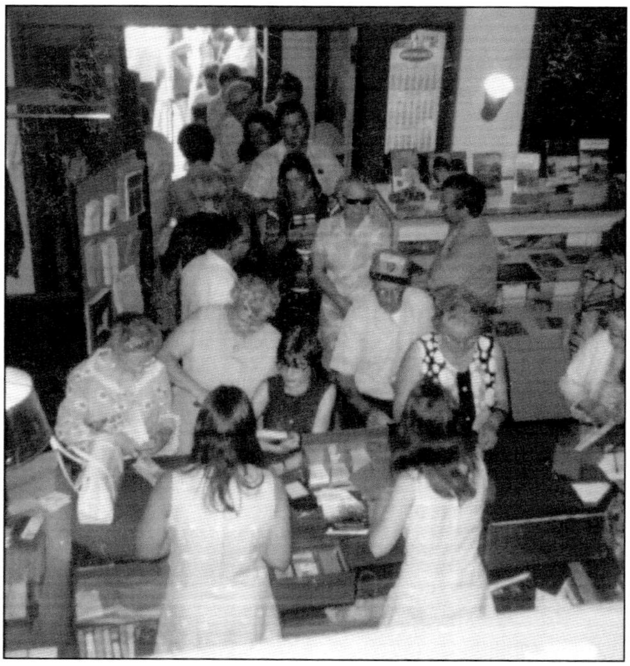

Steele Library is back in action. Patrons are lining up to buy a *Star-Gazette* booklet about the flood of 1972. (AB.)

Four

A History of Flooding

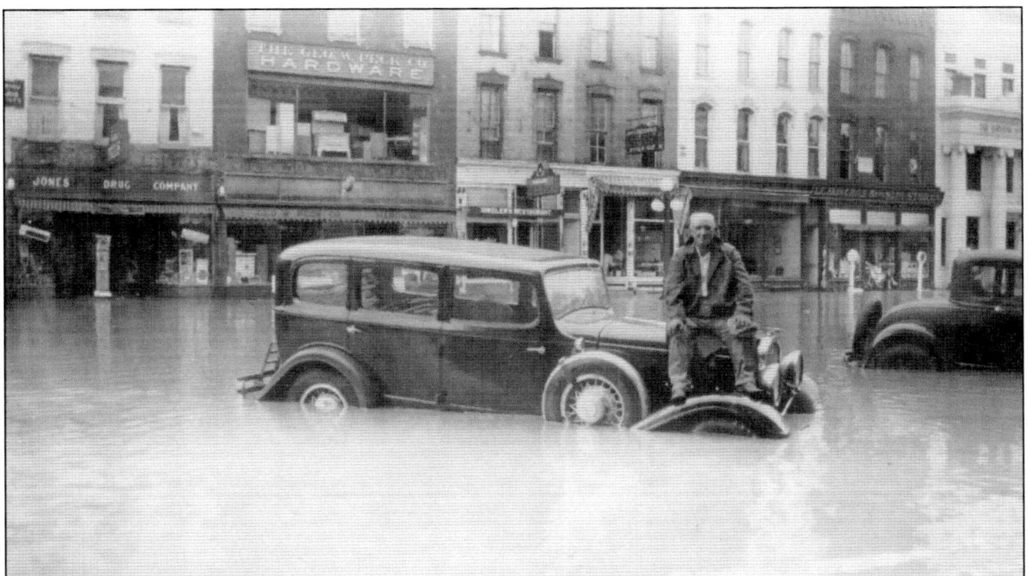

Flooding has long been a fact of life in the central Southern Tier of New York. One study identifies 86 significant regional floods between 1784 (the Ice Flood) and January 1999. The New Deal began taming the rivers after 1935, which has done a world of good. But nature is mighty big, and from time to time, it still gets the better of residents. And it will again. (SCHS.)

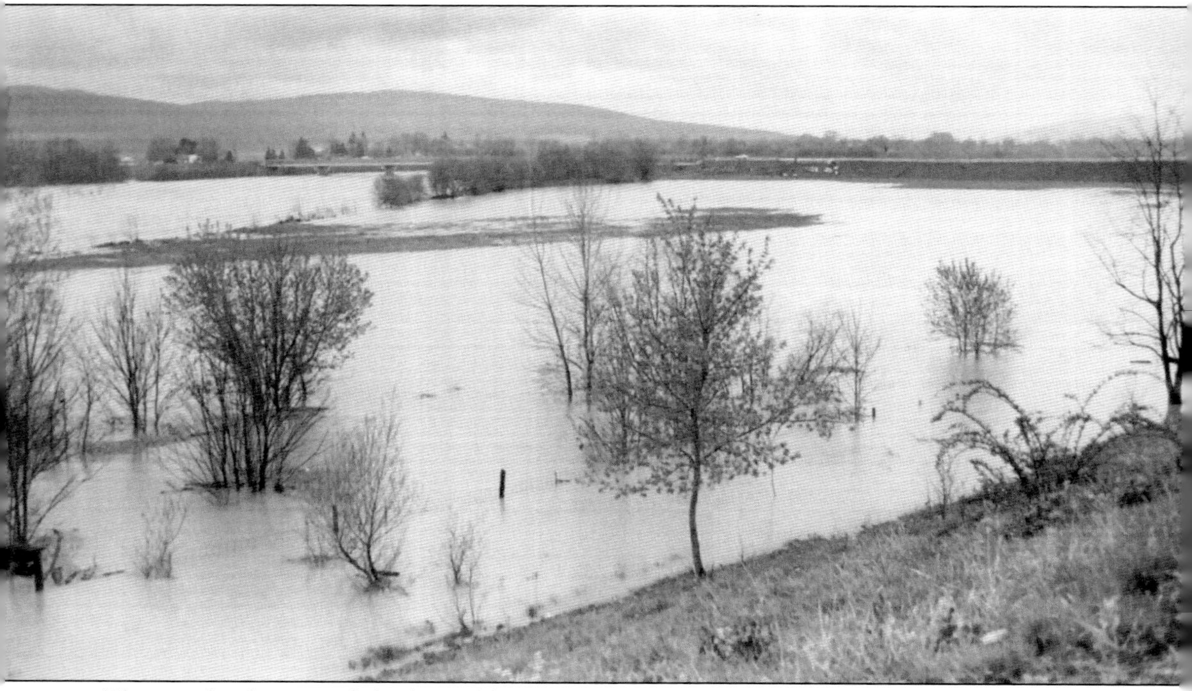

The stands of trees and the line of fence posts running lower left to upper right show just how widely the Susquehanna River near Owego had overflowed its banks in 1972. (TC.)

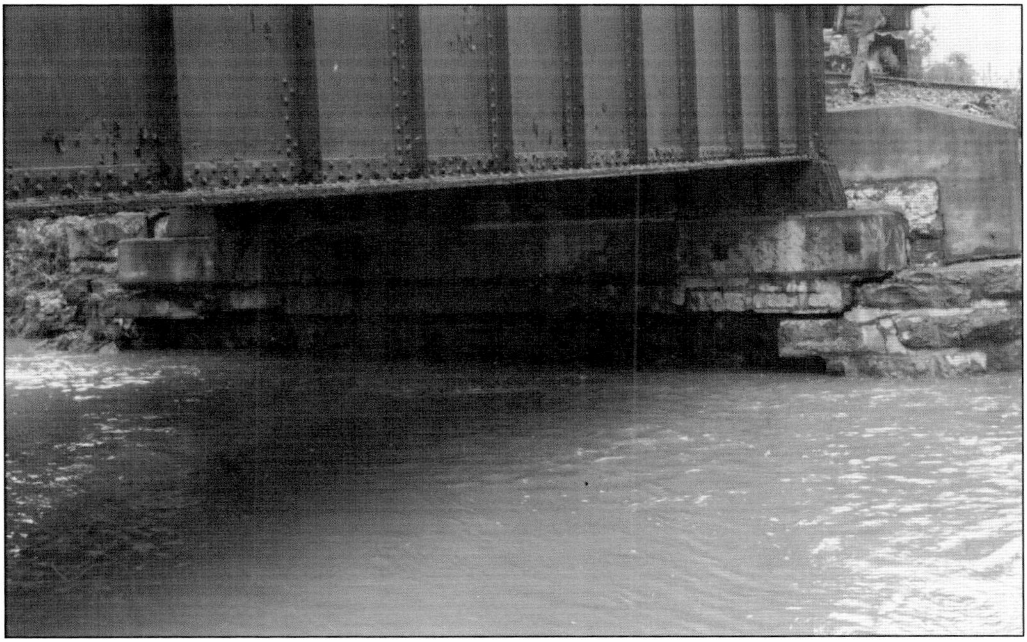

While the Chemung River flows roughly west to east across Steuben and Chemung Counties and then drops down into Pennsylvania, the Susquehanna runs east to west across Broome and Tioga Counties, dropping into Pennsylvania to receive the Chemung River. With both streams involved in the flood, the river rolled a tide of destruction through Pennsylvania and Maryland before emptying into Chesapeake Bay. This Erie Lackawanna Railroad Bridge east of Owego (Tioga County) was thrown out of alignment in 1972. (EL.)

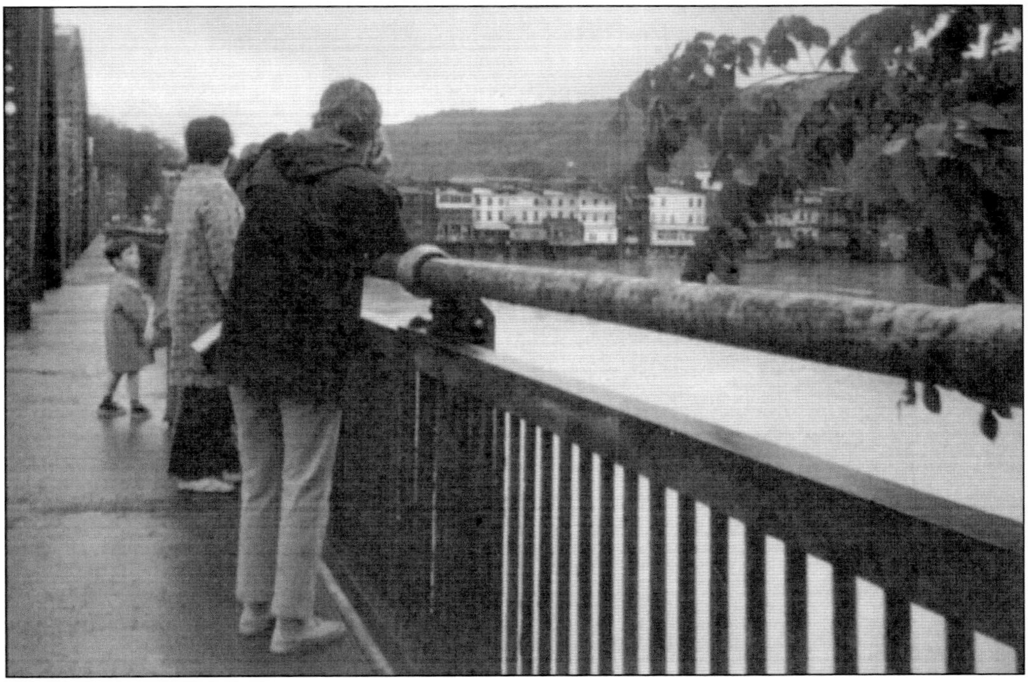

These 1972 spectators are looking across the Susquehanna River to the Riverrow in Owego, the seat of Tioga County. (TC.)

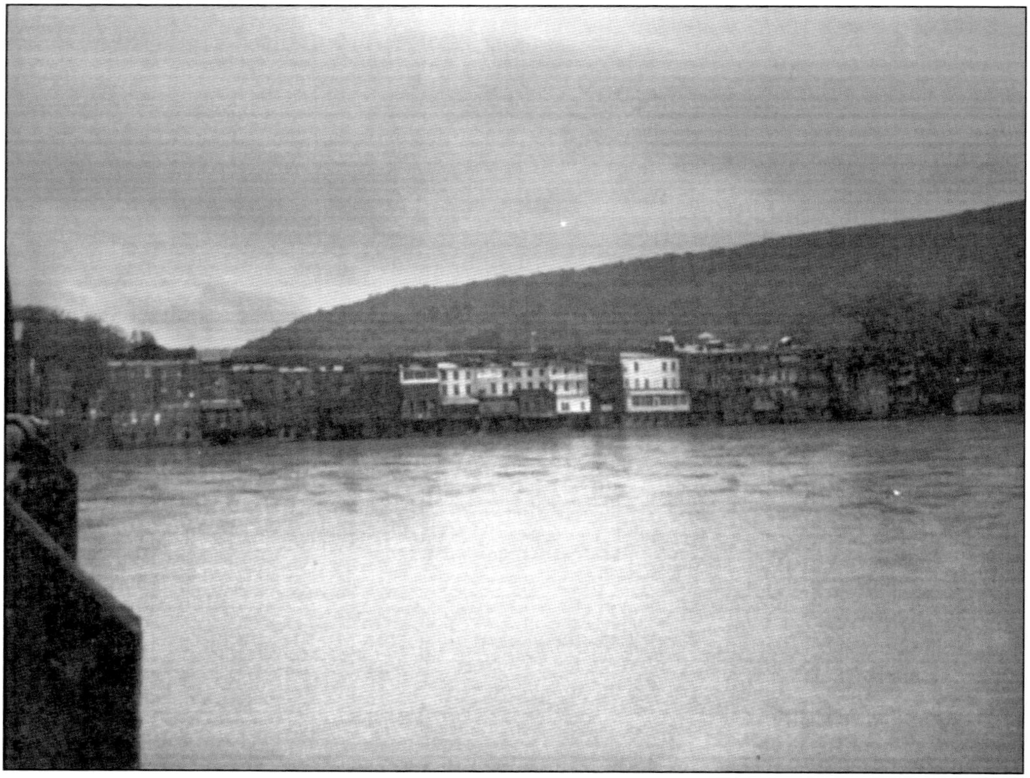

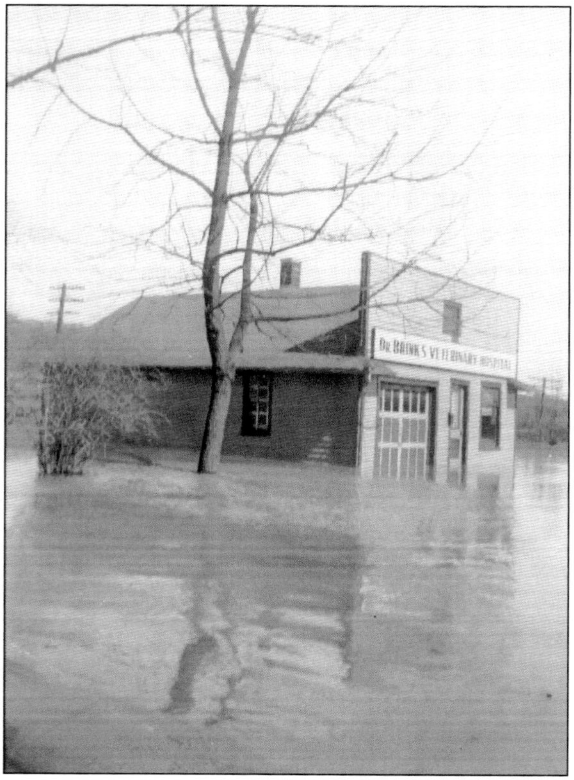

Riverrow suffered extensive damage in 1972. Flooding also damaged the town and the region, especially Broome and Tioga Counties, in 2011. (TC.)

For many years, flooding has been a perennial hazard in the region. This Tioga County flood apparently took place in the 1930s, but from the state of the trees, this is not the July disaster of 1935. (TC.)

Notice how still the waters and how perfect the reflections are in this companion photograph from Tioga County. (TC.)

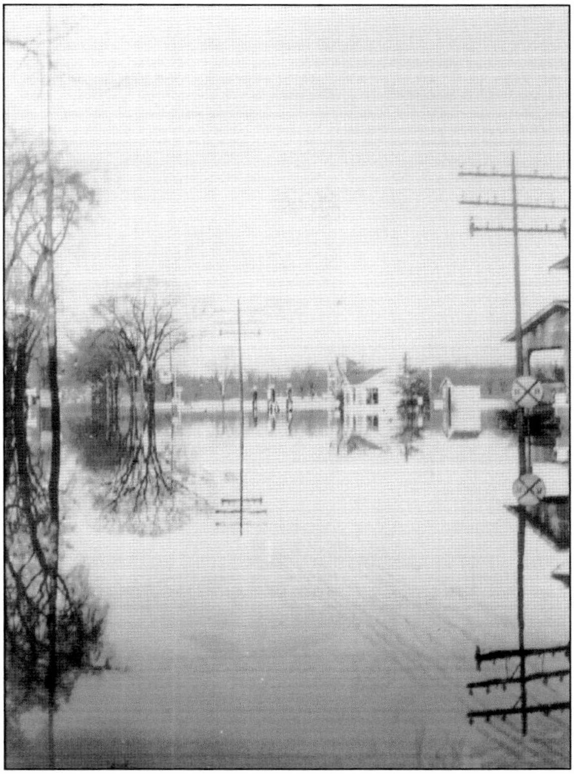

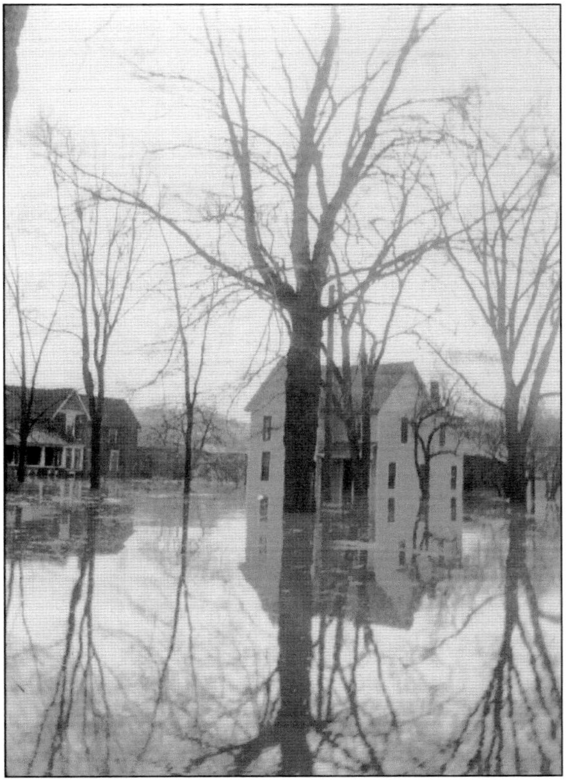

The photographer who made this photograph in the 1930s had an artist's eye. (TC.)

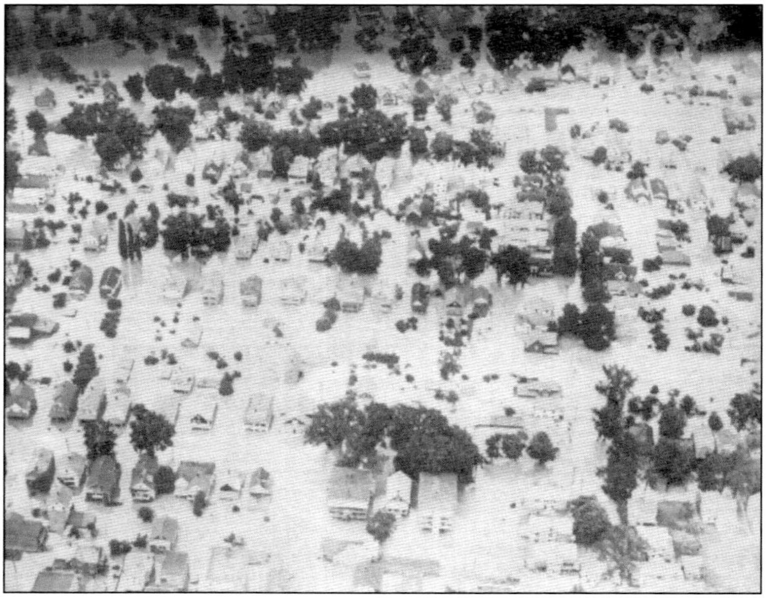

In Broome County, the Susquehanna River washes Binghamton, Vestal, Endicott, Endwell, and Johnson City. Much of Binghamton (along with its neighbors) was under the Susquehanna's waters in 1935 (shown here), not to mention in 1972, 2006, and 2011, when 20,000 people were evacuated. (SCHS.)

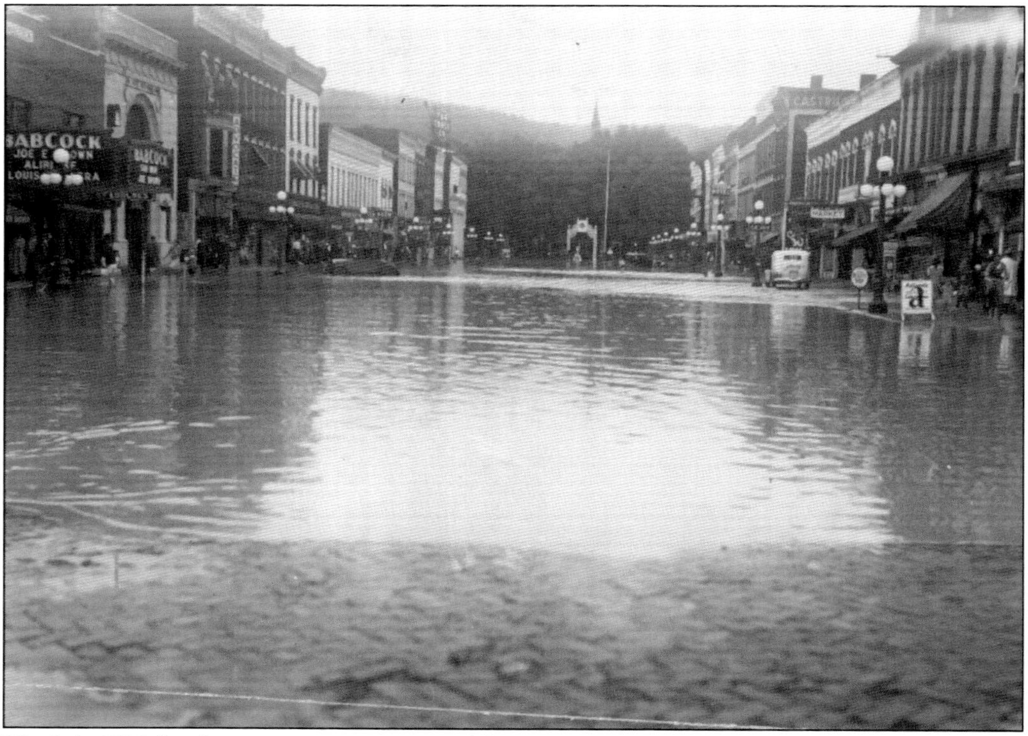

The July 1935 flood was an eerie precursor of the June 1972 flood. In both cases, days of pounding rain let loose murderous torrents. In 1935, the Conhocton River sprang from its banks to blanket the Steuben County seat of Bath. The wall art advertising Castrilli's (middle right) is still easily legible today after 75 years have passed. The *Advocate* (offices at middle left) was one of two weekly papers; the merged *Courier-Advocate* newspaper is published today. The Babcock Theater is playing Joe E. Brown in *Alibi Ike*. The theater is now part of the next-door Five Star Bank. (SCHS.)

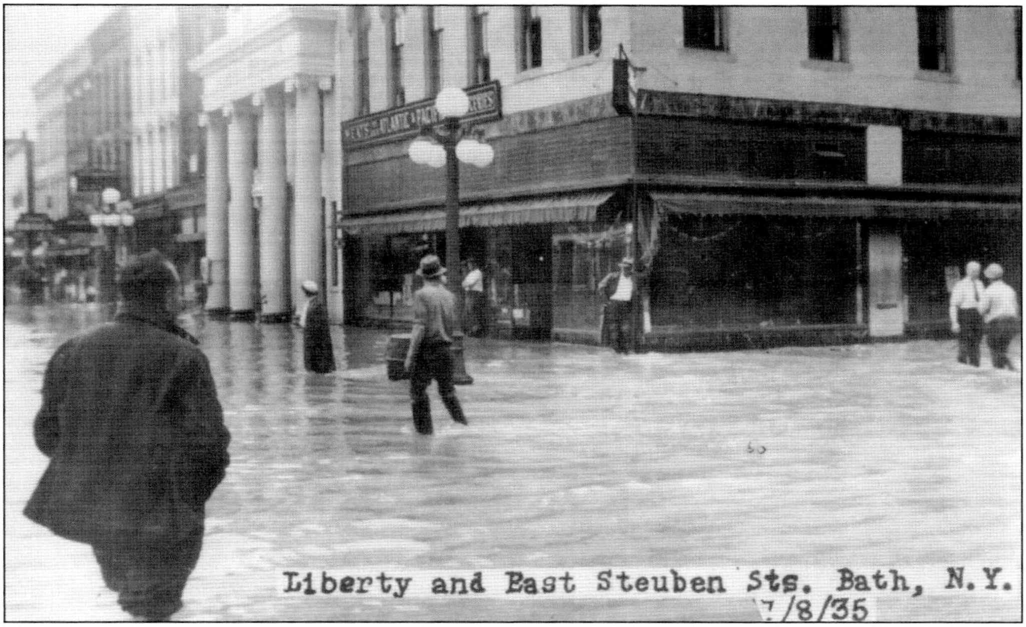

Those gents in front of the A&P seem pretty blasé about the whole thing, but over 40 people died region-wide. (SCHS.)

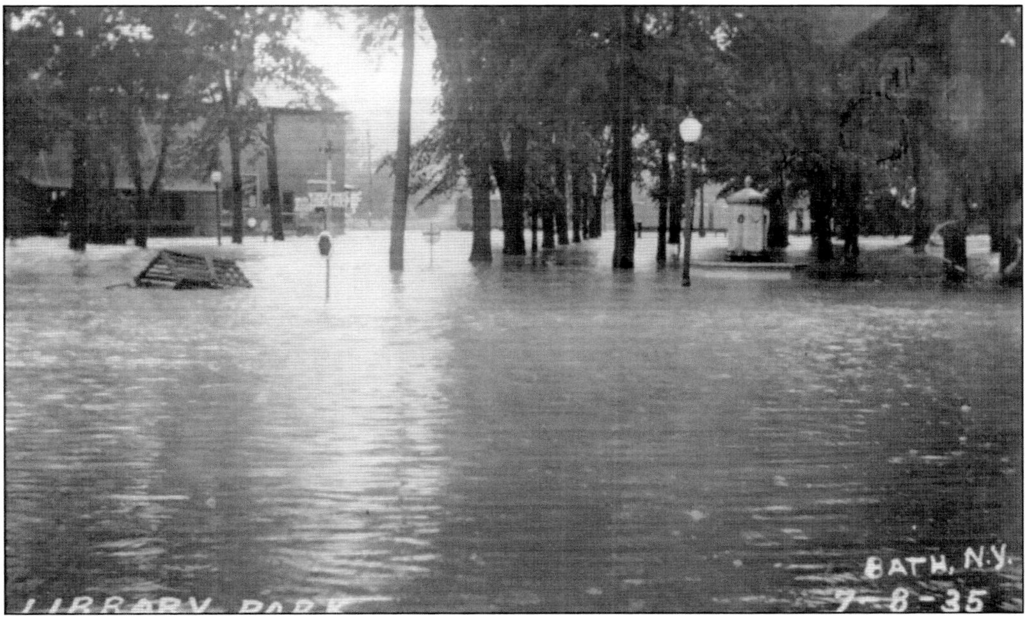

It looks as though the fountain has overflowed. The hydrologically complex 1935 flood was actually simultaneous separate events on the east-flowing Chemung River and its tributaries, the west-running Susquehanna and its lesser streams, and the north-flowing Genesee, with separate floods on northbound waters running into (and out of) Keuka, Seneca, and Cayuga Lakes. (SCHS.)

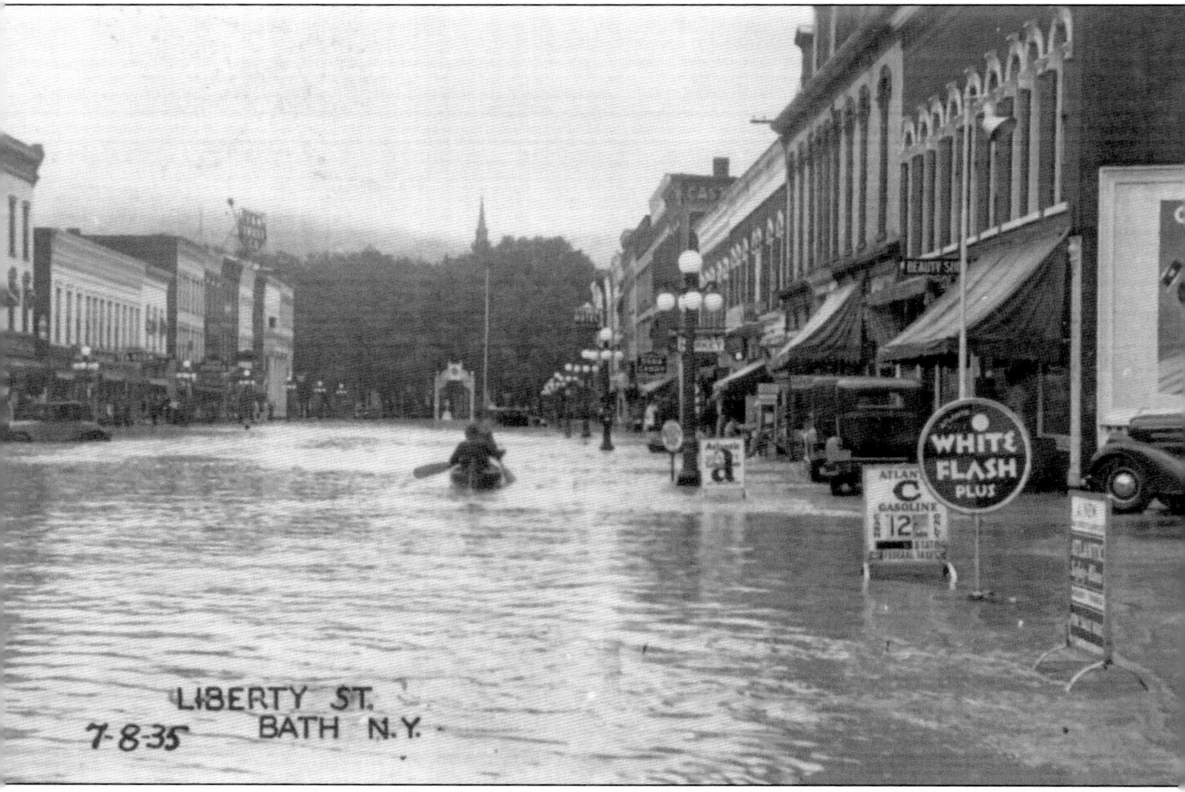

A canoe was a good way to get around. Notice that Atlantic gasoline was selling at 12¢ a gallon ("cash only"). (SCHS.)

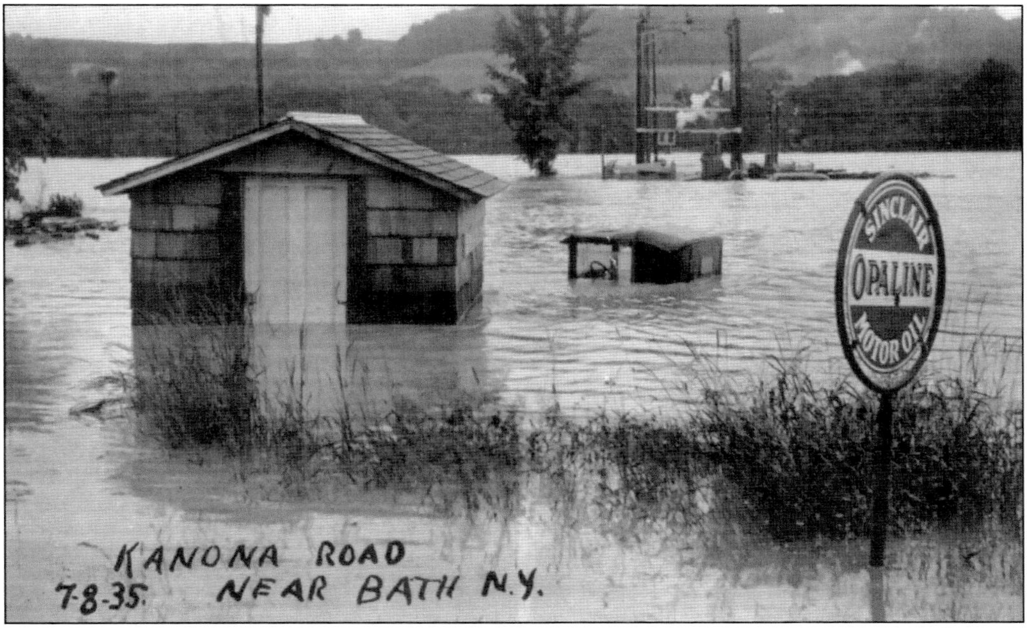

This photograph captures the damage to structures, fields, and property; the blockage of transportation; and the interruption of utility service. (SCH.)

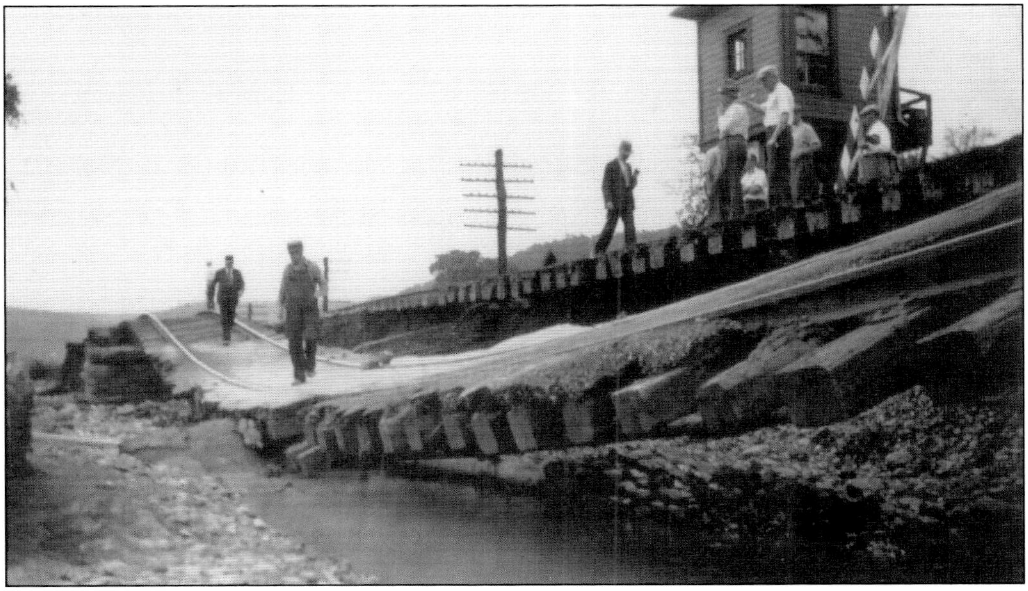

The Delaware, Lackawanna, & Western tracks (here at Belfast Street crossing in Bath) also suffered badly in the 1935 flood. In keeping with the styles of the day, everyone, including the worker risking his neck on the precarious tracks, wears a hat. This section flooded again in 1972, but Bath as a whole missed the worst of it then. (SCHS.)

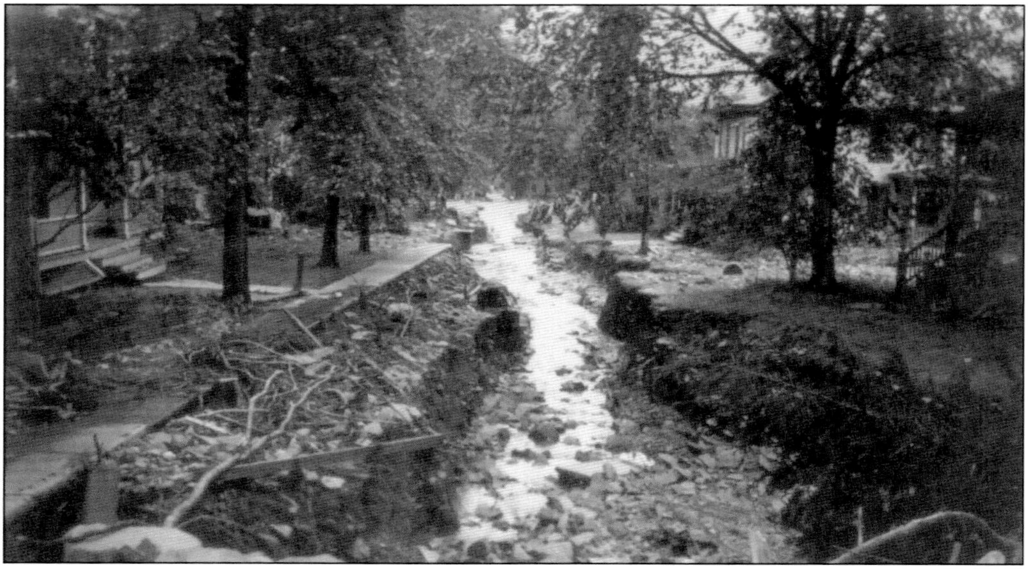

The 1935 waters tore streets away in Hammondsport, Steuben County, where the Glen Creek, Gulf Stream, Keuka Lake, and Keuka Inlet all flooded. As in 1972, the 1935 floods came up quickly, while people were sleeping. (SCHS.)

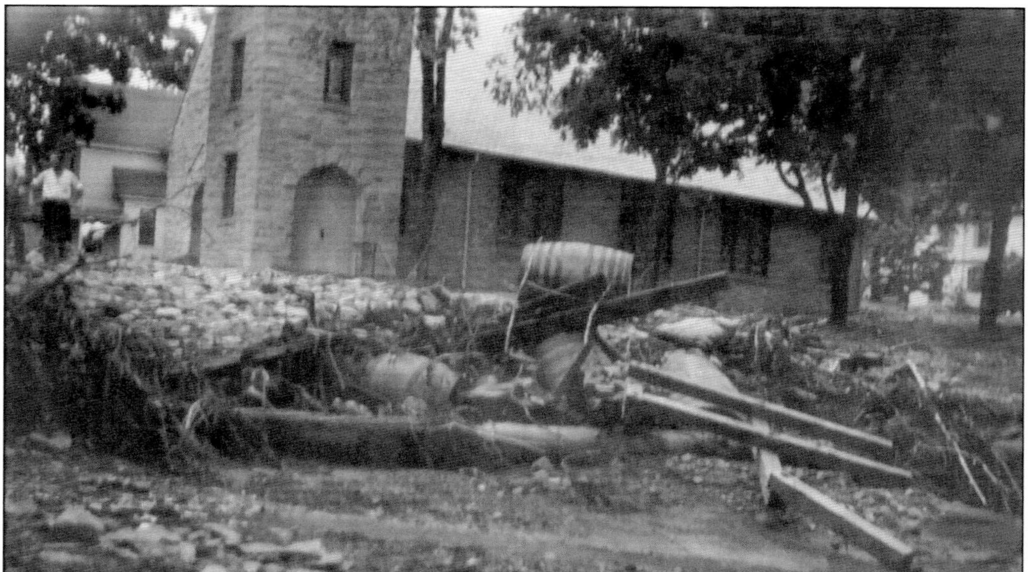

That same 1935 flood washed brandy casks from Roualet Winery's warehouse at the mouth of the Hammondsport Glen and dumped them all over town. In this scene, some are near the Episcopal church at Lake and Main Streets. Local families still tell tales about who recovered the casks and what they did with them. (SCHS.)

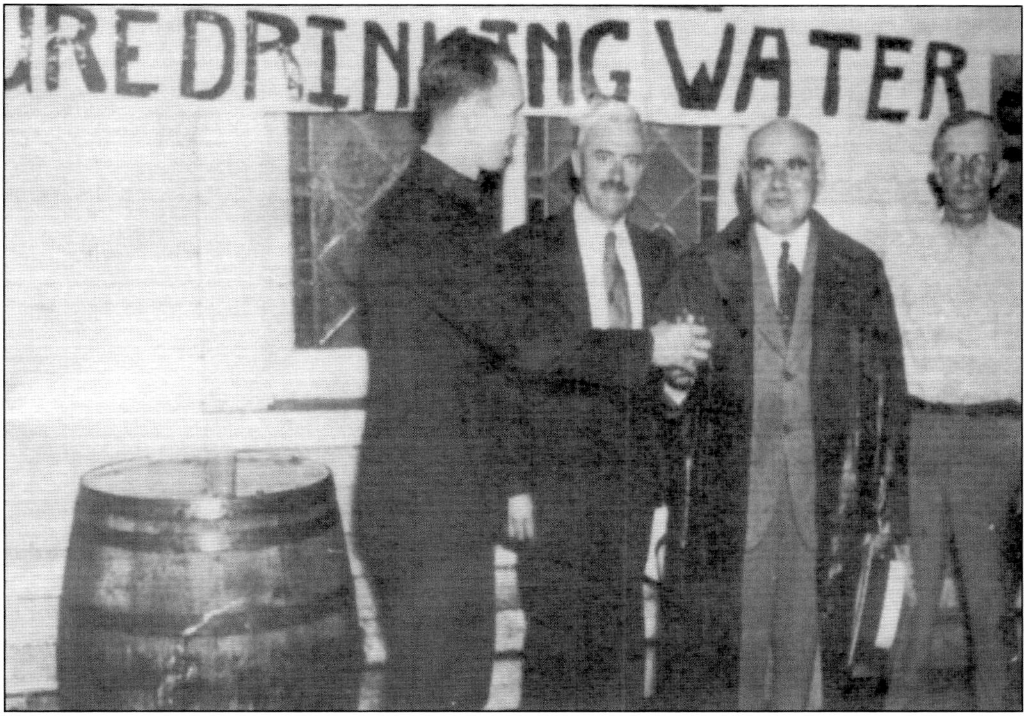

Gov. Herbert Lehman toured the region in the wake of the floods, and later governors, such as Nelson Rockefeller (1972) and Andrew Cuomo (2011), would repeat his pilgrimage. A Salvation Army officer in Hammondsport offers the governor the proverbial cup of water. (SCHS.)

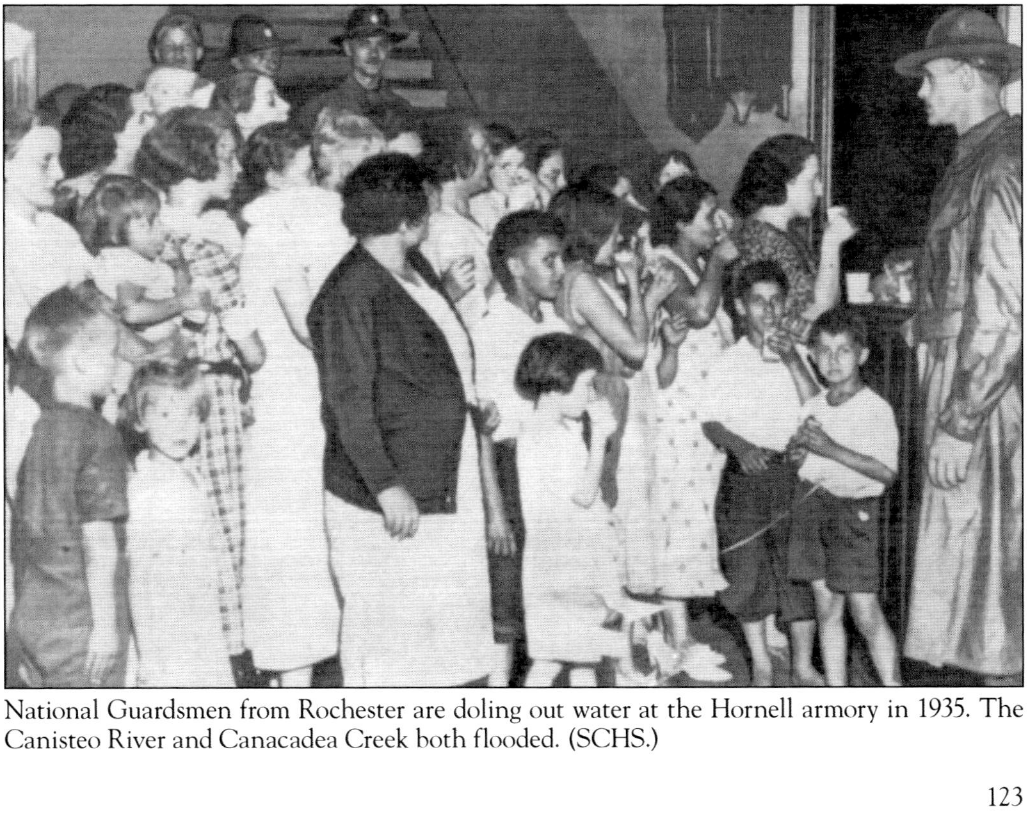

National Guardsmen from Rochester are doling out water at the Hornell armory in 1935. The Canisteo River and Canacadea Creek both flooded. (SCHS.)

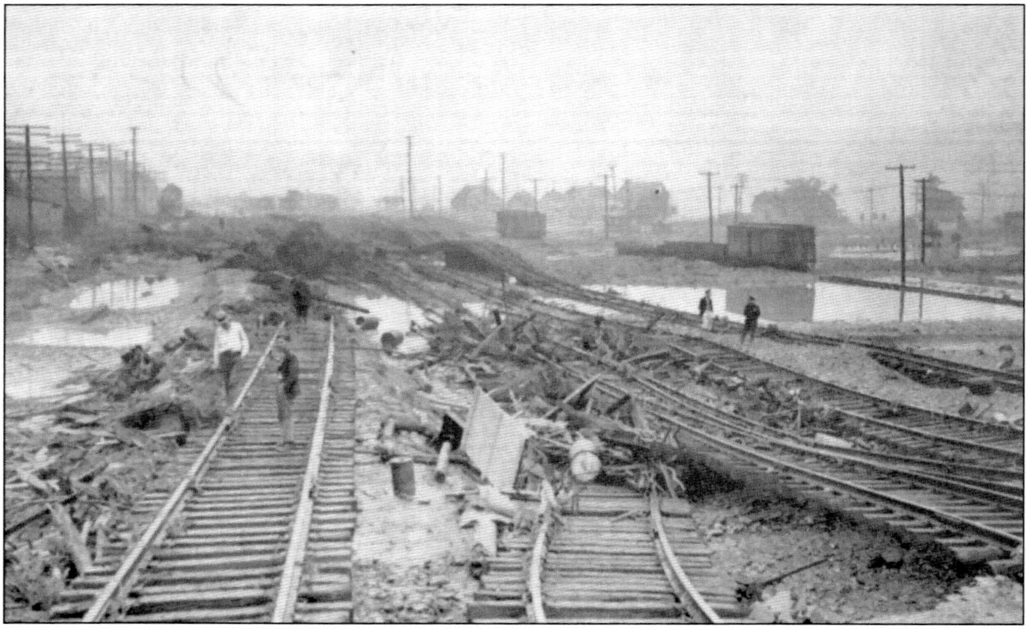

Hornell was home to the Erie Railroad's main repair shops. Damage to the Erie foreshadowed fatal damage to the Erie Lackawanna Railroad in 1972. (SCH.)

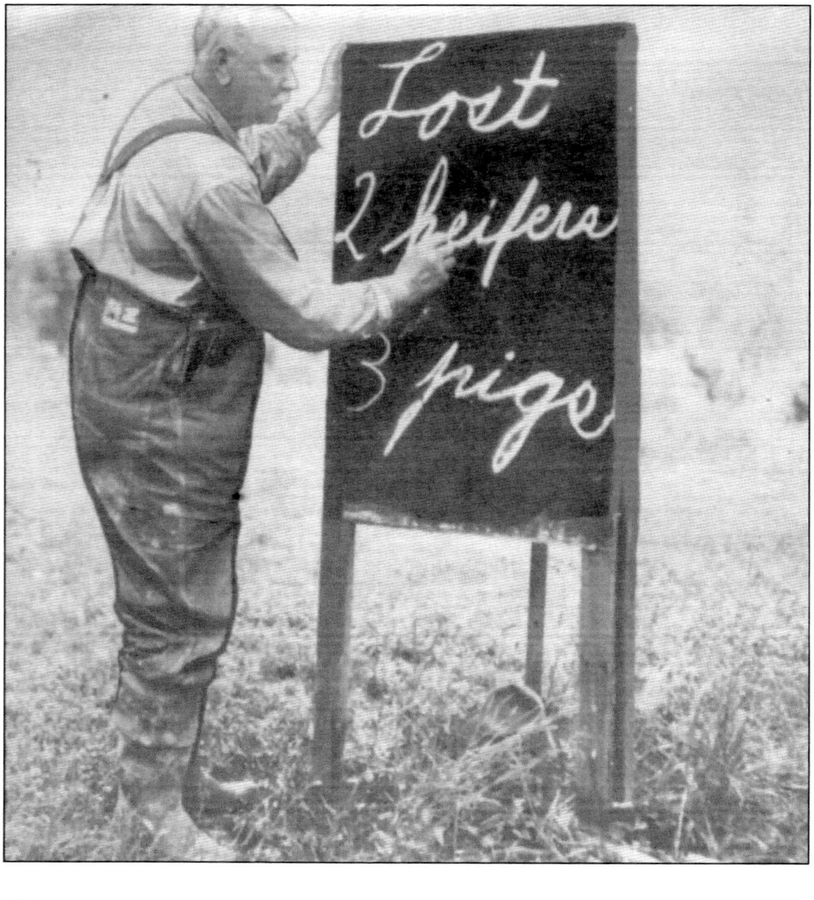

Such a livestock loss could have meant bankruptcy during the Great Depression. But J.J. Baker of Cooper's Plains in Steuben County, where the Conhocton River flooded in 1935, was not a man to give up easily. (SCHS.)

Likewise, this solitary cyclist in Painted Post is not about to quit. In the 1935 flood, as in 1972, the Chemung, Tioga, and Conhocton Rivers all inundated Painted Post. (SCHS.)

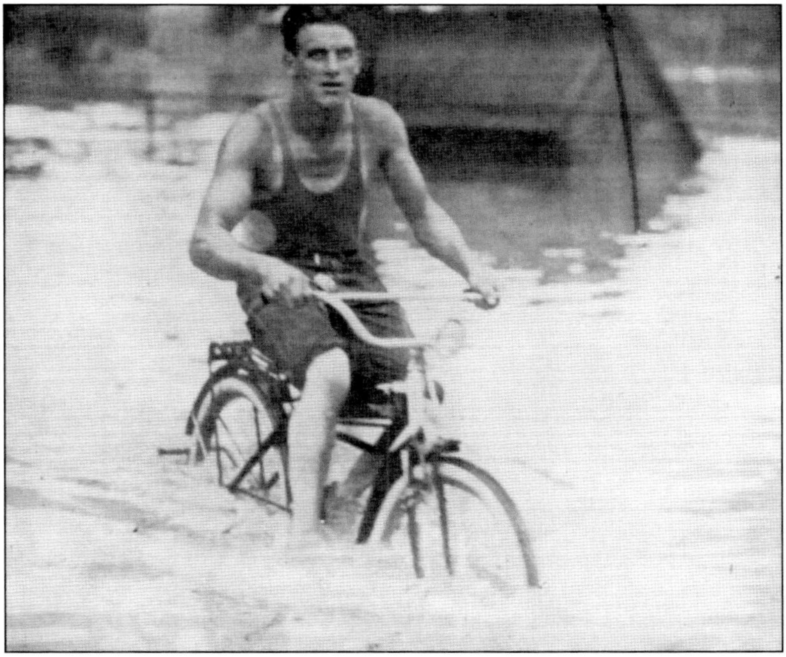

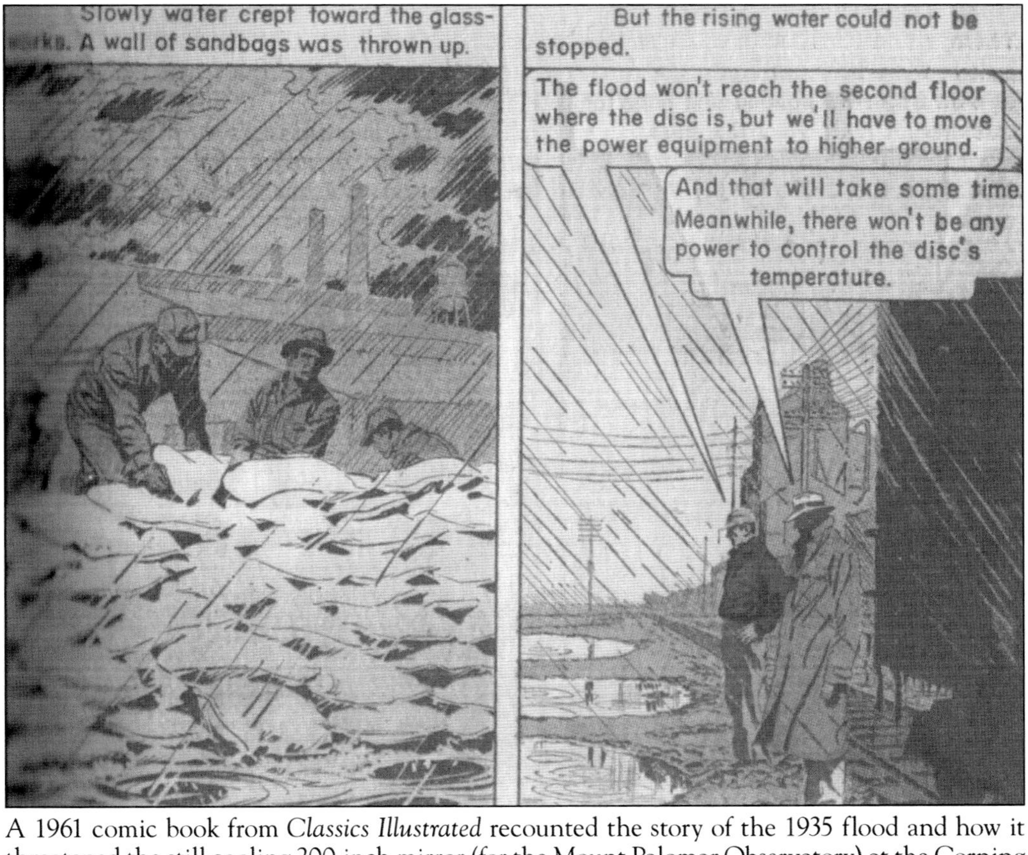

A 1961 comic book from *Classics Illustrated* recounted the story of the 1935 flood and how it threatened the still cooling 200-inch mirror (for the Mount Palomar Observatory) at the Corning Glass Works. (Author's collection.)

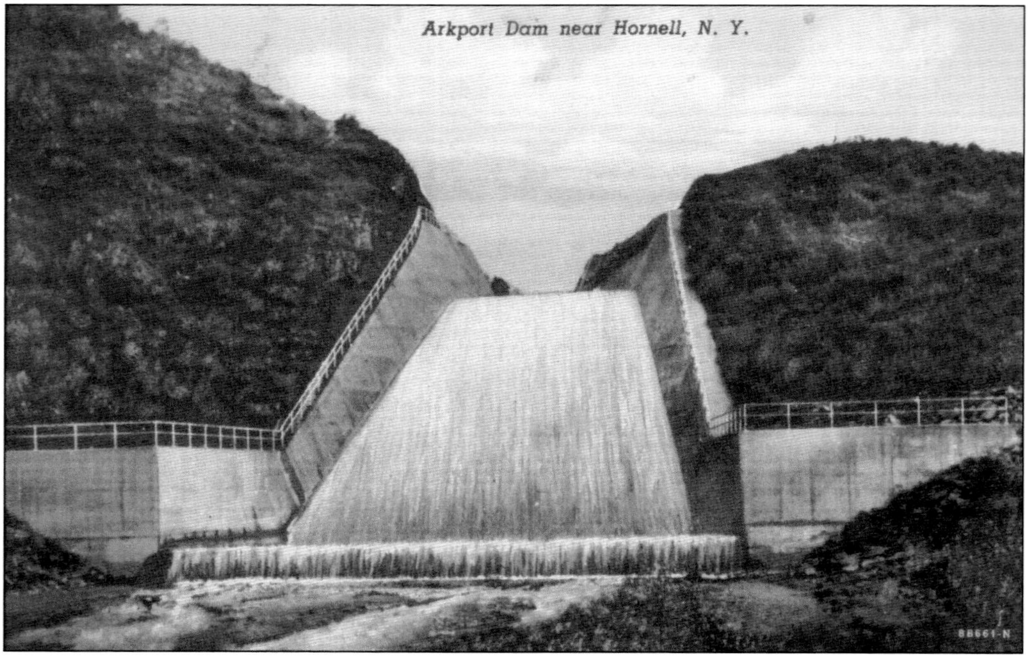

New Deal projects after 1935 and later works improved matters but would never completely control the ravages of nature. (SCHS.)

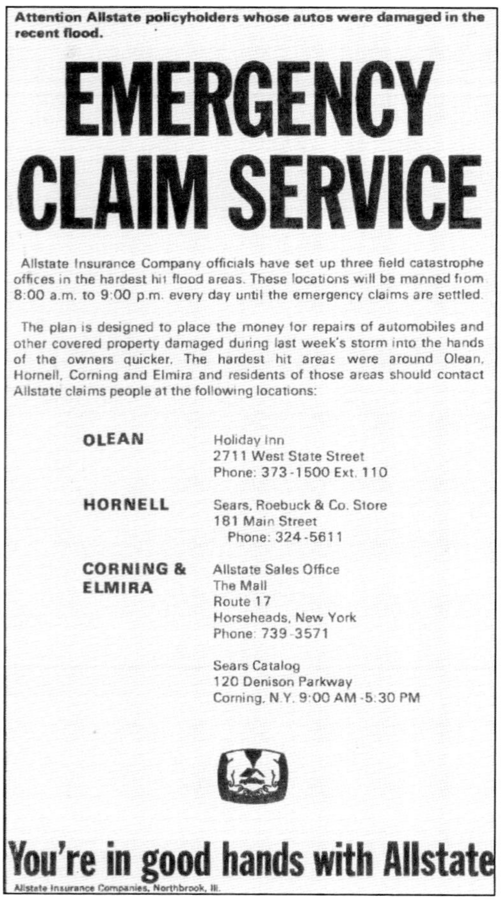

Outside help would always be needed. In this case, after the 1972 flood, the first challenge was connecting with displaced policyholders. (SCHS.)

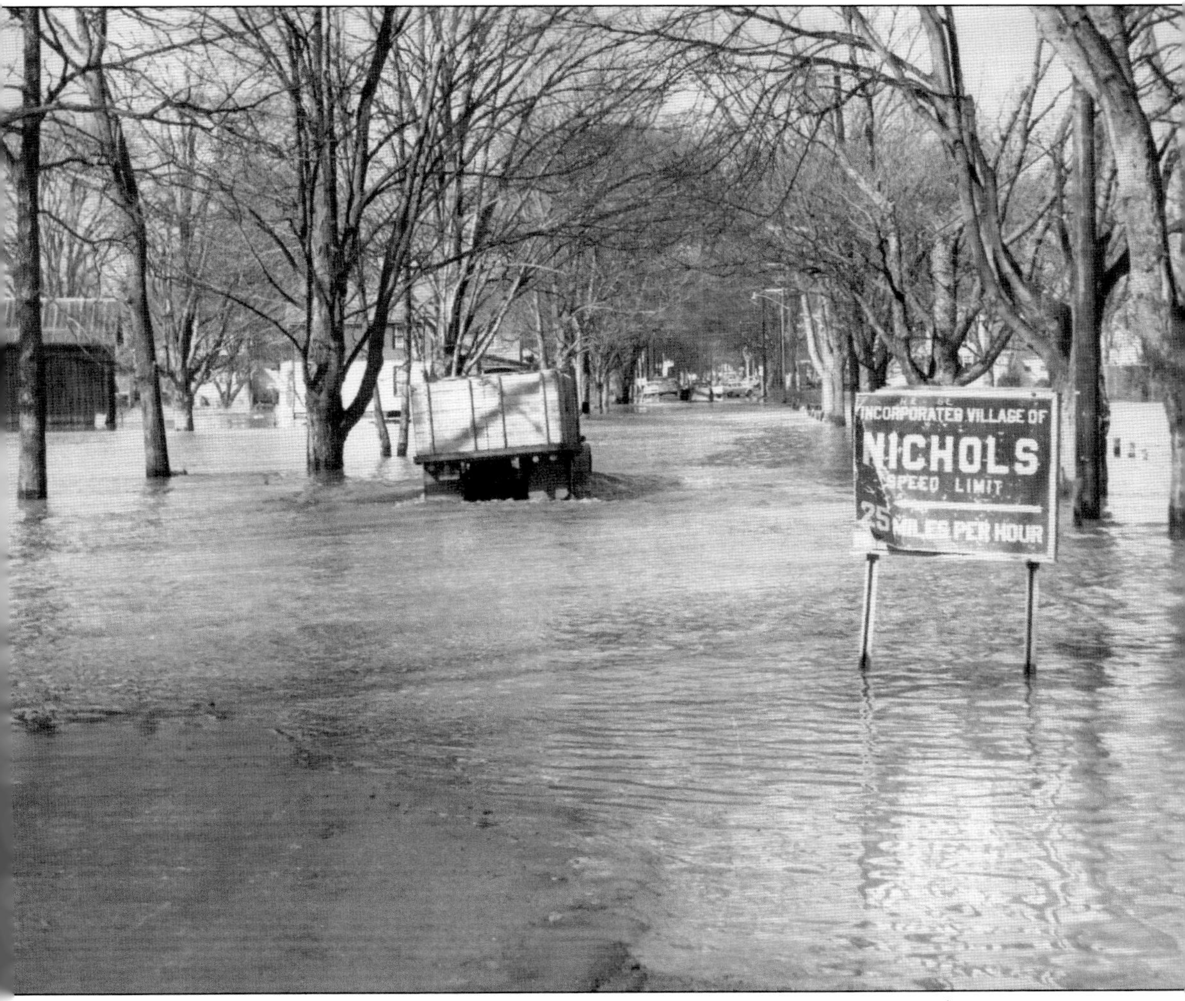

This truck seems unlikely to exceed the posted speed limit. Nichols, near the state line in Tioga County, is a village on the Susquehanna River—or, at times like these, in the Susquehanna. It flooded in 1935, in 1972, and in 2011 and will probably flood again. With hard work, and with help from the neighbors, Nichols and the other riverside towns will come back every time. (TC.)

Consistent with our mission to preserve history on a local level, this book was printed in South Carolina on American-made paper and manufactured entirely in the United States. Products carrying the accredited Forest Stewardship Council (FSC) label are printed on 100 percent FSC-certified paper.

MADE IN THE USA